# TENNYSON

## FIFTY POEMS

## 1830–1864

# TENNYSON

## FIFTY POEMS

## 1830–1864

Edited by
J. H. LOBBAN, M.A.

Cambridge:
at the University Press
1927

# CAMBRIDGE
## UNIVERSITY PRESS

University Printing House, Cambridge CB2 8BS, United Kingdom

Published in the United States of America by Cambridge University Press, New York

Cambridge University Press is part of the University of Cambridge.

It furthers the University's mission by disseminating knowledge in the pursuit of education, learning and research at the highest international levels of excellence.

www.cambridge.org
Information on this title: www.cambridge.org/9781107678736

© Cambridge University Press 1927

First edition 1910
Reprinted 1924 (twice), 1927
First published 1927
First paperback edition 2014

A catalogue record for this publication is available from the British Library

ISBN 978-1-107-67873-6 Paperback

# PREFACE

THE fifty poems contained in this selection range, with one exception, from *Poems, chiefly Lyrical* of 1830, to the *Enoch Arden* volume of 1864. The exception is the *Northern Farmer—New Style*, which was inserted through inadvertence, and appears here by the kind permission of Messrs Macmillan & Co., Ltd.

To contend that the outside limit imposed by the law of copyright does not in the case of Tennyson exclude some of his best work would be neither sound criticism nor good taste. It is, I hope, quite a different matter to venture the opinion that within these dates it is possible to represent Tennyson at his very best in every important department of his work. The present selection, therefore, and not its prescribed scope, is at fault if it fails to display Tennyson's mastery over lyric, narrative, elegiac, epic and occasional verse. Of the poems subsequent to 1864, no higher praise could be given to any than to say they reached the standard which the poet himself had earlier set.

In the notes I have recorded many debts to various editors and commentators and to the indispensable *Memoir* and Eversley Edition of the Poems.

J. H. L.

LONDON,
30 *May* 1910.

# CONTENTS

# INTRODUCTION

THAT the critical estimate of Tennyson should at the present time be an uncertain one is precisely what the history of English poetry would lead us to expect. His contemporary fame has in due course been followed by a reaction, and his position is still too close to permit of the forming of any convincing historical estimate. A supreme instance of this oscillation of fame is seen in the case of Pope. Half a century of almost unquestioned preeminence was followed by half a century of growing disaffection, until the question was raised whether Pope was a poet at all. That this question can ever be raised with regard to Tennyson is impossible, but it is none the less true and evident that at least a very large portion of his work is not of that supreme and indisputable kind that rides serene above the storms that assail most poetical achievements. The comparison of Tennyson and Pope—great artists both, working under two entirely different conceptions of their art—suggests yet another consideration bearing on the current estimate of Tennyson. For most poets—all, indeed, except the sublime few who have written "not for an age but for all time"—have two distinct sources of appeal. Their work interests us either by its essentially poetical quality or by its reflection of its time. Those who are repelled by the brilliant glitter

of *The Rape of the Lock* may yet be profoundly in-
terested in its pictures of a social order that is no more.
It is certain that no writer equals Tennyson as the
general interpreter of the Victorian age. If it be
counted to him as a defect that he was not in advance
of his age, the defect only adds to the historical value
of his interpretation.

The poet was born on August 6, 1809, at Somersby
Rectory, Lincolnshire. He was the fourth son of the
Rev. George Clayton Tennyson, and two of his elder
brothers won distinction as poets. As a child of five it
is recorded that Tennyson revealed the poetic impulse,
and of his work as a boy we have his own interesting
account. "I suppose I was nearer thirty than twenty
before I was anything of an artist, and in my earliest
teens I wrote an Epic—between 5000 and 6000 verses,
chiefly *à la* Scott, and full of battles, dealing too with
sea and savage mountain scenery. I used to compose
sixty or seventy lines all at once and shout them about
the fields as I leapt over the hedges. I never felt so
inspired, tho' of course the poem was not worth pre-
serving and into the fire it went." From the village
school Tennyson went to Louth Grammar School, but
after his eleventh year he was educated at home by
his father and tutors. In 1827, less from love of fame
than from the desire to augment their pocket-money,
Charles and Alfred collected their verses and had the
good fortune to induce a Louth bookseller to publish
them and to pay ten pounds for the copyright. The
little volume called *Poems by Two Brothers* (it contained at least four poems by Frederick Tennyson) is
said to have been noticed only by one unimportant
review. It is certainly of more importance now than

in its own day, because it reveals with certainty the
poet's earliest models. Byron, Scott, and Moore are
seen to be the chief influences, but particularly Byron
whose death had powerfully impressed the boy of
fifteen. It is amusing to note with what zeal the
young poet affects the master's pessimism and reck-
less despair, *e.g.*

> Oh! 'tis a fearful thing to glance
> Back on the gloom of misspent years:
> What shadowy forms of guilt advance,
> And fill me with a thousand fears!
> The vices of my life arise,
> Pourtray'd in shapes, alas! too true;
> And not one beam of hope breaks through,
> To cheer my old and aching eyes:

or

> Ah! yes, the lip may faintly smile,
> The eye may sparkle for a while;
> But never from that wither'd heart
> The consciousness of ill shall part!

And it is with the metres as with the thought.
*Marmion, The Destruction of Sennacherib,* and many
familiar *Irish Melodies* are repeatedly echoed. In one
poem, *Midnight,* however, there are lines giving distinct promise of the music and the pictorial power
to come:

> 'Tis midnight o'er the dim mere's lonely bosom,
> Dark, dusky, windy midnight: swift are driven
> The swelling vapours onward   .   .   .
> A wan, dull lengthen'd sheet of swimming light
> Lies the broad lake.

In 1828 Tennyson matriculated at Trinity College,
Cambridge, where his powers were speedily recognised
by his admission into the society of 'The Apostles'—at

that time a brilliant circle including James Spedding, Monckton Milnes, Henry Alford, and R. C. Trench. And one of his earliest friendships at Cambridge was with Arthur Henry Hallam whose untimely death he was later to bewail in the most elaborate of English elegies. In 1829 Tennyson won the Chancellor's prize for English verse, defeating both Hallam and Milnes. The subject was *Timbuctoo*, and Tennyson's victory was the more remarkable because, contrary to precedent, he adopted blank verse. The ruling influences of the earlier volume are no longer apparent and have given way to Milton and Wordsworth. But there are many lines of an "unborrowed cast" that point forward to the music of Tennyson's later blank verse.

> I saw
> The smallest grain that dappled the dark earth,
> The indistinctest atom in deep air,
> The Moon's white cities, and the opal width
> Of her small glowing lakes, her silver heights
> Unvisited with dew of vagrant cloud,
> And the unsounded, undescended depth
> Of her black hollows. The clear galaxy
> Shorn of its hoary lustre, wonderful,
> Distinct and vivid with sharp points of light,
> Blaze within blaze, an unimagin'd depth
> And harmony of planet-girded suns
> And moon-encircled planets, wheel in wheel,
> Arch'd the wan sapphire.

With the publication in 1830 of *Poems, chiefly Lyrical* Tennyson made his real entry into literature. Nearly thirty of the poems, revised and altered in the poet's usual way, were retained in the collected works, but more than twenty were not republished. The volume once more revealed Tennyson under a new influence. This time it was that of Shelley and Keats. But the striking feature of the poems was their marked originality and the beauty and boldness of their metrical effects. Hallam, who reviewed the poems with a friendly enthusiasm that stirred the wrath of Christopher North, was in this respect at least justified in asserting that "the author imitates nobody." This is true of the intricate rhyme of *Recollections of the Arabian Nights* and of the simpler form of *Mariana,* the latter poem a notable example of Tennyson's genius for evolving new and striking harmonies by apparently simple modifications of familiar stanzas. The three measures here combined produce a melody then new to English verse:

> Her tears fell with the dews at even ;
>   Her tears fell ere the dews were dried ;
> She could not look on the sweet heaven,
>   Either at morn or eventide.
> After the flitting of the bats,
>   When thickest dark did trance the sky,
>   She drew her casement-curtain by,
> And glanced athwart the glooming flats.
>     She only said, "The night is dreary,
>       He cometh not," she said ;
>     She said, "I am aweary, aweary,
>       I would that I were dead."

The novelty of the style was proved by the bewilderment of some of the critics, and this found amusing expression later in Coleridge's advice to the poet. "He has begun to write verses without very well understanding what metre is....To deal in new metres without considering what metre means and requires is preposterous. What I would, with many wishes of success, prescribe to Tennyson—indeed without it he can never be a poet in art—is to write for the next two or three years in none but one or two well-known and strictly-defined metres; such as the heroic couplet, the octave stanza, or the octosyllabic measures of the *Allegro* and *Penseroso*. He would probably thus get imbued with a sensation, if not a sense of metre, just as Eton boys get to write such good Latin verses by conning Ovid and Tibullus. As it is, I can scarcely scan his verses."

Even the most sanguine of Tennyson's friends could not have looked for so triumphant a vindication of their faith in him as he afforded in the wonderful collection of thirty *Poems* published at the end of 1832. Of the thirty, ten were ultimately cancelled by the poet, and those that were retained underwent in most cases the usual process of drastic revision. "All in all, a more original and beautiful volume of minor poetry never was added to our literature." In more than one way the most notable item in the volume is *The Lady of Shalott*. For this was Tennyson's first handling of Arthurian romance, and his method of treating it anticipated the theory of the pre-Raphaelite school. And it is certain that even Tennyson never drew a picture of purer loveliness, nor mated sound and sense with more subtle wizardry.

> Willows whiten, aspens quiver,
> Little breezes dusk and shiver
> Thro' the waves that run for ever
> By the island in the river
> Flowing down to Camelot.
> Four gray walls, and four gray towers,
> Overlook a space of flowers,
> And the silent isle imbowers
> The Lady of Shalott.

Part of the magic of the poem is the way in which familiar details of English landscape are utilised to give reality to romance and are themselves transfigured in the act.

> Only reapers, reaping early
> In among the bearded barley,
> Hear a song that echoes cheerly
> From the river winding clearly,
>         Down to tower'd Camelot:
> And by the moon the reaper weary,
> Piling sheaves in uplands airy,
> Listening, whispers, "'Tis the fairy
>         Lady of Shalott."

This first essay in Arthurian romance has qualities that distinguish it from Tennyson's more elaborate handling of the subject in the *Idylls*. As the poet went farther and farther away from Malory, so did he lose the charm of atmosphere that for ever haunts the prose-poem, *The Morte d'Arthur*. But in the case of *The Lady of Shalott*, he went beyond Malory to an Italian version of a story based on the same original source as Malory's great translation. "The Italian story," says Professor Ker, "like the English poem, is detached from its context; it is not like the Idyll of *Elaine*, part of a large and complicated history. The Italian story has no ties and dependencies; it is a thing by itself, in the old clear language, one of the beautiful small things of medieval art....Great part of the beauty of Tennyson's poem comes from the mystery of its story. It is a lyrical romance, and its setting is in a visionary land; there is no burden of historical substance in it as there is in the *Idylls of the King*. This strange isolation of the story, making

its own world, is part of the old Italian *novella*; and it
is this quality which makes the greatest distinction in
the new order of romantic poetry to which Tennyson's
poem belongs."

Among the other notable poems of the 1832 volume
is *Œnone*, the scenery of which was inspired by Tennyson's journey with Hallam to the Pyrenees in 1830,
when the two friends went to join the rebel forces in
the war of Spanish Independence. The development
of Tennyson's characteristic blank verse and of his
mastery of alliteration and phrase is seen in such lines
as these :—

> It was the deep midnoon : one silvery cloud
> Had lost his way between the piney sides
> Of this long glen. Then to the bower they came,
> Naked they came to that smooth-swarded bower,
> And at their feet the crocus brake like fire,
> Violet, amaracus, and asphodel,
> Lotos and lilies : and a wind arose,
> And overhead the wandering ivy and vine,
> This way and that, to many a wild festoon
> Ran riot, garlanding the gnarled boughs
> With branch and berry and flower thro' and thro'.

The "Quarterly Review" condemned *Œnone* for its
nineteen repetitions (with variants) of

> "O mother, hear me yet before I die."

Christopher North in "Blackwood" came nearer to
pointing out a real danger that was to beset the poet
in what, with the uncritical violence of his time, he
called his "puerile partiality for particular forms of
expression."

In *The Palace of Art* and *A Dream of Fair Women*
we have two stately examples of poetical pageantry.

The description of the palace is the fitting comment for the poem:

> Full of long-sounding corridors it was,
> That over-vaulted grateful gloom,
> Thro' which the livelong day my soul did pass,
> Well pleased from room to room.
>
> Full of great rooms and small the palace stood,
> All various, each a perfect whole
> From living nature, fit for every mood
> And charge of my still soul.

In *A Dream of Fair Women* there are many notable instances of Tennyson's genius for perfect phrasing which gives him rank with the foremost of those who have contributed to the stock of classical quotation:

> The spacious times of great Elizabeth.

> Those far-renowned brides of ancient song.

> A daughter of the gods, divinely tall,
> And most divinely fair.

> Saw God divide the night with flying flame,
> And thunder on the everlasting hills.

> As when a great thought strikes along the brain,
> And flushes all the cheek.

And for the wonderful impressiveness of its enumeration, as well as for its vowel-music and finely contrasted alliterative effects, it would not be easy to match this verse:

> Squadrons and squares of men in brazen plates,
> Scaffolds, still sheets of water, divers woes,
> Ranges of glimmering vaults with iron grates,
> And hush'd seraglios.

With this verse we might contrast the line,

> And clattering flints batter'd with clanging hoofs.

Here the alliteration has scarcely enough art to conceal its art, and this "particular form of expression" in time became with the poet a mannerism rather than an ornament.

The chief remaining poem of the 1832 volume is *The Lotos-Eaters*. With sure perception Tennyson chose for the opening of the poem the slow vehicle of the Spenserian stanza, which is changed for an irregular and melodious medley when the recreant mariners, in the glory of their shameful resolution, summon up sufficient energy to break into their choric song of sloth. The first two lines of the poem exhibit a nice stroke of art.

> "Courage!" he said, and pointed toward the land,
> "This mounting wave will roll us shoreward soon."

And with this note of courage and vigour in our ears, we pass straightway in the next line into a "land of drowsy head"—

> In the afternoon they came unto a land,
> In which it seemed always afternoon.
> All round the coast the languid air did swoon,
> Breathing like one that hath a weary dream.
> Full-faced above the valley stood the moon ;
> And like a downward smoke, the slender stream
> Along the cliff to fall and pause and fall did seem.

Finally mention may be made of two other poems in this volume as instances of Tennyson's limitations. To use the term, limitations, is indeed to beg the question, and in matters respecting humour and sentiment criticism can aim at nothing higher than the expression of personal opinion. Probably readers of Tennyson are equally divided in finding *The May*

*Queen* touching or mawkish and *The Goose* diverting or somewhat inept. If *The Goose* were all we had to judge by, the merits of Tennyson's *lyra jocosa* might be considered an open question. But there were other birds even heavier in the wing that were discreetly withdrawn from public view, so that there is reason for sharing the opinion of the poet's true friend and critic, FitzGerald, when he said, "Alfred, whatever he may think, cannot trifle. His smile is rather a grim one." And it is the more permissible to share that opinion, seeing that the defect, even if it exists, would not in itself disqualify Tennyson from ranking with Milton and Wordsworth.

Ten years passed before Tennyson again ventured on publication. In 1833 he suffered a shock that profoundly affected his attitude to life and art in the death of his friend and prospective brother-in-law, Arthur Henry Hallam. Soon he was at work on the series of elegies which seventeen years later he shaped into *In Memoriam.* During all this time the poet lived in London, cheered by the friendship of FitzGerald, Spedding, Milnes and many new acquaintances, notable among whom was Thomas Carlyle. Even in the days at Cambridge Tennyson had shown his extreme susceptibility to criticism, and he had felt deeply the ungenerous reception generally given to his first two volumes. It was well-known to his intimate circle that he was busily recasting old work and writing new poems of splendid achievement, but for long he resisted all their entreaties to publish, and a few poems contributed to various ephemeral magazines were the only sign given to the world of the poet's activity. At last in 1842 the long silence was triumphantly broken, and the poet's restraint and severe self-criticism met their due reward in the chorus of critical approval that hailed the appearance of the two new volumes of *Poems.* Carlyle, Emerson, Poe, Dickens, Elizabeth Barrett were only a few of the eminent writers who endorsed what even the "Quarterly Review" at last had to admit, that the poems were "a real addition to our literature." And Wordsworth himself, soon after his appointment as laureate, described his defeated younger rival as "the first of our living poets."

Of the contents of these volumes, the first of which contained the portions of his earlier work that the poet thought fit to retain (with the wonted revision and pruning), the most important poem is the *Morte d'Arthur. The Lady of Shalott,* as has been pointed out, differs from the rest of Tennyson's handling of Arthurian romance by virtue of its detachment and self-centred isolation of theme. The *Morte d'Arthur,* on the contrary, was to find its place later in the completed scheme of the *Idylls,* and yet, it, too, has generally been felt to be something of a thing apart. For in the *Idylls* we become increasingly aware of an incongruity and an alien note, and the medieval chivalry is almost lost sight of under the paint of Victorian sentiment.

The poem reveals the maturity of Tennyson's blank verse, free as yet from overloaded prettiness and happily capturing the flavour of Malory's prose. There is nothing in the later *Idylls* to surpass in pictorial power and in beauty of diction the memorable closing lines:

"But now farewell. I am going a long way
With these thou seëst—if indeed I go—
(For all my mind is clouded with a doubt)
To the island-valley of Avilion;
Where falls not hail, or rain, or any snow,
Nor ever wind blows loudly; but it lies
Deep-meadow'd, happy, fair with orchard-lawns
And bowery hollows crown'd with summer sea,
Where I will heal me of my grievous wound."
    So said he, and the barge with oar and sail
Moved from the brink, like some full-breasted swan
That, fluting a wild carol ere her death,
Ruffles her pure cold plume, and takes the flood
With swarthy webs. Long stood Sir Bedivere
Revolving many memories, till the hull
Look'd one black dot against the verge of dawn,
And on the mere the wailing died away.

The fidelity with which Tennyson recreates the atmosphere of Malory may to some extent be seen even by comparing these few lines with the closing sentences of the prose romance.

And so then they rowed from the land, and sir Bedivere beheld al those ladies goe from him; then sir Bedivere cried, "Ah, my lord Arthur, what shall become of mee now ye goe from me, and leave me here alone among mine enemies?" "Comfort thy selfe," said king Arthur, "and do as well as thou maiest, for in mee is no trust for to trust in; for I wil into the vale of Avilion for to heale me of my greivous wound; and if thou never heere more of mee, pray for my soule." But evermore the queenes and the ladies wept and shriked that it was pittie for to heare them. And as soon as sir Bedivere had lost the sight of the barge, hee wept and wailed, and so tooke the forrest.

"It [Malory's *Morte d'Arthur*] remains," says Professor Hales, "the most delightful version of the Arthurian legends; and we think it will be esteemed and read

long after many other versions, largely founded upon
it, have ceased to be esteemed and read. One may
confidently predict that Malory will outlive Tennyson
as a teller of the Arthurian tale. If any one of the
*Idylls of the King* lives on, we think it will be the one
that is most directly and fully taken from Malory—
that known in its latest issue, with some inferior
additions, as the *Passing of Arthur*." The freedom
and the beauty and the essential fidelity of the interpretation are such as to give it a true originality,
and in comparison with it one is tempted to apply
to the later *Idylls* what Bentley said of Pope's *Iliad*:
"a pretty poem, Mr Pope, but you must not call it
Homer."

In domestic idylls such as *Dora* and *The Gardener's
Daughter* Tennyson shows the influence of Crabbe, but
the sternness and the "worsted stockings" of the old
realist are discarded for things more becoming to the
boudoir. In *St Simeon Stylites* and *Ulysses* he developed the dramatic monologue of which he had
already given an example in *Œnone*. *Ulysses* has
interesting connexions with other poems, as it is to
some extent a sequel to *The Lotos-Eaters,* and Tennyson himself tells us that it was written in the first tide
of his grief for the death of Arthur Hallam. And just
as *The Lady of Shalott* is his finest and most single-
minded reproduction of the magic of medieval romance,
*Ulysses* marks his loftiest embodiment of the Hellenic
spirit. The noble lines that follow reveal an austerity
and a studied simplicity that are too often wanting, and
it will be noted with how fine an effect he introduces
in one famous line a familiar ornament from his own
metrical paradise of dainty devices.

My mariners,
Souls that have toil'd, and wrought, and thought with me—
That ever with a frolic welcome took
The thunder and the sunshine, and opposed
Free hearts, free foreheads—you and I are old;
Old age hath yet his honour and his toil;
Death closes all: but something ere the end,
Some work of noble note, may yet be done,
Not unbecoming men that strove with Gods.
The lights begin to twinkle from the rocks:
The long day wanes: the slow moon climbs: the deep
Moans round with many voices. Come, my friends,
'Tis not too late to seek a newer world.
Push off, and sitting well in order smite
The sounding furrows; for my purpose holds
To sail beyond the sunset, and the baths
Of all the western stars, until I die.

Though it has fared hardly in the hands of critics
*Locksley Hall* shares with a song from *Maud* the
greatest popularity won by any of Tennyson's poems.
The quality that has given it this distinction is its
voicing of the protest of youth against its first en-
counter with the thraldom and insincerity of social
conventions, and had the poem presented a deeper
and more coherent philosophy it would doubtless have
forfeited this fame. In its shallowness lies its truth.
And this appeal of its subject is re-enforced by its
swinging trochaic rhyme, though on close inspection
it will be noticed that Tennyson uses the metre with
quite unusual laxity. The secret of the poem's fascina-
tion is seen in such lines as these:

Yearning for the large excitement that the coming years
    would yield,
Eager-hearted as a boy when first he leaves his father's field,

And at night along the dusky highway near and nearer drawn,
Sees in heaven the light of London flaring like a dreary dawn;

And his spirit leaps within him to be gone before him then,
Underneath the light he looks at, in among the throngs of
men.

This passage must have awakened and shaped many a
life's ambition, even as *Pendennis* has done.

Many poets as well as Goldsmith have found themselves "rich in fame but short of money." The success
of the 1842 volumes, however, was not one-sided.
Tennyson won friends in every department of literary
and social eminence, and according to the story the
merits of *Locksley Hall* and *Ulysses* so impressed Sir
Robert Peel that he granted the poet a Civil List
pension of £200. Soon after this official recognition
appeared *The Princess* (1847), well described as
"a medley." The poem is faintly satirical, faintly
humorous, and finally didactic, but its enduring parts
are the songs added by an afterthought, just as Pope
strengthened *The Rape of the Lock* by adding the
"Rosicrucian machinery" contrary to Mr Addison's
advice. And allowing for the vast difference of their
poetical medium, there is not a little in common between these two poems. In their polish and artificiality
they are both "classical," and while the modern poet
approaches the problem with all the politeness and
delicacy of the Victorian age, it may be doubted if
there is any profound or radical difference between
Tennyson's views as to the mission of "the fair sex"
and those held by Milton and Swift and Addison and
Pope. There still lurks in Tennyson something of
Addison's "condescension towards his pretty pupils,"

and the Princess Ida's dream of emancipation ends
in her being asked by the Prince to

> Look up, and let thy nature strike on mine   .   .   .
> Lay thy sweet hands in mine and trust to me.

The candid and captious FitzGerald went the length
of calling the poem "accursed" and "a wretched waste
of power at a time of life when a man ought to be
doing his best."

In the beginning of 1850 Tennyson published *In
Memoriam*: in June he was married to Miss Emily
Sellwood, whose younger sister had fourteen years
before been married to his brother, Charles Tennyson;
and in the November of the same year he was appointed poet-laureate in succession to Wordsworth, two
of the "candidates" mentioned by the press being
Samuel Rogers, whose *Pleasures of Memory* was now
a far distant memory of 1792, and Leigh Hunt, whose
*Juvenilia* appeared in 1801 and whose critical charity
had long ago brought solace to Shelley and Keats and
to Tennyson himself in his earliest endeavours. It was
a remarkable coincidence that Tennyson had won his
way to the laurel at the very moment when his long
labour of love and thought had reached its fulness in
*In Memoriam*.

From the first there has been acute difference of
opinion in the critical estimate of *In Memoriam*. None
of Tennyson's poems has been so carefully analysed
and interpreted by a long succession of scholarly and
zealous commentators who have striven to show its
underlying unity of thought. Composed over a long
number of years, the poem consists of a series of
elegies and reflective monologues which the poet

finally shaped into a more or less orderly and
systematic grouping. So far all are agreed: most,
too, would agree with Professor Elton that *In Memoriam* "is one of the hardest poems in the modern
English language; it is set with small thorns for the
interpreter; and it calls for no intelligence less fine
and serious, and for no scholarship less nicely-dividing,
than have been bestowed on it by Professor Bradley."
When Professor Elton goes on to speak of the poem as
"Tennyson's methodized grief," he reaches the point
where criticism finds itself in antagonism with the
popular estimate of Tennyson's contemporaries which is
still maintained by a loyal following and which found
its best known expression in Queen Victoria's avowal,
"Next to the Bible *In Memoriam* is my comfort."
"*Lycidas*," said FitzGerald, when he heard of the
poem in the making, "is the utmost length an elegiac
should reach." It is a bold but impossible endeavour
to state definite limits for the poetical expression of
a personal sorrow, and it is certain that the brevity
of *Lycidas* brings to its readers little conviction of its
emotional sincerity. But there is a profound truth in
FitzGerald's objection which lies at the root of all the
difference of opinion manifested towards *In Memoriam*
The natural and convincing medium of a deeply-felt
sorrow is not the long-drawn-out elegy but the brief
and poignant lyric of Cowper and Burns. It is merci-
fully impossible in human nature for sorrow to "keep
his own wounds green" for so long a period as that
occupied in the making of this poem. The mourner
gives place slowly to the artist. That Tennyson re-
cognized this himself seems clear from his note on
*Ulysses* which, he says, "was written soon after Arthur

Hallam's death, and gives the feeling about the need of going forward and braving the struggle of life perhaps more simply than anything in *In Memoriam*." There are, in fact, two distinct elements in *In Memoriam*. There are the few sections of personal and lyrical significance: the rest is the work of the brilliant successor of what we may call the churchyard school of eighteenth-century poetry, begun by Young and Blair and culminating magnificently in Gray.

Passing over the interesting additions made from time to time to the various new editions of the *Poems* of 1842, we come to the *Maud* volume of 1855. The title-poem was built round the stanzas beginning with the famous lines,

> O, that 'twere possible
> After long grief and pain
> To find the arms of my true love
> Round me once again!

These lines had been written as early as 1836 when they appeared in *The Tribute*, a miscellany made for a charitable object which enlisted the sympathy of his friend, Monckton Milnes. Tennyson at first somewhat gruffly refused his aid, whereupon his friend rejoined tartly. The incident is thus commented on by Professor Ker. "Out of the Life of Tennyson I take one thing which is not altogether trifling, and which seems to me to be characteristic and memorable, though it is not part of the common tradition, the things that are generally repeated about the poet....Milnes was offended and wrote an angry letter. Tennyson's reply (given in the two biographies, Lord Houghton's and his own) brings out the character, temper and humour of a very remarkable man dealing with a very severe trial of his patience. His friend had lost his head, but kept his talent for language, and in some of his carefully chosen phrases (like 'piscatory vanity') had shown that he meant not only to quarrel but to wound. Tennyson's answer is a proof of the virtue of imagination in dealing with practical affairs. Milnes's sharpened phrases have their full effect, and Tennyson suffers the pain that was intended. Anger comes also, not mere resentment, but the passion that would have destroyed all vestiges of friendship. That can be made out from Tennyson's words: 'I put down my pipe and stared at the fire for ten minutes till the stranger vanished up the chimney.'...He stares the stranger out of countenance and up the chimney; the friendship remains unbroken because Tennyson is magnanimous; and one need not require any more convincing proof of the largeness and generosity of his nature and his mind; of his intellectual virtue, if I may use the term freely and in no restricted or scholastic sense."

*Maud* like *The Princess* is a medley and a curious mingling of failure and achievement. Strenuous self-critic as he was, the history of literature forbids our accepting too fully the poet's own preference for the poem. Its "wild and wandering cries" give it affinity with *Locksley Hall*, but here the rhetoric is more apparent and the indignation more hollow and declamatory. The poem, however, contains in itself conclusive evidence of Tennyson's genius for metrical effects. The lovely lyric, "Come into the garden, Maud," belongs indisputably to that rare order of verse from which years of ignoble use cannot rub the freshness and the bloom.

Leaving aside the *Idylls of the King*, which range

from 1859 to 1885 and of which we have already seen
the important beginnings in *The Lady of Shalott* and
the *Morte d'Arthur*, we come to the *Enoch Arden*
volume of 1864, the last from which the poems in this
selection are drawn. In the title-poem and in *Aylmer's
Field* Tennyson reverts to the narrative style of *Dora*,
and again appears to disadvantage as a narrator in
comparison with the homelier style of Crabbe. Un-
doubtedly Archbishop Trench was right when he said
of *The Northern Farmer*, "It is a wonderful revelation
of the heathenism still in the land, and quite the most
valuable thing in the book." It is impossible to read
*The Northern Farmer* without some regret for the
might-have-been—without some regret for the sheltered
and secluded life. There is always in Tennyson the
hint of a volcanic force that never found its vent. Had
the course of his life been less ideally poetic, the
hidden fires, which only fostered the too luxuriant
verdure of the mountain slopes, might have issued in
the lava of scathing satire. His earliest friends had
always that feeling of unfulfilment. FitzGerald longed
to see "old Hallam" and Tennyson fighting against
the French in a Martello tower—the latter "a more
heroic figure to lead the defenders of his country could
not be."

The present selection of Tennyson's poems spans
the entire period of his development as a poet. In
the twenty-eight years after the publication of *Enoch
Arden* Tennyson made no new departure except in his
preoccupation with the drama. In this matter one feels
that he lacked the help of a reliable counsellor such
as Fanny Burney had in Daddy Crisp. For such a
mentor would never have allowed Tennyson to write

for the stage and would have given him the encouragement he needed to add to the glory of English lyric. As it was, the great things in the production of Tennyson's later years were returns to his earlier triumphs. The long years given to the drama were almost nugatory: the long years given to the *Idylls* never produced the equal of the *Morte d'Arthur.* But the latest years of Tennyson's life revealed one marvel— his imperishable gift of song. It was in his seventy-sixth year that Tennyson wrote the noble lines on Virgil, the poet whose music he so often and so finely echoed, and in summing whose achievement the eulogist sang his own:

Wielder of the stateliest measure ever moulded by the lips of
    man . . .
All the charm of all the Muses often flowering in a lonely
    word.

And in his eightieth year the old lyric splendour of phrase flashed forth in *Crossing the Bar.* The magic potency of "wisdom married to immortal verse" was manifested by the complaint of a famous thinker, a contemporary of Tennyson, that the poet in a few lines could bring more conviction to the public than could the results of a lifetime given to philosophy. But that is the poet's peculiar reward, never so finely described as by the poets' poet:

> For deeds do die, however nobly done,
> And thoughts of men do as themselves decay:
> But wise words taught in numbers for to run,
> Recorded by the Muses, live for aye.

Most of the excellences and characteristics of Tennyson's verse have been referred to or have been briefly exemplified in the foregoing pages. It remains but to call attention to three points—the merit of his occasional verse, his wonderful delineation of nature, and his historical position.

The most widely read poet in the eighteenth century was John Pomfret, and his successor on the throne of popularity and dulness was Martin Tupper. The mention of these names prepares one for the shock of investigating the list of our poets-laureate. Spenser, Ben Jonson, and Dryden appear, with more or less doubtful credentials, at the head of the list, but the undeniably authentic record contains the unfamiliar names of Eusden, Whitehead, and Pye—names unknown to readers of modern anthologies and reprints. The office regained its dignity in the person of Southey, and the laurel grew greener as it passed to Wordsworth and then to Tennyson. But Tennyson alone, in a true sense, deserved the title. For there never came the occasion to which he failed to give dignified and supremely felicitous expression. His lines *To the Queen* as fitly precede the magnificent body of his verse as the personal lyric, *Crossing the Bar*, comes, by its author's wish, at the rear. And the verses that immediately precede that closing triumph—the lines on *The Death of the Duke of Clarence and Avondale*—remind us of the fidelity and brilliancy with which Tennyson discharged this minor duty. But on one—and it chanced to be the first—occasion on which he was called upon to "write to order," he turned it to glorious use in the *Ode on the Death of the Duke of Wellington*. It is one of the puzzles of literature that this splendid poem was coldly received by contemporary critics. It echoes marvellously the processional music of a great funeral pageant with all its attendant circumstance—the hush of a mighty crowd, the tolling of bells, the drum-beat, and the roar of cannon. And never was Tennyson's dramatic skill more happily shown than in the lines where our greatest Admiral is made to welcome the hero of a hundred fights. The poem is vibrant with a lofty and passionate patriotism, and above all its skilfully concerted harmonies one note rings out insistently and true:

> Not once or twice in our rough island story,
> The path of duty was the way to glory.

The wonderful accuracy of Tennyson's descriptions of nature are known to all of his readers. The mere hearing of certain passages would convey a vivid picture to the blind. The familiar and classical examples, and they are typical of hundreds, are the lines so highly praised by Mr Holbrook in *Cranford*,

> The cedar spreads his dark green layers of shade,

and (of Alice's hair)

> More dark than ashbuds in the front of March.

Another brilliant descriptive line is

> Laburnums, dropping-wells of fire.

But of all Tennyson's masterpieces of observation and subtly phrased descriptions there is none to surpass *The Eagle*. Once read, it is a lifetime's treasure. By its six lines alone Tennyson would have found his way to immortality by the postern gate of the anthologies.

> He clasps the crag with hooked hands:
> Close to the sun in lonely lands,
> Ring'd with the azure world, he stands.
> The wrinkled sea beneath him crawls;
> He watches from his mountain walls,
> And like a thunderbolt he falls.

When Tennyson's career began, the so-called Romantic Triumph had run its course. The name of the movement is misleading, as the triumph was the result not of revolution but of a quite usual and natural process of evolution. The "classical" school of English poetry began with Milton and Waller and Dryden: it culminated in Pope: it reached its nadir with Erasmus Darwin. The heroic couplet lost all its heroism when it was called upon to celebrate *The Loves of the Plants*. The protest of Wordsworth and Coleridge against the old order of things exaggerated the novelty of their innovation, and neglected the fact that from the time of Pope onwards there was a steady growth of a romantic school. Keats and Shelley did much to bridge the apparent gap; especially Keats, who did not disdain to write the new poetry in the old heroic couplet. But it was left to Tennyson to be the reconciler of the old antagonisms. Milton and Gray surpassed him in knowledge, but Tennyson, beyond all rivals, proved himself the heir of all the ages of song. He rifled the ancient classics, he borrowed freely from Shakespeare and Milton, he practised every precept of Pope, he did not disdain to use the hempen fibre of Crabbe. He made a full and catholic and understanding use, as no previous poet had done, of all his predecessors. And in all his borrowings he displayed the Shakespearean genius for appropriating and transmuting all he stole. "Orpheus with his lute can hardly have worked greater wonders in savage places than has Tennyson with the haunting refrains of his song-snatches, the yearnful music of his love-plaints, the forlorn sadness of his elegies, or the 'mellow lin-lan-lone' of his evening chimes."

# POEMS BY TENNYSON

## TO THE QUEEN

Revered, beloved—O you that hold
  A nobler office upon earth
  Than arms, or power of brain, or birth
Could give the warrior kings of old,

Victoria,—since your Royal grace
  To one of less desert allows
  This laurel greener from the brows
Of him that utter'd nothing base;

And should your greatness, and the care
  That yokes with empire, yield you time    10
  To make demand of modern rhyme
If aught of ancient worth be there;

Then—while a sweeter music wakes,
  And thro' wild March the throstle calls,
  Where all about your palace-walls
The sun-lit almond-blossom shakes—

Take, Madam, this poor book of song;
    For tho' the faults were thick as dust
    In vacant chambers, I could trust
Your kindness. May you rule us long,     20

And leave us rulers of your blood
    As noble till the latest day!
    May children of our children say,
"She wrought her people lasting good;

"Her court was pure; her life serene;
    God gave her peace; her land reposed;
    A thousand claims to reverence closed
In her as Mother, Wife and Queen;

"And statesmen at her council met
    Who knew the seasons, when to take     30
    Occasion by the hand, and make
The bounds of freedom wider yet

"By shaping some august decree,
    Which kept her throne unshaken still,
    Broad-based upon her people's will,
And compass'd by the inviolate sea."


## THE KRAKEN

Below the thunders of the upper deep;
Far, far beneath in the abysmal sea,
His ancient, dreamless, uninvaded sleep
The Kraken sleepeth: faintest sunlights flee
About his shadowy sides: above him swell
Huge sponges of millennial growth and height;

And far away into the sickly light,
From many a wondrous grot and secret cell
Unnumber'd and enormous polypi
Winnow with giant arms the slumbering green. 10
There hath he lain for ages and will lie
Battening upon huge seaworms in his sleep,
Until the latter fire shall heat the deep;
Then once by man and angels to be seen,
In roaring he shall rise and on the surface die.

## MARIANA

"Mariana in the moated grange."
*Measure for Measure.*

With blackest moss the flower-plots
  Were thickly crusted, one and all:
The rusted nails fell from the knots
  That held the peach to the garden-wall.
The broken sheds look'd sad and strange:
  Unlifted was the clinking latch;
  Weeded and worn the ancient thatch
Upon the lonely moated grange.
    She only said, "My life is dreary,
      He cometh not," she said;          10
    She said, "I am aweary, aweary,
      I would that I were dead!"

Her tears fell with the dews at even;
  Her tears fell ere the dews were dried;
She could not look on the sweet heaven,
  Either at morn or eventide.

After the flitting of the bats,
 When thickest dark did trance the sky,
 She drew her casement-curtain by,
And glanced athwart the glooming flats.  20
  She only said, "The night is dreary,
   He cometh not," she said;
  She said, "I am aweary, aweary,
   I would that I were dead!"

Upon the middle of the night,
 Waking she heard the night-fowl crow:
The cock sung out an hour ere light:
 From the dark fen the oxen's low
Came to her: without hope of change,
 In sleep she seem'd to walk forlorn,  30
 Till cold winds woke the gray-eyed morn
About the lonely moated grange.
  She only said, "The day is dreary,
   He cometh not," she said;
  She said, "I am aweary, aweary,
   I would that I were dead!"

About a stone-cast from the wall
 A sluice with blacken'd waters slept,
And o'er it many, round and small,
 The cluster'd marish-mosses crept.  40
Hard by a poplar shook alway,
 All silver-green with gnarled bark:
For leagues no other tree did mark
The level waste, the rounding gray.
  She only said, "My life is dreary,
   He cometh not," she said;
  She said, "I am aweary, aweary,
   I would that I were dead!"

And ever when the moon was low,
  And the shrill winds were up and away,     50
In the white curtain, to and fro,
  She saw the gusty shadow sway.
But when the moon was very low,
  And wild winds bound within their cell,
  The shadow of the poplar fell
Upon her bed, across her brow.
    She only said, "The night is dreary,
      He cometh not," she said;
    She said, "I am aweary, aweary,
      I would that I were dead!"     60

All day within the dreamy house,
  The doors upon their hinges creak'd;
The blue fly sung in the pane; the mouse
  Behind the mouldering wainscot shriek'd,
Or from the crevice peer'd about.
  Old faces glimmer'd thro' the doors,
  Old footsteps trod the upper floors,
Old voices called her from without.
    She only said, "My life is dreary,
      He cometh not," she said;     70
    She said, "I am aweary, aweary,
      I would that I were dead!"

The sparrow's chirrup on the roof,
  The slow clock ticking, and the sound
Which to the wooing wind aloof
  The poplar made, did all confound
Her sense; but most she loathed the hour
  When the thick-moted sunbeam lay
  Athwart the chambers, and the day
Was sloping toward his western bower.     80

Then, said she, "I am very dreary,
  He will not come," she said;
She wept, "I am aweary, aweary,
  Oh God, that I were dead!"

## RECOLLECTIONS OF THE ARABIAN NIGHTS

When the breeze of a joyful dawn blew free
In the silken sail of infancy,
The tide of time flow'd back with me,
  The forward-flowing tide of time;
And many a sheeny summer-morn,
Adown the Tigris I was borne,
By Bagdat's shrines of fretted gold,
High-walled gardens green and old;
True Mussulman was I and sworn,
  For it was in the golden prime          10
    Of good Haroun Alraschid.

Anight my shallop, rustling thro'
The low and bloomed foliage, drove
The fragrant, glistening deeps, and clove
The citron-shadows in the blue:
By garden porches on the brim,
The costly doors flung open wide,
Gold glittering thro' lamplight dim,
And broider'd sofas on each side:
  In sooth it was a goodly time,          20
  For it was in the golden prime
    Of good Haroun Alraschid.

Often, where clear-stemm'd platans guard
The outlet, did I turn away
The boat-head down a broad canal
From the main river sluiced, where all
The sloping of the moon-lit sward
Was damask-work, and deep inlay
Of braided blooms unmown, which crept
Adown to where the water slept.                        30
   A goodly place, a goodly time,
    For it was in the golden prime
      Of good Haroun Alraschid.

A motion from the river won
Ridged the smooth level, bearing on
My shallop thro' the star-strown calm,
Until another night in night
I enter'd, from the clearer light,
Imbower'd vaults of pillar'd palm,
Imprisoning sweets, which, as they clomb      40
Heavenward, were stay'd beneath the dome
   Of hollow boughs.—A goodly time,
    For it was in the golden prime
      Of good Haroun Alraschid.

Still onward; and the clear canal
Is rounded to as clear a lake.
From the green rivage many a fall
Of diamond rillets musical,
Thro' little crystal arches low
Down from the central fountain's flow      50
Fall'n silver-chiming, seem'd to shake
The sparkling flints beneath the prow.
   A goodly place, a goodly time,
    For it was in the golden prime
      Of good Haroun Alraschid.

Above thro' many a bowery turn
A walk with vary-colour'd shells
Wander'd engrain'd. On either side
All round about the fragrant marge
From fluted vase, and brazen urn                    60
In order, eastern flowers large,
Some dropping low their crimson bells
Half-closed, and others studded wide
  With disks and tiars, fed the time
  With odour in the golden prime
    Of good Haroun Alraschid.

Far off, and where the lemon-grove
In closest coverture upsprung,
The living airs of middle night
Died round the bulbul as he sung;                   70
Not he: but something which possess'd
The darkness of the world, delight,
Life, anguish, death, immortal love,
Ceasing not, mingled, unrepress'd,
  Apart from place, withholding time,
  But flattering the golden prime
    Of good Haroun Alraschid.

Black the garden-bowers and grots
Slumber'd: the solemn palms were ranged
Above, unwoo'd of summer wind:                      80
A sudden splendour from behind
Flush'd all the leaves with rich gold-green,
And, flowing rapidly between
Their interspaces, counterchanged
The level lake with diamond-plots
  Of dark and bright. A lovely time,
  For it was in the golden prime
    Of good Haroun Alraschid.

Dark-blue the deep sphere overhead,
Distinct with vivid stars inlaid,                    90
Grew darker from that under-flame:
So, leaping lightly from the boat,
With silver anchor left afloat,
In marvel whence that glory came
Upon me, as in sleep I sank
In cool soft turf upon the bank,
  Entranced with that place and time,
  So worthy of the golden prime
    Of good Haroun Alraschid.

Thence thro' the garden I was drawn—          100
A realm of pleasance, many a mound,
And many a shadow-chequer'd lawn
Full of the city's stilly sound,
And deep myrrh-thickets blowing round
The stately cedar, tamarisks,
Thick rosaries of scented thorn,
Tall orient shrubs, and obelisks
  Graven with emblems of the time,
  In honour of the golden prime
    Of good Haroun Alraschid.                    110

With dazed vision unawares
From the long alley's latticed shade
Emerged, I came upon the great
Pavilion of the Caliphat.
Right to the carven cedarn doors,
Flung inward over spangled floors,
Broad-based flights of marble stairs
Ran up with golden balustrade,
  After the fashion of the time,
  And humour of the golden prime          120
    Of good Haroun Alraschid.

The fourscore windows all alight
As with the quintessence of flame,
A million tapers flaring bright
From twisted silvers look'd to shame
The hollow-vaulted dark, and stream'd
Upon the mooned domes aloof
In inmost Bagdat, till there seem'd
Hundreds of crescents on the roof
   Of night new-risen, that marvellous time,   130
   To celebrate the golden prime
      Of good Haroun Alraschid.

Then stole I up, and trancedly
Gazed on the Persian girl alone,
Serene with argent-lidded eyes
Amorous, and lashes like to rays
Of darkness, and a brow of pearl
Tressed with redolent ebony,
In many a dark delicious curl,
Flowing beneath her rose-hued zone;   140
   The sweetest lady of the time,
   Well worthy of the golden prime
      Of good Haroun Alraschid.

Six columns, three on either side,
Pure silver, underpropt a rich
Throne of the massive ore, from which
Down-droop'd, in many a floating fold,
Engarlanded and diaper'd
With inwrought flowers, a cloth of gold.
Thereon, his deep eye laughter-stirr'd   150
With merriment of kingly pride,
   Sole star of all that place and time,
   I saw him—in his golden prime,
      THE GOOD HAROUN ALRASCHID!

## THE POET

The poet in a golden clime was born,
  With golden stars above;
Dower'd with the hate of hate, the scorn of scorn,
  The love of love.

He saw thro' life and death, thro' good and ill,
  He saw thro' his own soul.
The marvel of the everlasting will,
  An open scroll,

Before him lay: with echoing feet he threaded
  The secretest walks of fame:                    10
The viewless arrows of his thoughts were headed
  And wing'd with flame.

Like Indian reeds blown from his silver tongue,
  And of so fierce a flight,
From Calpe unto Caucasus they sung,
  Filling with light

And vagrant melodies the winds which bore
  Them earthward till they lit;
Then, like the arrow-seeds of the field flower,
  The fruitful wit                                20

Cleaving, took root, and springing forth anew
  Where'er they fell, behold,
Like to the mother plant in semblance, grew
  A flower all gold,

And bravely furnish'd all abroad to fling
　　The winged shafts of truth,
To throng with stately blooms the breathing spring
　　Of Hope and Youth.

So many minds did gird their orbs with beams,
　　Tho' one did fling the fire.　　　　　　　　30
Heaven flow'd upon the soul in many dreams
　　Of high desire.

Thus truth was multiplied on truth, the world
　　Like one great garden show'd,
And thro' the wreaths of floating dark upcurl'd,
　　Rare sunrise flow'd.

And Freedom rear'd in that august sunrise
　　Her beautiful bold brow,
When rites and forms before his burning eyes
　　Melted like snow.　　　　　　　　　　40

There was no blood upon her maiden robes
　　Sunn'd by those orient skies;
But round about the circles of the globes
　　Of her keen eyes

And in her raiment's hem was traced in flame
　　WISDOM, a name to shake
All evil dreams of power—a sacred name.
　　And when she spake,

Her words did gather thunder as they ran,
　　And as the lightning to the thunder　　　50
Which follows it, riving the spirit of man,
　　Making earth wonder,

So was their meaning to her words. No sword
    Of wrath her right arm whirl'd,
But one poor poet's scroll, and with *his* word
    She shook the world.

## THE POET'S MIND

### 1

  Vex not thou the poet's mind
    With thy shallow wit:
  Vex not thou the poet's mind;
    For thou canst not fathom it.
  Clear and bright it should be ever,
  Flowing like a crystal river;
  Bright as light, and clear as wind.

### 2

  Dark-brow'd sophist, come not anear;
    All the place is holy ground;
  Hollow smile and frozen sneer      10
      Come not here.
  Holy water will I pour
  Into every spicy flower
Of the laurel-shrubs that hedge it around.
The flowers would faint at your cruel cheer.
  In your eye there is death,
  There is frost in your breath
  Which would blight the plants.
    Where you stand you cannot hear
      From the groves within      20
      The wild-bird's din.

In the heart of the garden the merry bird chants,
It would fall to the ground if you came in.
  In the middle leaps a fountain
    Like sheet lightning,
    Ever brightening
  With a low melodious thunder;
All day and all night it is ever drawn
    From the brain of the purple mountain
    Which stands in the distance yonder:    30
It springs on a level of bowery lawn,
And the mountain draws it from Heaven above,
And it sings a song of undying love;
And yet, tho' its voice be so clear and full,
You never would hear it; your ears are so dull;
So keep where you are: you are foul with sin;
It would shrink to the earth if you came in.


## THE SEA-FAIRIES

Slow sailed the weary mariners, and saw,
Between the green brink and the running foam,
White limbs unrobèd in a chrystal air,
Sweet faces, rounded arms, and bosoms prest
To little harps of gold: and while they mused,
Whispering to each other half in fear,
Shrill music reached them on the middle sea.

### Song.

Whither away, whither away, whither away?  Fly no
    more:
Whither away wi' the singing sail? whither away wi'
    the oar?

Whither away from the high green field and the happy
    blossoming shore ? 10
  Weary mariners, hither away,
    One and all, one and all,
  Weary mariners come and play;
  We will sing to you all the day;
    Furl the sail and the foam will fall
    From the prow!  One and all
    Furl the sail! drop the oar!
        Leap ashore!
Know danger and trouble and toil no more.
Whither away wi' the sail and the oar ? 20
      Drop the oar,
      Leap ashore,
      Fly no more!
Whither away wi' the sail? whither away wi' the oar ?

Day and night to the billow the fountain calls:
Down shower the gambolling waterfalls
  From wandering over the lea;
They freshen the silvery-crimson shells,
And thick with white bells the clover-hill swells
  High over the full-toned sea. 30
Merrily carol the revelling gales
  Over the islands free:
From the green sea-banks the rose down-trails
  To the happy brimmèd sea.
Come hither, come hither, and be our lords,
  For merry brides are we:
We will kiss sweet kisses, and speak sweet words:
  Oh listen, listen, your eyes shall glisten
    With pleasure and love and revelry;
    Oh listen, listen, your eyes shall glisten, 40

When the sharp clear twang of the golden chords
    Runs up the ridgèd sea.
  Ye will not find so happy a shore,
Weary mariners! all the world o'er;
        Oh! fly no more!
Harken ye, harken ye, sorrow shall darken ye,
    Danger and trouble and toil no more;
          Whither away?
            Drop the oar;
            Hither away,                    50
            Leap ashore;
      Oh fly no more—no more.
Whither away, whither away, whither away with the
    sail and the oar?




## THE BALLAD OF ORIANA

My heart is wasted with my woe,
        Oriana.
There is no rest for me below,
        Oriana.
When the long dun wolds are ribb'd with snow
And loud the Norland whirlwinds blow,
        Oriana,
Alone I wander to and fro,
        Oriana.

Ere the light on dark was growing,          10
        Oriana,
At midnight the cock was crowing,
        Oriana:

Winds were blowing, waters flowing,
We heard the steeds to battle going,
      Oriana;
Aloud the hollow bugle blowing,
      Oriana.

In the yew-wood black as night,
      Oriana,              20
Ere I rode into the fight,
      Oriana,
While blissful tears blinded my sight
By star-shine and by moonlight,
      Oriana,
I to thee my troth did plight,
      Oriana.

She stood upon the castle wall,
      Oriana:
She watch'd my crest among them all,     30
      Oriana:
She saw me fight, she heard me call,
When forth there stept a foeman tall,
      Oriana,
Atween me and the castle wall,
      Oriana.

The bitter arrow went aside,
      Oriana:
The false, false arrow went aside,
      Oriana:             40
The damned arrow glanced aside,
And pierced thy heart, my love, my bride,
      Oriana!
Thy heart, my life, my love, my bride,
      Oriana!

Oh! narrow, narrow was the space,
　　　Oriana.
Loud, loud rung out the bugle's brays,
　　　Oriana.
Oh! deathful stabs were dealt apace,　　　50
The battle deepen'd in its place,
　　　Oriana;
But I was down upon my face,
　　　Oriana.

They should have stabb'd me where I lay,
　　　Oriana!
How could I rise and come away,
　　　Oriana?
How could I look upon the day?
They should have stabb'd me where I lay,　　　60
　　　Oriana—
They should have trod me into clay,
　　　Oriana.

O breaking heart that will not break,
　　　Oriana!
O pale, pale face so sweet and meek,
　　　Oriana!
Thou smilest, but thou dost not speak,
And then the tears run down my cheek,
　　　Oriana:　　　70
What wantest thou? whom dost thou seek,
　　　Oriana?

I cry aloud: none hear my cries,
　　　Oriana.
Thou comest atween me and the skies,
　　　Oriana.

I feel the tears of blood arise
Up from my heart unto my eyes,
        Oriana.
Within thy heart my arrow lies,        80
        Oriana.

O cursed hand! O cursed blow!
        Oriana!
O happy thou that liest low,
        Oriana!
All night the silence seems to flow
Beside me in my utter woe,
        Oriana.
A weary, weary way I go,
        Oriana.        90

When Norland winds pipe down the sea,
        Oriana,
I walk, I dare not think of thee,
        Oriana.
Thou liest beneath the greenwood tree,
I dare not die and come to thee,
        Oriana.
I hear the roaring of the sea,
        Oriana.

## THE MERMAN

### 1

Who would be
A merman bold,
Sitting alone,
Singing alone
Under the sea,
With a crown of gold,
On a throne?

### 2

I would be a merman bold;
I would sit and sing the whole of the day;
I would fill the sea-halls with a voice of power;　10
But at night I would roam abroad and play
With the mermaids in and out of the rocks,
Dressing their hair with the white sea-flower;
And holding them back by their flowing locks
I would kiss them often under the sea,
And kiss them again till they kiss'd me
　　Laughingly, laughingly;
And then we would wander away, away
To the pale-green sea-groves straight and high,
　　Chasing each other merrily.　20

### 3

There would be neither moon nor star;
But the wave would make music above us afar—
Low thunder and light in the magic night—
　　Neither moon nor star.

We would call aloud in the dreamy dells,
  Call to each other and whoop and cry
     All night, merrily, merrily;
They would pelt me with starry spangles and shells,
  Laughing and clapping their hands between,
     All night, merrily, merrily:                    30
But I would throw to them back in mine
Turkis and agate and almondine:
Then leaping out upon them unseen
I would kiss them often under the sea,
And kiss them again till they kiss'd me
     Laughingly, laughingly.
Oh! what a happy life were mine
Under the hollow-hung ocean green!
Soft are the moss-beds under the sea;
We would live merrily, merrily.                    40


## THE MERMAID

### 1

Who would be
A mermaid fair,
Singing alone,
Combing her hair
Under the sea,
In a golden curl
With a comb of pearl
On a throne?

## 2

I would be a mermaid fair;
I would sing to myself the whole of the day;     10
With a comb of pearl I would comb my hair;
And still as I comb'd I would sing and say,
"Who is it loves me? who loves not me?"
I would comb my hair till my ringlets would fall,
      Low adown, low adown,
From under my starry sea-bud crown
      Low adown and around,
And I should look like a fountain of gold
      Springing alone
        With a shrill inner sound,     20
      Over the throne
      In the midst of the hall;
Till that great sea-snake under the sea
From his coiled sleeps in the central deeps
Would slowly trail himself sevenfold
Round the hall where I sate, and look in at the gate
With his large calm eyes for the love of me.
And all the mermen under the sea
Would feel their immortality
Die in their hearts for the love of me.     30

## 8

But at night I would wander away, away,
  I would fling on each side my low-flowing locks,
And lightly vault from the throne and play
  With the mermen in and out of the rocks;
We would run to and fro, and hide and seek,
  On the broad sea-wolds in the crimson shells,
  Whose silvery spikes are nighest the sea.

But if any came near I would call, and shriek,
And adown the steep like a wave I would leap
  From the diamond-ledges that jut from the dells;
For I would not be kiss'd by all who would list, 41
Of the bold merry mermen under the sea;
They would sue me, and woo me, and flatter me,
In the purple twilights under the sea;
But the king of them all would carry me,
Woo me, and win me, and marry me,
In the branching jaspers under the sea;
Then all the dry pied things that be
In the hueless mosses under the sea
Would curl round my silver feet silently,     50
All looking up for the love of me.
And if I should carol aloud, from aloft
All things that are forked, and horned, and soft
Would lean out from the hollow sphere of the sea,
All looking down for the love of me.


## THE LADY OF SHALOTT

### PART I

On either side the river lie
Long fields of barley and of rye,
That clothe the wold and meet the sky;
And thro' the field the road runs by
      To many-tower'd Camelot;
And up and down the people go,
Gazing where the lilies blow
Round an island there below,
      The island of Shalott.

Willows whiten, aspens quiver,　　　10
Little breezes dusk and shiver
Thro' the wave that runs for ever
By the island in the river
　　　Flowing down to Camelot.
Four gray walls, and four gray towers,
Overlook a space of flowers,
And the silent isle imbowers
　　　The Lady of Shalott.

By the margin, willow-veil'd,
Slide the heavy barges trail'd　　　20
By slow horses; and unhail'd
The shallop flitteth silken-sail'd
　　　Skimming down to Camelot:
But who hath seen her wave her hand?
Or at the casement seen her stand?
Or is she known in all the land,
　　　The Lady of Shalott?

Only reapers, reaping early
In among the bearded barley,
Hear a song that echoes cheerly　　　30
From the river winding clearly,
　　　Down to tower'd Camelot:
And by the moon the reaper weary,
Piling sheaves in uplands airy,
Listening, whispers "'Tis the fairy
　　　Lady of Shalott."

## PART II

There she weaves by night and day
A magic web with colours gay,
She has heard a whisper say,

A curse is on her if she stay                    40
    To look down to Camelot.
She knows not what the curse may be,
And so she weaveth steadily,
And little other care hath she,
    The Lady of Shalott.


And moving thro' a mirror clear
That hangs before her all the year,
Shadows of the world appear.
There she sees the highway near
    Winding down to Camelot:         50
There the river eddy whirls,
And there the surly village-churls,
And the red cloaks of market girls,
    Pass onward from Shalott.


Sometimes a troop of damsels glad,
An abbot on an ambling pad,
Sometimes a curly shepherd-lad,
Or long-hair'd page in crimson clad,
    Goes by to tower'd Camelot;
And sometimes thro' the mirror blue         60
The knights come riding two and two:
She hath no loyal knight and true,
    The Lady of Shalott.


But in her web she still delights
To weave the mirror's magic sights,
For often thro' the silent nights
A funeral, with plumes and lights,
    And music, went to Camelot:

Or when the moon was overhead,
Came two young lovers lately wed;  70
"I am half-sick of shadows," said
    The Lady of Shalott.

## PART III

A bow-shot from her bower-eaves,
He rode between the barley-sheaves,
The sun came dazzling thro' the leaves,
And flamed upon the brazen greaves
    Of bold Sir Lancelot.
A redcross knight for ever kneel'd
To a lady in his shield,
That sparkled on the yellow field,  80
    Beside remote Shalott.

The gemmy bridle glitter'd free,
Like to some branch of stars we see
Hung in the golden Galaxy.
The bridle bells rang merrily
    As he rode down to Camelot:
And from his blazon'd baldric slung
A mighty silver bugle hung,
And as he rode his armour rung,
    Beside remote Shalott.  90

All in the blue unclouded weather
Thick-jewell'd shone the saddle-leather,
The helmet and the helmet-feather
Burn'd like one burning flame together,
    As he rode down to Camelot.
As often thro' the purple night,
Below the starry clusters bright,
Some bearded meteor, trailing light,
    Moves over still Shalott.

His broad clear brow in sunlight glow'd;     100
On burnish'd hooves his war-horse trode;
From underneath his helmet flow'd
His coal-black curls as on he rode,
     As he rode down to Camelot.
From the bank and from the river
He flash'd into the crystal mirror,
"Tirra lirra," by the river
     Sang Sir Lancelot.

She left the web, she left the loom,
She made three paces thro' the room,     110
She saw the water-lily bloom,
She saw the helmet and the plume,
     She look'd down to Camelot.
Out flew the web and floated wide;
The mirror crack'd from side to side;
"The curse is come upon me," cried
     The Lady of Shalott.

## Part IV

In the stormy east-wind straining,
The pale yellow woods were waning,
The broad stream in his banks complaining,     120
Heavily the low sky raining
     Over tower'd Camelot;
Down she came and found a boat
Beneath a willow left afloat,
And round about the prow she wrote
     *The Lady of Shalott.*

And down the river's dim expanse—
Like some bold seër in a trance,
Seeing all his own mischance—
With a glassy countenance                                    130
          Did she look to Camelot.
And at the closing of the day
She loosed the chain, and down she lay;
The broad stream bore her far away,
          The Lady of Shalott.

Lying, robed in snowy white
That loosely flew to left and right—
The leaves upon her falling light—
Thro' the noises of the night
          She floated down to Camelot:                       140
And as the boat-head wound along
The willowy hills and fields among,
They heard her singing her last song,
          The Lady of Shalott.

Heard a carol, mournful, holy,
Chanted loudly, chanted lowly,
Till her blood was frozen slowly,
And her eyes were darken'd wholly,
          Turn'd to tower'd Camelot;
For ere she reach'd upon the tide                            150
The first house by the water-side,
Singing in her song she died,
          The Lady of Shalott.

Under tower and balcony,
By garden-wall and gallery,
A gleaming shape she floated by,
A corse between the houses high,
          Silent into Camelot.

Out upon the wharfs they came,
Knight and burgher, lord and dame,    160
And round the prow they read her name,
    *The Lady of Shalott.*

Who is this? and what is here?
And in the lighted palace near
Died the sound of royal cheer;
And they cross'd themselves for fear,
        All the knights at Camelot:
But Lancelot mused a little space;
He said, "She has a lovely face;
God in His mercy lend her grace,    170
        The Lady of Shalott."


## THE TWO VOICES

A still small voice spake unto me,
"Thou art so full of misery,
Were it not better not to be?"

Then to the still small voice I said
"Let me not cast in endless shade
What is so wonderfully made."

To which the voice did urge reply;
"To-day I saw the dragon-fly
Come from the wells where he did lie.

"An inner impulse rent the veil    10
Of his old husk: from head to tail
Came out clear plates of sapphire mail.

"He dried his wings: like gauze they grew;
Thro' crofts and pastures wet with dew
A living flash of light he flew."

I said, "When first the world began,
Young Nature thro' five cycles ran,
And in the sixth she moulded man.

"She gave him mind, the lordliest
Proportion, and, above the rest,                    20
Dominion in the head and breast."

Thereto the silent voice replied;
"Self-blinded are you by your pride:
Look up thro' night: the world is wide.

"This truth within thy mind rehearse,
That in a boundless universe
Is boundless better, boundless worse.

"Think you this mould of hopes and fears
Could find no statelier than his peers
In yonder hundred million spheres?"                 30

It spake, moreover, in my mind:
"Tho' thou wert scatter'd to the wind,
Yet is there plenty of the kind."

Then did my response clearer fall:
"No compound of this earthly ball
Is like another, all in all."

To which he answer'd scoffingly;
"Good soul! suppose I grant it thee,
Who'll weep for thy deficiency?

"Or will one beam be less intense,                  40
When thy peculiar difference
Is cancell'd in the world of sense?"

I would have said, "Thou canst not know,"
But my full heart, that work'd below,
Rain'd thro' my sight its overflow.

Again the voice spake unto me:
"Thou art so steep'd in misery,
Surely 'twere better not to be.

"Thine anguish will not let thee sleep,
Nor any train of reason keep:                    50
Thou canst not think, but thou wilt weep."

I said, "The years with change advance:
If I make dark my countenance,
I shut my life from happier chance.

"Some turn this sickness yet might take,
Ev'n yet." But he: "What drug can make
A wither'd palsy cease to shake?"

I wept, "Tho' I should die, I know
That all about the thorn will blow
In tufts of rosy-tinted snow;                    60

"And men, thro' novel spheres of thought
Still moving after truth long sought,
Will learn new things when I am not."

"Yet," said the secret voice, "some time,
Sooner or later, will gray prime
Make thy grass hoar with early rime.

"Not less swift souls that yearn for light,
Rapt after heaven's starry flight,
Would sweep the tracts of day and night.

"Not less the bee would range her cells,           70
The furzy prickle fire the dells,
The foxglove cluster dappled bells."

I said that "all the years invent;
Each month is various to present
The world with some development.

"Were this not well, to bide mine hour,
Tho' watching from a ruin'd tower
How grows the day of human power?"

"The highest-mounted mind," he said,
"Still sees the sacred morning spread        80
The silent summit overhead.

"Will thirty seasons render plain
Those lonely lights that still remain,
Just breaking over land and main?

"Or make that morn, from his cold crown
And crystal silence creeping down,
Flood with full daylight glebe and town?

"Forerun thy peers, thy time, and let
Thy feet, millenniums hence, be set
In midst of knowledge, dream'd not yet.        90

"Thou hast not gain'd a real height,
Nor art thou nearer to the light,
Because the scale is infinite.

"'Twere better not to breathe or speak,
Than cry for strength, remaining weak,
And seem to find, but still to seek.

"Moreover, but to seem to find
Asks what thou lackest, thought resign'd,
A healthy frame, a quiet mind."

I said, "When I am gone away,        100
'He dared not tarry,' men will say,
Doing dishonour to my clay."

"This is more vile," he made reply,
"To breathe and loathe, to live and sigh,
Than once from dread of pain to die.

"Sick art thou—a divided will
Still heaping on the fear of ill
The fear of men, a coward still.

"Do men love thee?  Art thou so bound
To men, that how thy name may sound    110
Will vex thee lying underground?

"The memory of the wither'd leaf
In endless time is scarce more brief
Than of the garner'd Autumn-sheaf.

"Go, vexed Spirit, sleep in trust;
The right ear, that is fill'd with dust,
Hears little of the false or just."

"Hard task, to pluck resolve," I cried,
"From emptiness and the waste wide
Of that abyss, or scornful pride!    120

"Nay—rather yet that I could raise
One hope that warm'd me in the days
While still I yearn'd for human praise.

"When, wide in soul and bold of tongue,
Among the tents I paused and sung,
The distant battle flash'd and rung.

"I sung the joyful Pæan clear,
And, sitting, burnish'd without fear
The brand, the buckler, and the spear—

"Waiting to strive a happy strife,    130
To war with falsehood to the knife,
And not to lose the good of life—

"Some hidden principle to move,
To put together, part and prove,
And mete the bounds of hate and love—

"As far as might be, to carve out
Free space for every human doubt,
That the whole mind might orb about—

"To search thro' all I felt or saw,
The springs of life, the depths of awe,     140
And reach the law within the law:

"At least, not rotting like a weed,
But, having sown some generous seed,
Fruitful of further thought and deed,

"To pass, when Life her light withdraws,
Not void of righteous self-applause,
Nor in a merely selfish cause—

"In some good cause, not in mine own,
To perish, wept for, honour'd, known,
And like a warrior overthrown;     150

"Whose eyes are dim with glorious tears,
When, soil'd with noble dust, he hears
His country's war-song thrill his ears:

"Then dying of a mortal stroke,
What time the foeman's line is broke,
And all the war is roll'd in smoke."

"Yea!" said the voice, "thy dream was good,
While thou abodest in the bud.
It was the stirring of the blood.

"If Nature put not forth her power     160
About the opening of the flower,
Who is it that could live an hour?

"Then comes the check, the change, the fall.
Pain rises up, old pleasures pall.
There is one remedy for all.

"Yet hadst thou, thro' enduring pain,
Link'd month to month with such a chain
Of knitted purport, all were vain.

"Thou hadst not between death and birth
Dissolved the riddle of the earth.                    170
So were thy labour little-worth.

"That men with knowledge merely play'd,
I told thee—hardly nigher made,
Tho' scaling slow from grade to grade;

"Much less this dreamer, deaf and blind,
Named man, may hope some truth to find,
That bears relation to the mind.

"For every worm beneath the moon
Draws different threads, and late and soon
Spins, toiling out his own cocoon.                    180

"Cry, faint not: either Truth is born
Beyond the polar gleam forlorn,
Or in the gateways of the morn.

"Cry, faint not, climb: the summits slope
Beyond the furthest flights of hope,
Wrapt in dense cloud from base to cope.

"Sometimes a little corner shines,
As over rainy mist inclines
A gleaming crag with belts of pines.

"I will go forward, sayest thou,                      190
I shall not fail to find her now.
Look up, the fold is on her brow.

"If straight thy track, or if oblique,
Thou know'st not.  Shadows thou dost strike,
Embracing cloud, Ixion-like;

"And owning but a little more
Than beasts, abidest lame and poor,
Calling thyself a little lower

"Than angels.  Cease to wail and brawl!
Why inch by inch to darkness crawl?                    200
There is one remedy for all."

"O dull, one-sided voice," said I,
"Wilt thou make everything a lie,
To flatter me that I may die?

"I know that age to age succeeds,
Blowing a noise of tongues and deeds,
A dust of systems and of creeds.

"I cannot hide that some have striven,
Achieving calm, to whom was given
The joy that mixes man with Heaven:                    210

"Who, rowing hard against the stream,
Saw distant gates of Eden gleam,
And did not dream it was a dream;

"But heard, by secret transport led,
Ev'n in the charnels of the dead,
The murmur of the fountain-head—

"Which did accomplish their desire,
Bore and forbore, and did not tire,
Like Stephen, an unquenched fire.

"He heeded not reviling tones,                         220
Nor sold his heart to idle moans,
Tho' cursed and scorn'd, and bruised with stones:

"But looking upward, full of grace,
He pray'd, and from a happy place
God's glory smote him on the face."

The sullen answer slid betwixt:
"Not that the grounds of hope were fix'd,
The elements were kindlier mix'd."

I said, "I toil beneath the curse,
But, knowing not the universe,                    230
I fear to slide from bad to worse.

"And that, in seeking to undo
One riddle, and to find the true,
I knit a hundred others new:

"Or that this anguish fleeting hence,
Unmanacled from bonds of sense,
Be fix'd and froz'n to permanence:

"For I go, weak from suffering here;
Naked I go, and void of cheer:
What is it that I may not fear?"                   240

"Consider well," the voice replied,
"His face, that two hours since hath died;
Wilt thou find passion, pain or pride?

"Will he obey when one commands?
Or answer should one press his hands?
He answers not, nor understands.

"His palms are folded on his breast:
There is no other thing express'd
But long disquiet merged in rest.

"His lips are very mild and meek:                  250
Tho' one should smite him on the cheek,
And on the mouth, he will not speak.

"His little daughter, whose sweet face
He kiss'd, taking his last embrace,
Becomes dishonour to her race—

"His sons grow up that bear his name,
Some grow to honour, some to shame,—
But he is chill to praise or blame.

"He will not hear the north-wind rave,
Nor, moaning, household shelter crave          260
From winter rains that beat his grave.

"High up the vapours fold and swim:
About him broods the twilight dim:
The place he knew forgetteth him."

"If all be dark, vague voice," I said,
"These things are wrapt in doubt and dread,
Nor canst thou show the dead are dead.

"The sap dries up: the plant declines.
A deeper tale my heart divines.
Know I not Death? the outward signs?          270

"I found him when my years were few;
A shadow on the graves I knew,
And darkness in the village yew.

"From grave to grave the shadow crept:
In her still place the morning wept:
Touch'd by his feet the daisy slept.

"The simple senses crown'd his head:
'Omega! thou art Lord,' they said,
'We find no motion in the dead.'

"Why, if man rot in dreamless ease,          280
Should that plain fact, as taught by these,
Not make him sure that he shall cease?

"Who forged that other influence,
That heat of inward evidence,
By which he doubts against the sense?

"He owns the fatal gift of eyes,
That read his spirit blindly wise,
Not simple as a thing that dies.

"Here sits he shaping wings to fly:
His heart forebodes a mystery:          29
He names the name Eternity.

"That type of Perfect in his mind
In Nature can he nowhere find.
He sows himself on every wind.

"He seems to hear a Heavenly Friend,
And thro' thick veils to apprehend
A labour working to an end.

"The end and the beginning vex
His reason: many things perplex,
With motions, checks, and counterchecks.    300

"He knows a baseness in his blood
At such strange war with something good,
He may not do the thing he would.

"Heaven opens inward, chasms yawn,
Vast images in glimmering dawn,
Half shown, are broken and withdrawn.

"Ah! sure within him and without,
Could his dark wisdom find it out,
There must be answer to his doubt.

"But thou canst answer not again.          310
With thine own weapon art thou slain,
Or thou wilt answer but in vain.

"The doubt would rest, I dare not solve.
In the same circle we revolve.
Assurance only breeds resolve."

As when a billow, blown against,
Falls back, the voice with which I fenced
A little ceased, but recommenced.

"Where wert thou when thy father play'd
In his free field, and pastime made,          320
A merry boy in sun and shade?

"A merry boy they called him then.
He sat upon the knees of men
In days that never come again.

"Before the little ducts began
To feed thy bones with lime, and ran
Their course, till thou wert also man:

"Who took a wife, who rear'd his race,
Whose wrinkles gather'd on his face,
Whose troubles number with his days:          330

"A life of nothings, nothing-worth,
From that first nothing ere his birth
To that last nothing under earth!"

"These words," I said, "are like the rest,
No certain clearness, but at best
A vague suspicion of the breast:

"But if I grant, thou might'st defend
The thesis which thy words intend—
That to begin implies to end;

"Yet how should I for certain hold,            340
Because my memory is so cold,
That I first was in human mould?

"I cannot make this matter plain,
But I would shoot, howe'er in vain,
A random arrow from the brain.

"It may be that no life is found,
Which only to one engine bound
Falls off, but cycles always round.

"As old mythologies relate,
Some draught of Lethe might await          350
The slipping thro' from state to state.

"As here we find in trances, men
Forget the dream that happens then,
Until they fall in trance again.

"So might we, if our state were such
As one before, remember much,
For those two likes might meet and touch.

"But, if I lapsed from nobler place,
Some legend of a fallen race
Alone might hint of my disgrace;          360

"Some vague emotion of delight
In gazing up an Alpine height,
Some yearning toward the lamps of night.

"Or if thro' lower lives I came—
Tho' all experience past became
Consolidate in mind and frame—

"I might forget my weaker lot;
For is not our first year forgot?
The haunts of memory echo not.

"And men, whose reason long was blind,     370
From cells of madness unconfined,
Oft lose whole years of darker mind.

"Much more, if first I floated free,
As naked essence, must I be
Incompetent of memory:

"For memory dealing but with time,
And he with matter, could she climb
Beyond her own material prime?

"Moreover, something is or seems,
That touches me with mystic gleams,     380
Like glimpses of forgotten dreams—

"Of something felt, like something here;
Of something done, I know not where;
Such as no language may declare."

The still voice laugh'd.  "I talk," said he,
"Not with thy dreams.  Suffice it thee
Thy pain is a reality."

"But thou," said I, "hast miss'd thy mark,
Who sought'st to wreck my mortal ark,
By making all the horizon dark.     390

"Why not set forth, if I should do
This rashness, that which might ensue
With this old soul in organs new?

"Whatever crazy sorrow saith,
No life that breathes with human breath
Has ever truly long'd for death.

"'Tis life, whereof our nerves are scant,
Oh life, not death, for which we pant;
More life, and fuller, that I want."

I ceased, and sat as one forlorn.     400
Then said the voice, in quiet scorn,
"Behold, it is the Sabbath morn."

And I arose, and I released
The casement, and the light increased
With freshness in the dawning east.

Like soften'd airs that blowing steal,
When meres begin to uncongeal,
The sweet church bells began to peal.

On to God's house the people prest:
Passing the place where each must rest,    410
Each enter'd like a welcome guest.

One walk'd between his wife and child,
With measur'd footfall firm and mild,
And now and then he gravely smiled.

The prudent partner of his blood
Lean'd on him, faithful, gentle, good,
Wearing the rose of womanhood.

And in their double love secure,
The little maiden walk'd demure,
Pacing with downward eyelids pure.    420

These three made unity so sweet,
My frozen heart began to beat,
Remembering its ancient heat.

I blest them, and they wander'd on:
I spoke, but answer came there none:
The dull and bitter voice was gone.

A second voice was at mine ear,
A little whisper silver-clear,
A murmur, "Be of better cheer."

As from some blissful neighbourhood    430
A notice faintly understood,
"I see the end, and know the good."

A little hint to solace woe,
A hint, a whisper breathing low,
"I may not speak of what I know."

Like an Æolian harp that wakes
No certain air, but overtakes
Far thought with music that it makes:

Such seem'd the whisper at my side:
"What is it thou knowest, sweet voice?" I cried.
"A hidden hope," the voice replied:          441

So heavenly-toned, that in that hour
From out my sullen heart a power
Broke, like the rainbow from the shower,

To feel, altho' no tongue can prove,
That every cloud, that spreads above
And veileth love, itself is love.

And forth into the fields I went,
And Nature's living motion lent
The pulse of hope to discontent.          450

I wonder'd at the bounteous hours,
The slow result of winter showers:
You scarce could see the grass for flowers.

I wonder'd, while I paced along:
The woods were fill'd so full with song,
There seem'd no room for sense of wrong.

So variously seem'd all things wrought,
I marvell'd how the mind was brought
To anchor by one gloomy thought;

And wherefore rather I made choice          460
To commune with that barren voice,
Than him that said, "Rejoice! rejoice!"

## THE MILLER'S DAUGHTER

I see the wealthy miller yet,
  His double chin, his portly size,
And who that knew him could forget
  The busy wrinkles round his eyes?
The slow wise smile that, round about
  His dusty forehead drily curl'd,
Seem'd half-within and half-without,
  And full of dealings with the world?

In yonder chair I see him sit,
  Three fingers round the old silver cup— 10
I see his gray eyes twinkle yet
  At his own jest—gray eyes lit up
With summer lightnings of a soul
  So full of summer warmth, so glad,
So healthy, sound, and clear and whole,
  His memory scarce can make me sad.

Yet fill my glass: give me one kiss:
  My own sweet Alice, we must die.
There's somewhat in this world amiss
  Shall be unriddled by and by. 20
There's somewhat flows to us in life,
  But more is taken quite away.
Pray, Alice, pray, my darling wife,
  That we may die the self-same day.

Have I not found a happy earth?
  I least should breathe a thought of pain.
Would God renew me from my birth
  I'd almost live my life again.

So sweet it seems with thee to walk,
    And once again to woo thee mine—    30
It seems in after-dinner talk
    Across the walnuts and the wine—

To be the long and listless boy
    Late-left an orphan of the squire,
Where this old mansion mounted high
    Looks down upon the village spire:
For even here, where I and you
    Have lived and loved alone so long,
Each morn my sleep was broken thro'
    By some wild skylark's matin song.    40

And oft I heard the tender dove
    In firry woodlands making moan;
But ere I saw your eyes, my love,
    I had no motion of my own.
For scarce my life with fancy play'd
    Before I dream'd that pleasant dream—
Still hither thither idly sway'd
    Like those long mosses in the stream.

Or from the bridge I lean'd to hear
    The milldam rushing down with noise,    50
And see the minnows everywhere
    In crystal eddies glance and poise,
The tall flag-flowers when they sprung
    Below the range of stepping-stones,
Or those three chestnuts near, that hung
    In masses thick with milky cones.

But, Alice, what an hour was that,
    When after roving in the woods
('Twas April then), I came and sat
    Below the chestnuts, when their buds    60

Were glistening to the breezy blue;
  And on the slope, an absent fool,
I cast me down, nor thought of you,
  But angled in the higher pool.

A love-song I had somewhere read,
  An echo from a measured strain,
Beat time to nothing in my head
  From some odd corner of the brain.
It haunted me, the morning long,
  With weary sameness in the rhymes, 70
The phantom of a silent song,
  That went and came a thousand times.

Then leapt a trout. In lazy mood
  I watch'd the little circles die;
They past into the level flood,
  And there a vision caught my eye:
The reflex of a beauteous form,
  A glowing arm, a gleaming neck,
As when a sunbeam wavers warm
  Within the dark and dimpled beck. 80

For you remember, you had set,
  That morning, on the casement's edge
A long green box of mignonette,
  And you were leaning from the ledge:
And when I raised my eyes, above
  They met with two so full and bright—
Such eyes! I swear to you, my love,
  That these have never lost their light.

I loved, and love dispell'd the fear
  That I should die an early death: 90
For love possess'd the atmosphere,
  And fill'd the breast with purer breath.

My mother thought, What ails the boy?
  For I was alter'd, and began
To move about the house with joy,
  And with the certain step of man.

I loved the brimming wave that swam
  Thro' quiet meadows round the mill,
The sleepy pool above the dam,
  The pool beneath it never still,          100
The meal-sacks on the whiten'd floor,
  The dark round of the dripping wheel,
The very air about the door
  Made misty with the floating meal.

And oft in ramblings on the wold,
  When April nights began to blow,
And April's crescent glimmer'd cold,
  I saw the village lights below;
I knew·your taper far away,
  And full at heart of trembling hope,      110
From off the wold I came, and lay
  Upon the freshly-flower'd slope.

The deep brook groan'd beneath the mill;
  And "by that lamp," I thought, "she sits!"
The white chalk-quarry from the hill
  Gleam'd to the flying moon by fits.
"O that I were beside her now!
  O will she answer if I call?
O would she give me vow for vow,
  Sweet Alice, if I told her all?"           120

Sometimes I saw you sit and spin;
  And, in the pauses of the wind,
Sometimes I heard you sing within;
  Sometimes your shadow cross'd the blind.

At last you rose and moved the light,
　　And the long shadow of the chair
Flitted across into the night,
　　And all the casement darken'd there.

But when at last I dared to speak,
　　The lanes, you know, were white with may, 130
Your ripe lips moved not, but your cheek
　　Flush'd like the coming of the day;
And so it was—half-sly, half-shy,
　　You would, and would not, little one!
Although I pleaded tenderly,
　　And you and I were all alone.

And slowly was my mother brought
　　To yield consent to my desire:
She wish'd me happy, but she thought
　　I might have look'd a little higher; 140
And I was young—too young to wed:
　　"Yet must I love her for your sake;
Go fetch your Alice here," she said:
　　Her eyelid quiver'd as she spake.

And down I went to fetch my bride:
　　But, Alice, you were ill at ease;
This dress and that by turns you tried,
　　Too fearful that you should not please.
I loved you better for your fears,
　　I knew you could not look but well; 150
And dews, that would have fall'n in tears,
　　I kiss'd away before they fell.

I watch'd the little flutterings,
　　The doubt my mother would not see;
She spoke at large of many things,
　　And at the last she spoke of me;

L. T.　　　　　　　　　　　　　　　　　　4

And turning look'd upon your face,
  As near this door you sat apart,
And rose, and, with a silent grace
  Approaching, press'd you heart to heart.    160

Ah, well—but sing the foolish song
  I gave you, Alice, on the day
When, arm in arm, we went along,
  A pensive pair, and you were gay
With bridal flowers—that I may seem,
  As in the nights of old, to lie
Beside the mill-wheel in the stream,
  While those full chestnuts whisper by.

     It is the miller's daughter,
      And she is grown so dear, so dear,    170
     That I would be the jewel
      That trembles at her ear:
     For hid in ringlets day and night,
     I'd touch her neck so warm and white.

     And I would be the girdle
      About her dainty dainty waist,
     And her heart would beat against me,
      In sorrow and in rest:
     And I should know if it beat right,
     I'd clasp it round so close and tight.    180

     And I would be the necklace,
      And all day long to fall and rise
     Upon her balmy bosom,
      With her laughter or her sighs,
     And I would lie so light, so light,
     I scarce should be unclasp'd at night.

A trifle, sweet! which true love spells—
  True love interprets—right alone.
His light upon the letter dwells,
  For all the spirit is his own.                    190
So, if I waste words now, in truth
  You must blame Love.  His early rage
Had force to make me rhyme in youth,
  And makes me talk too much in age.

And now those vivid hours are gone,
  Like mine own life to me thou art,
Where Past and Present, wound in one,
  Do make a garland for the heart:
So sing that other song I made,
  Half-anger'd with my happy lot,              200
The day, when in the chestnut shade
  I found the blue Forget-me-not.

          Love that hath us in the net,
          Can he pass, and we forget?
          Many suns arise and set.
          Many a chance the years beget.
          Love the gift is Love the debt.
                  Even so.

          Love is hurt with jar and fret.
          Love is made a vague regret.          210
          Eyes with idle tears are wet.
          Idle habit links us yet.
          What is love? for we forget:
                  Ah, no! no!

Look thro' mine eyes with thine.  True wife,
  Round my true heart thine arms entwine;
My other dearer life in life,
  Look thro' my very soul with thine!

Untouch'd with any shade of years,
  May those kind eyes for ever dwell!    220
They have not shed a many tears,
  Dear eyes, since first I knew them well.

Yet tears they shed: they had their part
  Of sorrow: for when time was ripe,
The still affection of the heart
  Became an outward breathing type,
That into stillness past again,
  And left a want unknown before;
Although the loss that brought us pain,
  That loss but made us love the more,    230

With farther lookings on.  The kiss,
  The woven arms, seem but to be
Weak symbols of the settled bliss,
  The comfort, I have found in thee:
But that God bless thee, dear—who wrought
  Two spirits to one equal mind—
With blessings beyond hope or thought,
  With blessings which no words can find.

Arise, and let us wander forth,
  To yon old mill across the wolds;    240
For look, the sunset, south and north,
  Winds all the vale in rosy folds,
And fires your narrow casement glass,
  Touching the sullen pool below:
On the chalk-hill the bearded grass
  Is dry and dewless.  Let us go.

## ŒNONE

There lies a vale in Ida, lovelier
Than all the valleys of Ionian hills.
The swimming vapour slopes athwart the glen,
Puts forth an arm, and creeps from pine to pine,
And loiters, slowly drawn. On either hand
The lawns and meadow-ledges midway down
Hang rich in flowers, and far below them roars
The long brook falling thro' the clov'n ravine
In cataract after cataract to the sea.
Behind the valley topmost Gargarus                                10
Stands up and takes the morning: but in front
The gorges, opening wide apart, reveal
Troas and Ilion's column'd citadel,
The crown of Troas.
                            Hither came at noon
Mournful Œnone, wandering forlorn
Of Paris, once her playmate on the hills.
Her cheek had lost the rose, and round her neck
Floated her hair or seem'd to float in rest.
She, leaning on a fragment twined with vine,
Sang to the stillness, till the mountain-shade              2
Sloped downward to her seat from the upper cliff.

"O mother Ida, many-fountain'd Ida,
Dear mother Ida, harken ere I die.
For now the noonday quiet holds the hill:
The grasshopper is silent in the grass:
The lizard, with his shadow on the stone,
Rests like a shadow, and the cicala sleeps.

The purple flowers droop: the golden bee
Is lily-cradled: I alone awake.
My eyes are full of tears, my heart of love,    30
My heart is breaking, and my eyes are dim,
And I am all aweary of my life.

"O mother Ida, many-fountain'd Ida,
Dear mother Ida, harken ere I die.
Hear me O Earth, hear me O Hills, O Caves
That house the cold crown'd snake! O mountain brooks,
I am the daughter of a River-God,
Hear me, for I will speak, and build up all
My sorrow with my song, as yonder walls
Rose slowly to a music slowly breathed,    40
A cloud that gather'd shape: for it may be
That, while I speak of it, a little while
My heart may wander from its deeper woe.

"O mother Ida, many-fountain'd Ida,
Dear mother Ida, harken ere I die.
I waited underneath the dawning hills,
Aloft the mountain lawn was dewy-dark,
And dewy-dark aloft the mountain pine:
Beautiful Paris, evil-hearted Paris,
Leading a jet-black goat white-horn'd, white-hooved,
Came up from reedy Simois all alone.    51

"O mother Ida, harken ere I die.
Far-off the torrent call'd me from the cleft:
Far up the solitary morning smote
The streaks of virgin snow. With down-dropt eyes
I sat alone: white-breasted like a star
Fronting the dawn he moved; a leopard skin
Droop'd from his shoulder, but his sunny hair

Cluster'd about his temples like a God's;
And his cheek brighten'd as the foam-bow brightens
When the wind blows the foam, and all my heart
Went forth to embrace him coming ere he came. 62

"Dear mother Ida, harken ere I die.
He smiled, and opening out his milk-white palm
Disclosed a fruit of pure Hesperian gold,
That smelt ambrosially, and while I look'd
And listen'd, the full-flowing river of speech
Came down upon my heart.
　　　　　　　　"'My own Œnone,
Beautiful-brow'd Œnone, my own soul,
Behold this fruit, whose gleaming rind ingrav'n　70
"For the most fair," would seem to award it thine,
As lovelier than whatever Oread haunt
The knolls of Ida, loveliest in all grace
Of movement, and the charm of married brows.'

"Dear mother Ida, harken ere I die.
He pressed the blossom of his lips to mine,
And added 'This was cast upon the board,
When all the full-faced presence of the Gods
Ranged in the halls of Peleus; whereupon
Rose feud, with question unto whom 'twere due:　80
But light-foot Iris brought it yester-eve,
Delivering, that to me, by common voice
Elected umpire, Herè comes to-day,
Pallas and Aphrodite, claiming each
This meed of fairest. Thou, within the cave
Behind yon whispering tuft of oldest pine,
Mayst well behold them unbeheld, unheard,
Hear all, and see thy Paris judge of Gods.'

"Dear mother Ida, harken ere I die.
It was the deep midnoon: one silvery cloud 90
Had lost his way between the piney sides
Of this long glen.  Then to the bower they came,
Naked they came to that smooth-swarded bower,
And at their feet the crocus brake like fire,
Violet, amaracus, and asphodel,
Lotos and lilies: and a wind arose,
And overhead the wandering ivy and vine,
This way and that, in many a wild festoon
Ran riot, garlanding the gnarled boughs
With bunch and berry and flower thro' and thro'.

"O mother Ida, harken ere I die. 101
On the tree-tops a crested peacock lit,
And o'er him flow'd a golden cloud, and lean'd
Upon him, slowly dropping fragrant dew.
Then first I heard the voice of her, to whom
Coming thro' Heaven, like a light that grows
Larger and clearer, with one mind the Gods
Rise up for reverence.  She to Paris made
Proffer of royal power, ample rule
Unquestion'd, overflowing revenue 110
Wherewith to embellish state, 'from many a vale
And river-sunder'd champaign clothed with corn,
Or labour'd mines undrainable of ore.
Honour,' she said, 'and homage, tax and toll,
From many an inland town and haven large,
Mast-throng'd beneath her shadowing citadel
In glassy bays among her tallest towers.'

"O mother Ida, harken ere I die.
Still she spake on and still she spake of power,
'Which in all action is the end of all; 120

Power fitted to the season; wisdom-bred
And throned of wisdom—from all neighbour crowns
Alliance and allegiance, till thy hand
Fail from the sceptre-staff. Such boon from me,
From me, Heaven's Queen, Paris, to thee king-born,
A shepherd all thy life but yet king-born,
Should come most welcome, seeing men, in power
Only, are likest gods, who have attain'd
Rest in a happy place and quiet seats
Above the thunder, with undying bliss          130
In knowledge of their own supremacy.'

"Dear mother Ida, harken ere I die.
She ceased, and Paris held the costly fruit
Out at arm's-length, so much the thought of power
Flatter'd his spirit; but Pallas where she stood
Somewhat apart, her clear and bared limbs
O'erthwarted with the brazen-headed spear
Upon her pearly shoulder leaning cold,
The while, above, her full and earnest eye
Over her snow-cold breast and angry cheek          140
Kept watch, waiting decision, made reply.

"'Self-reverence, self-knowledge, self-control,
These three alone lead life to sovereign power.
Yet not for power, (power of herself
Would come uncall'd for) but to live by law,
Acting the law we live by without fear;
And, because right is right, to follow right
Were wisdom in the scorn of consequence.'

"Dear mother Ida, harken ere I die.
Again she said: 'I woo thee not with gifts.          150

Sequel of guerdon could not alter me
To fairer. Judge thou me by what I am,
So shalt thou find me fairest.

                  Yet, indeed,
If gazing on divinity disrobed
Thy mortal eyes are frail to judge of fair,
Unbiass'd by self-profit, oh! rest thee sure
That I shall love thee well and cleave to thee,
So that my vigour, wedded to thy blood,
Shall strike within thy pulses, like a God's,
To push thee forward thro' a life of shocks,     160
Dangers, and deeds, until endurance grow
Sinew'd with action, and the full-grown will,
Circled thro' all experiences, pure law,
Commeasure perfect freedom.'

                "Here she ceased,
And Paris ponder'd, and I cried, 'O Paris,
Give it to Pallas!' but he heard me not,
Or hearing would not hear me, woe is me!

  "O mother Ida, many-fountain'd Ida,
Dear mother Ida, harken ere I die.
Idalian Aphrodite beautiful,     170
Fresh as the foam, new-bathed in Paphian wells,
With rosy slender fingers backward drew
From her warm brows and bosom her deep hair
Ambrosial, golden round her lucid throat
And shoulder: from the violets her light foot
Shone rosy-white, and o'er her rounded form
Between the shadows of the vine-bunches
Floated the glowing sunlights, as she moved.

  "Dear mother Ida, harken ere I die.
She with a subtle smile in her mild eyes,     180

The herald of her triumph, drawing nigh
Half-whisper'd in his ear, 'I promise thee
The fairest and most loving wife in Greece.'
She spoke and laugh'd: I shut my sight for fear :
But when I look'd, Paris had raised his arm,
And I beheld great Herè's angry eyes,
As she withdrew into the golden cloud,
And I was left alone within the bower;
And from that time to this I am alone,
And I shall be alone until I die.          190

"Yet, mother Ida, harken ere I die.
Fairest—why fairest wife? am I not fair?
My love hath told me so a thousand times.
Methinks I must be fair, for yesterday,
When I past by, a wild and wanton pard,
Eyed like the evening star, with playful tail
Crouch'd fawning in the weed.  Most loving is she?
Ah me, my mountain shepherd, that my arms
Were wound about thee, and my hot lips prest
Close, close to thine in that quick-falling dew    200
Of fruitful kisses, thick as Autumn rains
Flash in the pools of whirling Simois.

"O mother, hear me yet before I die.
They came, they cut away my tallest pines,
My dark tall pines, that plumed the craggy ledge
High over the blue gorge, and all between
The snowy peak and snow-white cataract
Foster'd the callow eaglet—from beneath
Whose thick mysterious boughs in the dark morn
The panther's roar came muffled, while I sat    210
Low in the valley.  Never, never more

Shall lone Œnone see the morning mist
Sweep thro' them; never see them overlaid
With narrow moon-lit slips of silver cloud,
Between the loud stream and the trembling stars.

"O mother, hear me yet before I die.
I wish that somewhere in the ruin'd folds,
Among the fragments tumbled from the glens,
Or the dry thickets, I could meet with her,
The Abominable, that uninvited came                220
Into the fair Peleïan banquet-hall,
And cast the golden fruit upon the board,
And bred this change; that I might speak my mind
And tell her to her face how much I hate
Her presence, hated both of Gods and men.

"O mother, hear me yet before I die.
Hath he not sworn his love a thousand times,
In this green valley, under this green hill,
Ev'n on this hand, and sitting on this stone?
Seal'd it with kisses? water'd it with tears?      230
O happy tears, and how unlike to these!
O happy Heaven, how canst thou see my face?
O happy earth, how canst thou bear my weight?
O death, death, death, thou ever-floating cloud,
There are enough unhappy on this earth,
Pass by the happy souls, that love to live:
I pray thee, pass before my light of life,
And shadow all my soul, that I may die.
Thou weighest heavy on the heart within,
Weigh heavy on my eyelids: let me die.             240

"O mother, hear me yet before I die.
I will not die alone, for fiery thoughts
Do shape themselves within me, more and more,
Whereof I catch the issue, as I hear
Dead sounds at night come from the inmost hills,
Like footsteps upon wool. I dimly see
My far-off doubtful purpose, as a mother
Conjectures of the features of her child
Ere it is born: her child!—a shudder comes
Across me: never child be born of me,                    250
Unblest, to vex me with his father's eyes!

"O mother, hear me yet before I die.
Hear me, O earth. I will not die alone,
Lest their shrill happy laughter come to me
Walking the cold and starless road of Death
Uncomforted, leaving my ancient love
With the Greek woman. I will rise and go
Down into Troy, and ere the stars came forth
Talk with the wild Cassandra, for she says
A fire dances before her, and a sound         260
Rings ever in her ears of armed men:
What this may be I know not, but I know
That, wheresoe'er I am by night and day,
All earth and air seem only burning fire."

## THE PALACE OF ART

I built my soul a lordly pleasure-house,
    Wherein at ease for aye to dwell.
I said, "O Soul, make merry and carouse,
    Dear soul, for all is well."

A huge crag-platform, smooth as burnish'd brass,
    I chose. The ranged ramparts bright
From level meadow-bases of deep grass
    Suddenly scaled the light.

Thereon I built it firm. Of ledge or shelf
    The rock rose clear, or winding stair.                    10
My soul would live alone unto herself
    In her high palace there.

And "while the world runs round and round," I said,
    "Reign thou apart, a quiet king,
Still as, while Saturn whirls, his stedfast shade
    Sleeps on his luminous ring."

To which my soul made answer readily:
    "Trust me, in bliss I shall abide
In this great mansion, that is built for me,
    So royal-rich and wide."                    20

      \*     \*     \*     \*
      \*     \*     \*     \*

Four courts I made, East, West and South and North,
    In each a squared lawn, wherefrom
The golden gorge of dragons spouted forth
    A flood of fountain-foam.

And round the cool green courts there ran a row
    Of cloisters, branch'd like mighty woods,
Echoing all night to that sonorous flow
    Of spouted fountain-floods.

And round the roofs a gilded gallery
    That lent broad verge to distant lands,    30
Far as the wild swan wings, to where the sky
    Dipt down to sea and sands.

From those four jets four currents in one swell
    Across the mountain stream'd below
In misty folds, that floating as they fell
    Lit up a torrent-bow.

And high on every peak a statue seem'd
    To hang on tiptoe, tossing up
A cloud of incense of all odour steam'd
    From out a golden cup.    40

So that she thought, "And who shall gaze upon
    My palace with unblinded eyes,
While this great bow will waver in the sun,
    And that sweet incense rise?"

For that sweet incense rose and never fail'd,
    And, while day sank or mounted higher,
The light aërial gallery, golden-rail'd,
    Burnt like a fringe of fire.

Likewise the deep-set windows, stain'd and traced,
    Would seem slow-flaming crimson fires    50
From shadow'd grots of arches interlaced,
    And tipt with frost-like spires.

      *       *       *       *
      *       *       *       *

Full of long-sounding corridors it was,
    That over-vaulted grateful gloom,
Thro' which the livelong day my soul did pass,
    Well-pleased, from room to room.

Full of great rooms and small the palace stood,
    All various, each a perfect whole
From living Nature, fit for every mood
    And change of my still soul.        60

For some were hung with arras green and blue,
    Showing a gaudy summer-morn,
Where with puff'd cheek the belted hunter blew
    His wreathed bugle-horn.

One seem'd all dark and red—a tract of sand,
    And some one pacing there alone,
Who paced for ever in a glimmering land,
    Lit with a low large moon.

One show'd an iron coast and angry waves.
    You seem'd to hear them climb and fall        70
And roar rock-thwarted under bellowing caves,
    Beneath the windy wall.

And one, a full-fed river winding slow
    By herds upon an endless plain,
The ragged rims of thunder brooding low,
    With shadow-streaks of rain.

And one, the reapers at their sultry toil.
    In front they bound the sheaves. Behind
Were realms of upland, prodigal in oil,
    And hoary to the wind.        80

And one, a foreground black with stones and slags,
  Beyond, a line of heights, and higher
All barr'd with long white cloud the scornful crags,
  And highest, snow and fire.

And one, an English home—gray twilight pour'd,
  On dewy pastures, dewy trees,
Softer than sleep—all things in order stored,
  A haunt of ancient Peace.

Nor these alone, but every landscape fair,
  As fit for every mood of mind,                    90
Or gay, or grave, or sweet, or stern, was there,
  Not less than truth design'd.

    \*      \*      \*      \*
    \*      \*      \*      \*

Or the maid-mother by a crucifix,
  In tracts of pasture sunny-warm,
Beneath branch-work of costly sardonyx
  Sat smiling, babe in arm.

Or in a clear-wall'd city on the sea,
  Near gilded organ-pipes, her hair
Wound with white roses, slept St Cecily:
  An angel look'd at her.                           100

Or thronging all one porch of Paradise,
  A group of Houris bow'd to see
The dying Islamite, with hands and eyes
  That said, We wait for thee.

Or mythic Uther's deeply-wounded son
  In some fair space of sloping greens
Lay, dozing in the vale of Avalon,
  And watch'd by weeping queens.

L. T.                                                 5

Or hollowing one hand against his ear,
　　To list a foot-fall, ere he saw　　　　110
The wood-nymph, stay'd the Ausonian king to hear
　　Of wisdom and of law.

Or over hills with peaky tops engrail'd,
　　And many a tract of palm and rice,
The throne of Indian Cama slowly sail'd
　　A summer fann'd with spice.

Or sweet Europa's mantle blew unclasp'd,
　　From off her shoulder backward borne:
From one hand droop'd a crocus: one hand grasp'd
　　The mild bull's golden horn.　　　　120

Or else flush'd Ganymede, his rosy thigh
　　Half-buried in the Eagle's down,
Sole as a flying star shot thro' the sky
　　Above the pillar'd town.

Nor these alone: but every legend fair
　　Which the supreme Caucasian mind
Carved out of Nature for itself, was there,
　　Not less than life, design'd.

＊　　　＊　　　＊　　　＊

＊　　　＊　　　＊　　　＊

Then in the towers I placed great bells that swung,
　　Moved of themselves, with silver sound;　　130
And with choice paintings of wise men I hung
　　The royal daïs round.

For there was Milton like a seraph strong,
　　Beside him Shakespeare bland and mild;
And there the world-worn Dante grasp'd his song,
　　And somewhat grimly smiled.

And there the Ionian father of the rest;
   A million wrinkles carved his skin;
A hundred winters snow'd upon his breast,
    From cheek and throat and chin.      140

Above, the fair hall-ceiling stately-set
   Many an arch high up did lift,
And angels rising and descending met
    With interchange of gift.

Below was all mosaic choicely plann'd
   With cycles of the human tale
Of this wide world, the times of every land
    So wrought, they will not fail.

The people here, a beast of burden slow,
   Toil'd onward, prick'd with goads and stings;   150
Here play'd, a tiger, rolling to and fro
    The heads and crowns of kings;

Here rose, an athlete, strong to break or bind
   All force in bonds that might endure,
And here once more like some sick man declined,
    And trusted any cure.

But over these she trod: and those great bells
   Began to chime. She took her throne:
She sat betwixt the shining Oriels,
    To sing her songs alone.      160

And thro' the topmost Oriels' colour'd flame
   Two godlike faces gazed below;
Plato the wise, and large-brow'd Verulam,
    The first of those who know.

And all those names, that in their motion were
  Full-welling fountain-heads of change,
Betwixt the slender shafts were blazon'd fair
    In diverse raiment strange:

Thro' which the lights, rose, amber, emerald, blue, 170
  Flush'd in her temples and her eyes,
And from her lips, as morn from Memnon, drew
    Rivers of melodies.

No nightingale delighteth to prolong
  Her low preamble all alone,
More than my soul to hear her echo'd song
    Throb thro' the ribbed stone;

Singing and murmuring in her feastful mirth,
  Joying to feel herself alive, 180
Lord over Nature, Lord of the visible earth,
    Lord of the senses five;

Communing with herself: "All these are mine,
  And let the world have peace or wars,
'Tis one to me." She—when young night divine
    Crown'd dying day with stars,

Making sweet close of his delicious toils—
  Lit light in wreaths and anadems,
And pure quintessences of precious oils
    In hollow'd moons of gems, 190

To mimic heaven; and clapt her hands and cried,
  "I marvel if my still delight
In this great house so royal-rich, and wide,
    Be flatter'd to the height.

"O all things fair to sate my various eyes!
  O shapes and hues that please me well!
O silent faces of the Great and Wise,
    My Gods, with whom I dwell!

"O God-like isolation which art mine,
  I can but count thee perfect gain,      200
What time I watch the darkening droves of swine
    That range on yonder plain.

"In filthy sloughs they roll a prurient skin,
  They graze and wallow, breed and sleep;
And oft some brainless devil enters in,
    And drives them to the deep."

Then of the moral instinct would she prate,
  And of the rising from the dead,
As hers by right of full-accomplished Fate;
    And at the last she said:      210

"I take possession of man's mind and deed.
  I care not what the sects may brawl.
I sit as God holding no form of creed,
    But contemplating all."

    *       *       *       *
    *       *       *       *

Full oft the riddle of the painful earth
  Flash'd thro' her as she sat alone,
Yet not the less held she her solemn mirth,
    And intellectual throne.

And so she throve and prosper'd: so three years
  She prosper'd: on the fourth she fell,      220
Like Herod, when the shout was in his ears,
    Struck thro' with pangs of hell.

Lest she should fail and perish utterly,
  God, before whom ever lie bare
The abysmal deeps of Personality,
    Plagued her with sore despair.

When she would think, where'er she turn'd her sight,
  The airy hand confusion wrought,
Wrote "Mene, mene," and divided quite
    The kingdom of her thought.               230

Deep dread and loathing of her solitude
  Fell on her, from which mood was born
Scorn of herself; again, from out that mood
    Laughter at her self-scorn.

"What! is not this my place of strength," she said,
  "My spacious mansion built for me,
Whereof the strong foundation-stones were laid
    Since my first memory?"

But in dark corners of her palace stood
  Uncertain shapes; and unawares           240
On white-eyed phantasms weeping tears of blood,
    And horrible nightmares,

And hollow shades enclosing hearts of flame,
  And, with dim fretted foreheads all,
On corpses three-months-old at noon she came,
    That stood against the wall.

A spot of dull stagnation, without light
  Or power of movement, seem'd my soul,
'Mid onward-sloping motions infinite
    Making for one sure goal.                250

A still salt pool, lock'd in with bars of sand;
   Left on the shore; that hears all night
The plunging seas draw backward from the land
    Their moon-led waters white.

A star that with the choral starry dance
   Join'd not, but stood, and standing saw
The hollow orb of moving Circumstance
    Roll'd round by one fix'd law.

Back on herself her serpent pride had curl'd.
   "No voice," she shriek'd in that lone hall,   260
"No voice breaks thro' the stillness of this world:
    One deep, deep silence all!"

She, mouldering with the dull earth's mouldering sod,
   Inwrapt tenfold in slothful shame,
Lay there exiled from eternal God,
    Lost to her place and name;

And death and life she hated equally,
   And nothing saw, for her despair,
But dreadful time, dreadful eternity,
    No comfort anywhere;    270

Remaining utterly confused with fears,
   And ever worse with growing time,
And ever unrelieved by dismal tears,
    And all alone in crime:

Shut up as in a crumbling tomb, girt round
   With blackness as a solid wall,
Far off she seem'd to hear the dully sound
    Of human footsteps fall.

As in strange lands a traveller walking slow,
  In doubt and great perplexity,                    280
A little before moon-rise hears the low
  Moan of an unknown sea;

And knows not if it be thunder or a sound
  Of rocks thrown down, or one deep cry
Of great wild beasts; then thinketh, "I have found
  A new land, but I die."

She howl'd aloud, "I am on fire within.
  There comes no murmur of reply.
What is it that will take away my sin,
  And save me lest I die?"                          290

So when four years were wholly finished,
  She threw her royal robes away.
"Make me a cottage in the vale," she said,
  "Where I may mourn and pray.

"Yet pull not down my palace towers, that are
  So lightly, beautifully built:
Perchance I may return with others there
  When I have purged my guilt."


## LADY CLARA VERE DE VERE

Lady Clara Vere de Vere,
  Of me you shall not win renown:
You thought to break a country heart
  For pastime, ere you went to town.
At me you smiled, but unbeguiled
  I saw the snare, and I retired:
The daughter of a hundred Earls,
  You are not one to be desired.

Lady Clara Vere de Vere,
  I know you proud to bear your name,     10
Your pride is yet no mate for mine,
  Too proud to care from whence I came.
Nor would I break for your sweet sake
  A heart that doats on truer charms.
A simple maiden in her flower
  Is worth a hundred coats-of-arms.

Lady Clara Vere de Vere,
  Some meeker pupil you must find,
For were you queen of all that is,
  I could not stoop to such a mind.     20
You sought to prove how I could love,
  And my disdain is my reply.
The lion on your old stone gates
  Is not more cold to you than I.

Lady Clara Vere de Vere,
  You put strange memories in my head.
Not thrice your branching limes have blown
  Since I beheld young Laurence dead.
Oh your sweet eyes, your low replies:
  A great enchantress you may be;     30
But there was that across his throat
  Which you had hardly cared to see.

Lady Clara Vere de Vere,
  When thus he met his mother's view,
She had the passions of her kind,
  She spake some certain truths of you.
Indeed I heard one bitter word
  That scarce is fit for you to hear;
Her manners had not that repose
  Which stamps the caste of Vere de Vere.     40

Lady Clara Vere de Vere,
  There stands a spectre in your hall:
The guilt of blood is at your door:
  You changed a wholesome heart to gall.
You held your course without remorse,
  To make him trust his modest worth,
And, last, you fix'd a vacant stare,
  And slew him with your noble birth.

Trust me, Clara Vere de Vere,
  From yon blue heavens above us bent          50
The grand old gardener and his wife
  Smile at the claims of long descent.
Howe'er it be, it seems to me,
  'Tis only noble to be good.
Kind hearts are more than coronets,
  And simple faith than Norman blood.

I know you, Clara Vere de Vere:
  You pine among your halls and towers:
The languid light of your proud eyes
  Is wearied of the rolling hours.          60
In glowing health, with boundless wealth,
  But sickening of a vague disease,
You know so ill to deal with time,
  You needs must play such pranks as these.

Clara, Clara Vere de Vere,
  If Time be heavy on your hands,
Are there no beggars at your gate,
  Nor any poor about your lands?
Oh! teach the orphan-boy to read,
  Or teach the orphan-girl to sew,          70
Pray Heaven for a human heart,
  And let the foolish yeoman go.

# THE LOTOS-EATERS

"Courage!" he said, and pointed toward the land,
"This mounting wave will roll us shoreward soon."
In the afternoon they came unto a land,
In which it seemed always afternoon.
All round the coast the languid air did swoon,
Breathing like one that hath a weary dream.
Full-faced above the valley stood the moon;
And like a downward smoke, the slender stream
Along the cliff to fall and pause and fall did seem.

A land of streams! some, like a downward smoke,   10
Slow-dropping veils of thinnest lawn, did go;
And some thro' wavering lights and shadows broke,
Rolling a slumbrous sheet of foam below.
They saw the gleaming river seaward flow
From the inner land: far off, three mountain-tops,
Three silent pinnacles of aged snow,
Stood sunset-flush'd: and, dew'd with showery drops,
Up-clomb the shadowy pine above the woven copse.

The charmed sunset linger'd low adown
In the red West: thro' mountain clefts the dale   20
Was seen far inland, and the yellow down
Border'd with palm, and many a winding vale
And meadow, set with slender galingale;
A land where all things always seem'd the same!
And round about the keel with faces pale,
Dark faces pale against that rosy flame,
The mild-eyed melancholy Lotos-eaters came.

Branches they bore of that enchanted stem,
Laden with flower and fruit, whereof they gave
To each, but whoso did receive of them,                    30
And taste, to him the gushing of the wave
Far far away did seem to mourn and rave
On alien shores; and if his fellow spake,
His voice was thin, as voices from the grave;
And deep-asleep he seem'd, yet all awake,
And music in his ears his beating heart did make.

They sat them down upon the yellow sand,
Between the sun and moon upon the shore;
And sweet it was to dream of Fatherland,
Of child, and wife, and slave; but evermore          40
Most weary seem'd the sea, weary the oar,
Weary the wandering fields of barren foam.
Then some one said, "We will return no more;"
And all at once they sang, "Our island home
Is far beyond the wave; we will no longer roam."

## CHORIC SONG

There is sweet music here that softer falls
Than petals from blown roses on the grass,
Or night-dews on still waters between walls
Of shadowy granite, in a gleaming pass;
Music that gentlier on the spirit lies,              50
Than tir'd eyelids upon tir'd eyes;
Music that brings sweet sleep down from the blissful
    skies.
Here are cool mosses deep,
And thro' the moss the ivies creep,
And in the stream the long-leaved flowers weep,
And from the craggy ledge the poppy hangs in sleep.

Why are we weigh'd upon with heaviness,
And utterly consumed with sharp distress,
While all things else have rest from weariness?
All things have rest: why should we toil alone,          60
We only toil, who are the first of things,
And make perpetual moan,
Still from one sorrow to another thrown:
Nor ever fold our wings,
And cease from wanderings,
Nor steep our brows in slumber's holy balm;
Nor harken what the inner spirit sings,
"There is no joy but calm!"
Why should we only toil, the roof and crown of things?

Lo! in the middle of the wood,                           70
The folded leaf is woo'd from out the bud
With winds upon the branch, and there
Grows green and broad, and takes no care,
Sun-steep'd at noon, and in the moon
Nightly dew-fed; and turning yellow
Falls, and floats adown the air.
Lo! sweeten'd with the summer light,
The full-juiced apple, waxing over-mellow,
Drops in a silent autumn night.
All its allotted length of days,                         80
The flower ripens in its place,
Ripens and fades, and falls, and hath no toil,
Fast-rooted in the fruitful soil.

Hateful is the dark-blue sky,
Vaulted o'er the dark-blue sea.
Death is the end of life; ah, why
Should life all labour be?

Let us alone. Time driveth onward fast,
And in a little while our lips are dumb.
Let us alone. What is it that will last?                    90
All things are taken from us, and become
Portions and parcels of the dreadful Past.
Let us alone. What pleasure can we have
To war with evil? Is there any peace
In ever climbing up the climbing wave?
All things have rest, and ripen toward the grave
In silence; ripen, fall and cease:
Give us long rest or death, dark death, or dreamful
     ease.

How sweet it were, hearing the downward stream,
With half-shut eyes ever to seem                          100
Falling asleep in a half-dream!
To dream and dream, like yonder amber light,
Which will not leave the myrrh-bush on the height;
To hear each other's whisper'd speech;
Eating the Lotos day by day,
To watch the crisping ripples on the beach,
And tender curving lines of creamy spray;
To lend our hearts and spirits wholly
To the influence of mild-minded melancholy;
To muse and brood and live again in memory,     110
With those old faces of our infancy
Heap'd over with a mound of grass,
Two handfuls of white dust, shut in an urn of brass!

Dear is the memory of our wedded lives,
And dear the last embraces of our wives
And their warm tears: but all hath suffer'd change;
For surely now our household hearths are cold:
Our sons inherit us: our looks are strange:

And we should come like ghosts to trouble joy.
Or else the island princes over-bold 120
Have eat our substance, and the minstrel sings
Before them of the ten-years' war in Troy,
And our great deeds, as half-forgotten things.
Is there confusion in the little isle?
Let what is broken so remain.
The Gods are hard to reconcile:
'Tis hard to settle order once again.
There *is* confusion worse than death,
Trouble on trouble, pain on pain,
Long labour unto aged breath, 130
Sore task to hearts worn out with many wars
And eyes grown dim with gazing on the pilot-stars.

But, propt on beds of amaranth and moly,
How sweet (while warm airs lull us, blowing lowly)
With half-dropt eyelids still,
Beneath a heaven dark and holy,
To watch the long bright river drawing slowly
His waters from the purple hill—
To hear the dewy echoes calling
From cave to cave thro' the thick-twined vine— 140
To watch the emerald-colour'd water falling
Thro' many a wov'n acanthus-wreath divine!
Only to hear and see the far-off sparkling brine,
Only to hear were sweet, stretch'd out beneath the pine.

The Lotos blooms below the barren peak:
The Lotos blows by every winding creek:
All day the wind breathes low with mellower tone:
Thro' every hollow cave and alley lone
Round and round the spicy downs the yellow Lotos-
    dust is blown.
We have had enough of action, and of motion we, 150

Roll'd to starboard, roll'd to larboard, when the surge
    was seething free,
Where the wallowing monster spouted his foam-
    fountains in the sea.
Let us swear an oath, and keep it with an equal mind,
In the hollow Lotos-land to live and lie reclined
On the hills like Gods together, careless of mankind.
For they lie beside their nectar, and the bolts are hurl'd
Far below them in the valleys, and the clouds are
    lightly curl'd
Round their golden houses, girdled with the gleaming
    world:
Where they smile in secret, looking over wasted lands,
Blight and famine, plague and earthquake, roaring
    deeps and fiery sands, 160
Clanging fights, and flaming towns, and sinking ships,
    and praying hands.
But they smile, they find a music centred in a doleful
    song
Steaming up, a lamentation and an ancient tale of
    wrong,
Like a tale of little meaning tho' the words are strong;
Chanted from an ill-used race of men that cleave the
    soil,
Sow the seed, and reap the harvest with enduring toil,
Storing yearly little dues of wheat, and wine and oil;
Till they perish and they suffer—some, 'tis whisper'd—
    down in hell
Suffer endless anguish, others in Elysian valleys dwell,
Resting weary limbs at last on beds of asphodel. 170
Surely, surely, slumber is more sweet than toil, the shore
Than labour in the deep mid-ocean, wind and wave
    and oar;
Oh rest ye, brother mariners, we will not wander more.

## A DREAM OF FAIR WOMEN

I read, before my eyelids dropt their shade,
  "*The Legend of Good Women,*" long ago
Sung by the morning star of song, who made
  His music heard below;

Dan Chaucer, the first warbler, whose sweet breath
  Preluded those melodious bursts, that fill
The spacious times of great Elizabeth
  With sounds that echo still.

And, for a while, the knowledge of his art
  Held me above the subject, as strong gales     10
Hold swollen clouds from raining, tho' my heart,
  Brimful of those wild tales,

Charged both mine eyes with tears. In every land
  I saw, wherever light illumineth,
Beauty and anguish walking hand in hand
  The downward slope to death.

Those far-renowned brides of ancient song
  Peopled the hollow dark, like burning stars,
And I heard sounds of insult, shame, and wrong,
  And trumpets blown for wars;     20

And clattering flints batter'd with clanging hoofs:
  And I saw crowds in column'd sanctuaries;
And forms that pass'd at windows and on roofs
  Of marble palaces;

Corpses across the threshold; heroes tall
    Dislodging pinnacle and parapet
Upon the tortoise creeping to the wall;
    Lances in ambush set;

And high shrine-doors burst thro' with heated blasts
    That run before the fluttering tongues of fire; 30
White surf wind-scatter'd over sails and masts,
    And ever climbing higher;

Squadrons and squares of men in brazen plates,
    Scaffolds, still sheets of water, divers woes,
Ranges of glimmering vaults with iron grates,
    And hush'd seraglios.

So shape chased shape as swift as, when to land
    Bluster the winds and tides the self-same way,
Crisp foam-flakes scud along the level sand,
    Torn from the fringe of spray.        40

I started once, or seem'd to start in pain,
    Resolved on noble things, and strove to speak,
As when a great thought strikes along the brain,
    And flushes all the cheek.

And once my arm was lifted to hew down
    A cavalier from off his saddle-bow,
That bore a lady from a leaguer'd town;
    And then, I know not how,

All those sharp fancies, by down-lapsing thought
    Stream'd onward, lost their edges, and did creep 50
Roll'd on each other, rounded, smooth'd, and brought
    Into the gulfs of sleep.

At last methought that I had wander'd far
    In an old wood: fresh-wash'd in coolest dew,
The maiden splendours of the morning star
    Shook in the steadfast blue.

Enormous elmtree-boles did stoop and lean
    Upon the dusky brushwood underneath
Their broad curved branches, fledged with clearest green,
    New from its silken sheath.       60

The dim red morn had died, her journey done,
    And with dead lips smiled at the twilight plain,
Half-fall'n across the threshold of the sun,
    Never to rise again.

There was no motion in the dumb dead air,
    Not any song of bird or sound of rill;
Gross darkness of the inner sepulchre
    Is not so deadly still

As that wide forest.  Growths of jasmine turn'd
    Their humid arms festooning tree to tree,    70
And at the root thro' lush green grasses burn'd
    The red anemone.

I knew the flowers, I knew the leaves, I knew
    The tearful glimmer of the languid dawn
On those long, rank, dark wood-walks drench'd in dew,
    Leading from lawn to lawn.

The smell of violets, hidden in the green,
    Pour'd back into my empty soul and frame
The times when I remember to have been
    Joyful and free from blame.    80

And from within me a clear under-tone
    Thrill'd thro' mine ears in that unblissful clime
"Pass freely thro': the wood is all thine own,
    Until the end of time."

At length I saw a lady within call,
    Stiller than chisell'd marble, standing there;
A daughter of the gods, divinely tall,
    And most divinely fair.

Her loveliness with shame and with surprise
    Froze my swift speech: she turning on my face   90
The star-like sorrows of immortal eyes,
    Spoke slowly in her place.

"I had great beauty: ask thou not my name:
    No one can be more wise than destiny.
Many drew swords and died. Where'er I came
    I brought calamity."

"No marvel, sovereign lady: in fair field
    Myself for such a face had boldly died,"
I answer'd free; and turning I appeal'd
    To one that stood beside.              100

But she, with sick and scornful looks averse,
    To her full height her stately stature draws;
"My youth," she said, "was blasted with a curse:
    This woman was the cause.

"I was cut off from hope in that sad place,
    Which yet to name my spirit loathes and fears:
My father held his hand upon his face;
    I, blinded with my tears,

"Still strove to speak: my voice was thick with sighs
    As in a dream.  Dimly I could descry    110
The stern black-bearded kings with wolfish eyes,
    Waiting to see me die.

"The high masts flicker'd as they lay afloat;
    The crowds, the temples, waver'd, and the shore;
The bright death quiver'd at the victim's throat;
    Touch'd; and I knew no more."

Whereto the other with a downward brow:
    "I would the white cold heavy-plunging foam,
Whirl'd by the wind, had roll'd me deep below,
    Then when I left my home."    120

Her slow full words sank thro' the silence drear,
    As thunder-drops fall on a sleeping sea:
Sudden I heard a voice that cried, "Come here,
    That I may look on thee."

I turning saw, throned on a flowery rise,
    One sitting on a crimson scarf unroll'd;
A queen, with swarthy cheeks and bold black eyes,
    Brow-bound with burning gold.

She, flashing forth a haughty smile, began:
    "I govern'd men by change, and so I sway'd    130
All moods. 'Tis long since I have seen a man.
    Once, like the moon, I made

"The ever-shifting currents of the blood
    According to my humour ebb and flow.
I have no men to govern in this wood:
    That makes my only woe.

"Nay—yet it chafes me that I could not bend
    One will; nor tame and tutor with mine eye
That dull cold-blooded Cæsar.  Prythee, friend,
    Where is Mark Antony?                                    140

"The man, my lover, with whom I rode sublime
    On Fortune's neck: we sat as God by God:
The Nilus would have risen before his time
    And flooded at our nod.

"We drank the Libyan Sun to sleep, and lit
    Lamps which outburn'd Canopus.  O my life
In Egypt!  O the dalliance and the wit,
    The flattery and the strife,

"And the wild kiss, when fresh from war's alarms,
    My Hercules, my Roman Antony,                            150
My mailed Bacchus leapt into my arms,
    Contented there to die!

"And there he died: and when I heard my name
    Sigh'd forth with life I would not brook my fear
Of the other: with a worm I balk'd his fame.
    What else was left? look here!"

(With that she tore her robe apart, and half
    The polish'd argent of her breast to sight
Laid bare.  Thereto she pointed with a laugh,
    Showing the aspick's bite)                               160

"I died a Queen.  The Roman soldier found
    Me lying dead, my crown about my brows,
A name for ever!—lying robed and crown'd,
    Worthy a Roman spouse."

Her warbling voice, a lyre of widest range
    Struck by all passion, did fall down and glance
From tone to tone, and glided thro' all change
    Of liveliest utterance.

When she made pause I knew not for delight;
    Because with sudden motion from the ground   170
She raised her piercing orbs, and fill'd with light
    The interval of sound.

Still with their fires Love tipt his keenest darts;
    As once they drew into two burning rings
All beams of Love, melting the mighty hearts
    Of captains and of kings.

Slowly my sense undazzled. Then I heard
    A noise of some one coming thro' the lawn,
And singing clearer than the crested bird,
    That claps his wings at dawn.     180

"The torrent brooks of hallow'd Israel
    From craggy hollows pouring, late and soon,
Sound all night long, in falling thro' the dell,
    Far-heard beneath the moon.

"The balmy moon of blessed Israel
    Floods all the deep-blue gloom with beams divine:
All night the splinter'd crags that wall the dell
    With spires of silver shine."

As one that museth where broad sunshine laves
    The lawn by some cathedral, thro' the door   190
Hearing the holy organ rolling waves
    Of sound on roof and floor

Within, and anthem sung, is charm'd and tied
    To where he stands,—so stood I, when that flow
Of music left the lips of her that died
    To save her father's vow;

The daughter of the warrior Gileadite,
    A maiden pure; as when she went along
From Mizpeh's tower'd gate with welcome light,
    With timbrel and with song.       200

My words leapt forth: "Heaven heads the count of
      crimes
    With that wild oath."    She render'd answer high:
"Not so, nor once alone; a thousand times
    I would be born and die.

"Single I grew, like some green plant, whose root
    Creeps to the garden water-pipes beneath,
Feeding the flower; but ere my flower to fruit
    Changed, I was ripe for death.

"My God, my land, my father—these did move
    Me from my bliss of life, that Nature gave,   210
Lower'd softly with a threefold cord of love
    Down to a silent grave.

"And I went mourning, 'No fair Hebrew boy
    Shall smile away my maiden blame among
The Hebrew mothers'—emptied of all joy,
    Leaving the dance and song,

"Leaving the olive-gardens far below,
    Leaving the promise of my bridal bower,
The valleys of grape-loaded vines that glow
    Beneath the battled tower.      220

"The light white cloud swam over us. Anon
   We heard the lion roaring from his den;
We saw the large white stars rise one by one,
   Or, from the darken'd glen,

"Saw God divide the night with flying flame,
   And thunder on the everlasting hills.
I heard Him, for He spake, and grief became
   A solemn scorn of ills.

"When the next moon was roll'd into the sky,
   Strength came to me that equall'd my desire.   230
How beautiful a thing it was to die
   For God and for my sire!

"It comforts me in this one thought to dwell,
   That I subdued me to my father's will;
Because the kiss he gave me, ere I fell,
   Sweetens the spirit still.

"Moreover it is written that my race
   Hew'd Ammon, hip and thigh, from Aroer
On Arnon unto Minneth." Here her face
   Glow'd, as I look'd at her.                     240

She lock'd her lips: she left me where I stood:
   "Glory to God," she sang, and past afar,
Thridding the sombre boskage of the wood,
   Toward the morning-star.

Losing her carol I stood pensively,
   As one that from a casement leans his head,
When midnight bells cease ringing suddenly,
   And the old year is dead.

"Alas! alas!" a low voice, full of care,
Murmur'd beside me: "Turn and look on me: 250
I am that Rosamond, whom men call fair,
If what I was I be.

"Would I had been some maiden coarse and poor!
O me, that I should ever see the light!
Those dragon eyes of anger'd Eleanor
Do hunt me, day and night."

She ceased in tears, fallen from hope and trust:
To whom the Egyptian: "O, you tamely died!
You should have clung to Fulvia's waist, and thrust
The dagger thro' her side." 260

With that sharp sound the white dawn's creeping beams,
Stol'n to my brain, dissolved the mystery
Of folded sleep. The captain of my dreams
Ruled in the eastern sky.

Morn broaden'd on the borders of the dark,
Ere I saw her, who clasp'd in her last trance
Her murder'd father's head, or Joan of Arc,
A light of ancient France;

Or her, who knew that Love can vanquish Death,
Who kneeling, with one arm about her king, 270
Drew forth the poison with her balmy breath,
Sweet as new buds in Spring.

No memory labours longer from the deep
Gold-mines of thought to lift the hidden ore
That glimpses, moving up, than I from sleep
To gather and tell o'er

Each little sound and sight. With what dull pain
   Compass'd, how eagerly I sought to strike
Into that wondrous track of dreams again!
   But no two dreams are like.      280

As when a soul laments, which hath been blest,
   Desiring what is mingled with past years,
In yearnings that can never be exprest
   By signs or groans or tears;

Because all words, tho' cull'd with choicest art,
   Failing to give the bitter of the sweet,
Wither beneath the palate, and the heart
   Faints, faded by its heat.


## THE BLACKBIRD

O Blackbird! sing me something well:
   While all the neighbours shoot thee round,
   I keep smooth plats of fruitful ground,
Where thou may'st warble, eat and dwell.

The espaliers and the standards all
   Are thine; the range of lawn and park:
   The unnetted black-hearts ripen dark,
All thine, against the garden wall.

Yet, tho' I spared thee all the spring,
   Thy sole delight is, sitting still,      10
   With that gold dagger of thy bill
To fret the summer jenneting.

A golden bill! the silver tongue,
   Cold February loved, is dry:
   Plenty corrupts the melody
That made thee famous once, when young:

And in the sultry garden-squares,
    Now thy flute-notes are changed to coarse,
    I hear thee not at all, or hoarse
As when a hawker hawks his wares.          20

Take warning! he that will not sing
    While yon sun prospers in the blue,
    Shall sing for want, ere leaves are new,
Caught in the frozen palms of Spring.


### FREEDOM

Of old sat Freedom on the heights,
    The thunders breaking at her feet:
Above her shook the starry lights:
    She heard the torrents meet.

There in her place she did rejoice,
    Self-gather'd in her prophet-mind,
But fragments of her mighty voice
    Came rolling on the wind.

Then stept she down thro' town and field
    To mingle with the human race,          10
And part by part to men reveal'd
    The fullness of her face—

Grave mother of majestic works,
    From her isle-altar gazing down,
Who, God-like, grasps the triple forks,
    And, King-like, wears the crown:

Her open eyes desire the truth.
    The wisdom of a thousand years
Is in them. May perpetual youth
    Keep dry their light from tears;          20

That her fair form may stand and shine,
    Make bright our days and light our dreams,
Turning to scorn with lips divine
    The falsehood of extremes!


## MORTE D'ARTHUR

So all day long the noise of battle roll'd
Among the mountains by the winter sea;
Until King Arthur's table, man by man,
Had fall'n in Lyonness about their Lord,
King Arthur: then, because his wound was deep,
The bold Sir Bedivere uplifted him,
Sir Bedivere, the last of all his knights,
And bore him to a chapel nigh the field,
A broken chancel with a broken cross,
That stood on a dark strait of barren land.          10
On one side lay the Ocean, and on one
Lay a great water, and the moon was full.
    Then spake King Arthur to Sir Bedivere:
"The sequel of to-day unsolders all
The goodliest fellowship of famous knights
Whereof this world holds record. Such a sleep
They sleep—the men I loved. I think that we
Shall never more, at any future time,
Delight our souls with talk of knightly deeds,
Walking about the gardens and the halls          20
Of Camelot, as in the days that were.
I perish by this people which I made,—
Tho' Merlin sware that I should come again
To rule once more—but let what will be, be,
I am so deeply smitten thro' the helm
That without help I cannot last till morn.

Thou therefore take my brand Excalibur,
Which was my pride: for thou rememberest how
In those old days, one summer noon, an arm
Rose up from out the bosom of the lake,    30
Clothed in white samite, mystic, wonderful,
Holding the sword—and how I row'd across
And took it, and have worn it, like a king:
And, wheresoever I am sung or told
In aftertime, this also shall be known:
But now delay not: take Excalibur,
And fling him far into the middle mere:
Watch what thou seëst, and lightly bring me word."

    To him replied the bold Sir Bedivere:
"It is not meet, Sir King, to leave thee thus,    40
Aidless, alone, and smitten thro' the helm—
A little thing may harm a wounded man.
Yet I thy hest will all perform at full,
Watch what I see, and lightly bring thee word."

    So saying, from the ruin'd shrine he stept
And in the moon athwart the place of tombs,
Where lay the mighty bones of ancient men,
Old knights, and over them the sea-wind sang
Shrill, chill, with flakes of foam. He, stepping down
By zig-zag paths, and juts of pointed rock,    50
Came on the shining levels of the lake.

    There drew he forth the brand Excalibur,
And o'er him, drawing it, the winter moon,
Brightening the skirts of a long cloud, ran forth
And sparkled keen with frost against the hilt:
For all the haft twinkled with diamond studs,
Myriads of topaz-lights, and jacinth-work
Of subtlest jewellery. He gazed so long
That both his eyes were dazzled, as he stood,

This way and that dividing the swift mind, 60
In act to throw: but at the last it seem'd
Better to leave Excalibur conceal'd
There in the many-knotted waterflags,
That whistled stiff and dry about the marge.
So strode he back slow to the wounded king.
  Then spake King Arthur to Sir Bedivere:
"Hast thou perform'd my mission which I gave?
What is it thou hast seen? or what hast heard?"
  And answer made the bold Sir Bedivere:
"I heard the ripple washing in the reeds, 70
And the wild water lapping on the crag."
  To whom replied King Arthur, faint and pale:
"Thou hast betray'd thy nature and thy name,
Not rendering true answer, as beseem'd
Thy fëalty, nor like a noble knight:
For surer sign had follow'd, either hand,
Or voice, or else a motion of the mere.
This is a shameful thing for men to lie.
Yet now, I charge thee, quickly go again
As thou art lief and dear, and do the thing 80
I bad thee, watch, and lightly bring me word."
  Then went Sir Bedivere the second time
Across the ridge, and paced beside the mere,
Counting the dewy pebbles, fix'd in thought;
But when he saw the wonder of the hilt,
How curiously and strangely chased, he smote
His palms together, and he cried aloud.
  "And if indeed I cast the brand away,
Surely a precious thing, one worthy note,
Should thus be lost for ever from the earth, 90
Which might have pleased the eyes of many men.
What good should follow this, if this were done?
What harm, undone? deep harm to disobey,

Seeing obedience is the bond of rule.
Were it well to obey then, if a king demand
An act unprofitable, against himself?
The King is sick, and knows not what he does.
What record, or what relic of my lord
Should be to aftertime, but empty breath
And rumours of a doubt? but were this kept,    100
Stored in some treasure-house of mighty kings,
Some one might show it at a joust of arms,
Saying, 'King Arthur's sword, Excalibur,
Wrought by the lonely maiden of the Lake.
Nine years she wrought it, sitting in the deeps
Upon the hidden bases of the hills.'
So might some old man speak in the aftertime
To all the people, winning reverence.
But now much honour and much fame were lost."

    So spake he, clouded with his own conceit,    110
And hid Excalibur the second time,
And so strode back slow to the wounded King.
    Then spoke King Arthur, breathing heavily:
"What is it thou hast seen? or what hast heard?"
    And answer made the bold Sir Bedivere:
"I heard the water lapping on the crag,
And the long ripple washing in the reeds."
    To whom replied King Arthur, much in wrath:
"Ah, miserable and unkind, untrue,
Unknightly, traitor-hearted! Woe is me!    120
Authority forgets a dying king,
Laid widow'd of the power in his eye
That bow'd the will. I see thee what thou art,
For thou, the latest-left of all my knights,
In whom should meet the offices of all,
Thou wouldst betray me for the precious hilt;
Either from lust of gold, or like a girl

Valuing the giddy pleasure of the eyes.
Yet, for a man may fail in duty twice,
And the third time may prosper, get thee hence: 130
But, if thou spare to fling Excalibur,
I will arise and slay thee with my hands."
   Then quickly rose Sir Bedivere, and ran,
And, leaping down the ridges lightly, plunged
Among the bulrush-beds, and clutch'd the sword,
And strongly wheel'd and threw it. The great brand
Made lightnings in the splendour of the moon,
And flashing round and round, and whirl'd in an arch,
Shot like a streamer of the northern morn,
Seen where the moving isles of winter shock      140
By night, with noises of the northern sea.
So flash'd and fell the brand Excalibur:
But ere he dipt the surface, rose an arm
Clothed in white samite, mystic, wonderful,
And caught him by the hilt, and brandish'd him
Three times, and drew him under in the mere.
And lightly went the other to the King.
   Then spoke King Arthur, drawing thicker breath:
"Now see I by thine eyes that this is done.
Speak out: what is it thou hast heard, or seen?" 150
   And answer made the bold Sir Bedivere:
"Sir King, I closed mine eyelids, lest the gems
Should blind my purpose, for I never saw,
Nor shall see, here or elsewhere, till I die,
Not tho' I live three lives of mortal men,
So great a miracle as yonder hilt.
Then with both hands I flung him, wheeling him;
But when I look'd again, behold an arm,
Clothed in white samite, mystic, wonderful,
That caught him by the hilt, and brandish'd him 160

Three times, and drew him under in the mere."
 And answer made King Arthur, breathing hard:
"My end draws nigh; 'tis time that I were gone.
Make broad thy shoulders to receive my weight,
And bear me to the margin; yet I fear
My wound hath taken cold, and I shall die."
 So saying, from the pavement he half rose,
Slowly, with pain, reclining on his arm,
And looking wistfully with wide blue eyes
As in a picture. Him Sir Bedivere                    170
Remorsefully regarded thro' his tears,
And would have spoken, but he found not words,
Then took with care, and kneeling on one knee,
O'er both his shoulders drew the languid hands,
And rising bore him thro' the place of tombs.
 But, as he walk'd, King Arthur panted hard,
Like one that feels a nightmare on his bed
When all the house is mute. So sigh'd the King,
Muttering and murmuring at his ear "Quick, quick!
I fear it is too late, and I shall die."               180
But the other swiftly strode from ridge to ridge,
Clothed with his breath, and looking, as he walk'd,
Larger than human on the frozen hills.
He heard the deep behind him, and a cry
Before. His own thought drove him like a goad.
Dry clash'd his harness in the icy caves
And barren chasms, and all to left and right
The bare black cliff clang'd round him, as he based
His feet on juts of slippery crag that rang
Sharp-smitten with the dint of armed heels—          190
And on a sudden, lo! the level lake,
And the long glories of the winter moon.
 Then saw they how there hove a dusky barge,

Dark as a funeral scarf from stem to stern,
Beneath them; and descending they were ware
That all the decks were dense with stately forms
Black-stoled, black-hooded, like a dream—by these
Three Queens with crowns of gold—and from them rose
A cry that shiver'd to the tingling stars,
And, as it were one voice, an agony  200
Of lamentation, like a wind, that shrills
All night in a waste land, where no one comes,
Or hath come, since the making of the world.
 Then murmur'd Arthur, "Place me in the barge,"
And to the barge they came. There those three Queens
Put forth their hands, and took the King, and wept.
But she, that rose the tallest of them all
And fairest, laid his head upon her lap,
And loosed the shatter'd casque, and chafed his hands,
And call'd him by his name, complaining loud, 210
And dropping bitter tears against his brow
Striped with dark blood: for all his face was white
And colourless, and like the wither'd moon
Smote by the fresh beam of the springing east;
And all his greaves and cuisses dash'd with drops
Of onset; and the light and lustrous curls—
That made his forehead like a rising sun
High from the daïs-throne—were parch'd with dust;
Or, clotted into points and hanging loose,
Mix'd with the knightly growth that fringed his lips. 220
So like a shatter'd column lay the King;
Not like that Arthur who, with lance in rest,
From spur to plume a star of tournament,
Shot thro' the lists at Camelot, and charged
Before the eyes of ladies and of kings.
 Then loudly cried the bold Sir Bedivere,

7—2

"Ah! my Lord Arthur, whither shall I go?
Where shall I hide my forehead and my eyes?
For now I see the true old times are dead,
When every morning brought a noble chance,     230
And every chance brought out a noble knight.
Such times have been not since the light that led
The holy Elders with the gift of myrrh.
But now the whole ROUND TABLE is dissolved
Which was an image of the mighty world;
And I, the last, go forth companionless,
And the days darken round me, and the years,
Among new men, strange faces, other minds."
  And slowly answer'd Arthur from the barge:
"The old order changeth, yielding place to new,     240
And God fulfils himself in many ways,
Lest one good custom should corrupt the world.
Comfort thyself: what comfort is in me?
I have lived my life, and that which I have done
May He within himself make pure! but thou,
If thou shouldst never see my face again,
Pray for my soul. More things are wrought by prayer
Than this world dreams of. Wherefore, let thy voice
Rise like a fountain for me night and day.
For what are men better than sheep or goats     250
That nourish a blind life within the brain,
If, knowing God, they lift not hands of prayer
Both for themselves and those who call them friend?
For so the whole round earth is every way
Bound by gold chains about the feet of God.
But now farewell. I am going a long way
With these thou seëst—if indeed I go—
(For all my mind is clouded with a doubt)
To the island-valley of Avilion;

Where falls not hail, or rain, or any snow,      260
Nor ever wind blows loudly; but it lies
Deep-meadow'd, happy, fair with orchard-lawns
And bowery hollows crown'd with summer sea,
Where I will heal me of my grievous wound."
  So said he, and the barge with oar and sail
Moved from the brink, like some full breasted swan
That, fluting a wild carol ere her death,
Ruffles her pure cold plume, and takes the flood
With swarthy webs.  Long stood Sir Bedivere
Revolving many memories, till the hull      270
Look'd one black dot against the verge of dawn,
And on the mere the wailing died away.


## THE GARDENER'S DAUGHTER;

### OR, THE PICTURES

This morning is the morning of the day,
When I and Eustace from the city went
To see the Gardener's Daughter; I and he,
Brothers in Art; a friendship so complete
Portion'd in halves between us, that we grew
The fable of the city where we dwelt.
  My Eustace might have sat for Hercules;
So muscular he spread, so broad of breast.
He, by some law that holds in love, and draws
The greater to the lesser, long desired      10
A certain miracle of symmetry,
A miniature of loveliness, all grace
Summ'd up and closed in little;—Juliet, she
So light of foot, so light of spirit—oh, she

To me myself, for some three careless moons,
The summer pilot of an empty heart
Unto the shores of nothing! Know you not
Such touches are but embassies of love,
To tamper with the feelings, ere he found
Empire for life? but Eustace painted her,     20
And said to me, she sitting with us then,
"When will *you* paint like this?" and I replied
(My words were half in earnest, half in jest,)
"'Tis not your work, but Love's. Love, unperceived,
A more ideal Artist he than all,
Came, drew your pencil from you, made those eyes
Darker than darkest pansies, and that hair
More black than ashbuds in the front of March."
And Juliet answer'd laughing, "Go and see
The Gardener's daughter: trust me, after that,     30
You scarce can fail to match his masterpiece."
And up we rose, and on the spur we went.

Not wholly in the busy world, nor quite
Beyond it, blooms the garden that I love.
News from the humming city comes to it
In sound of funeral or of marriage bells;
And, sitting muffled in dark leaves, you hear
The windy clanging of the minster clock;
Although between it and the garden lies
A league of grass, wash'd by a slow broad stream,     40
That, stirr'd with languid pulses of the oar,
Waves all its lazy lilies, and creeps on,
Barge-laden, to three arches of a bridge
Crown'd with the minster-towers.

                                    The fields between
Are dewy-fresh, browsed by deep-udder'd kine,
And all about the large lime feathers low,

The lime a summer home of murmurous wings.
  In that still place she, hoarded in herself,
Grew, seldom seen: not less among us lived
Her fame from lip to lip.  Who had not heard    50
Of Rose, the Gardener's daughter?  Where was he,
So blunt in memory, so old at heart,
At such a distance from his youth in grief,
That, having seen, forgot?  The common mouth,
So gross to express delight, in praise of her
Grew oratory.  Such a lord is Love,
And Beauty such a mistress of the world.
  And if I said that Fancy, led by Love,
Would play with flying forms and images,
Yet this is also true, that, long before    60
I look'd upon her, when I heard her name
My heart was like a prophet to my heart,
And told me I should love.  A crowd of hopes,
That sought to sow themselves like winged seeds,
Born out of everything I heard and saw,
Flutter'd about my senses and my soul;
And vague desires, like fitful blasts of balm
To one that travels quickly, made the air
Of Life delicious, and all kinds of thought,
That verged upon them, sweeter than the dream    70
Dream'd by a happy man, when the dark East,
Unseen, is brightening to his bridal morn.
  And sure this orbit of the memory folds
For ever in itself the day we went
To see her.  All the land in flowery squares,
Beneath a broad and equal-blowing wind,
Smelt of the coming summer, as one large cloud
Drew downward: but all else of Heaven was pure
Up to the Sun, and May from verge to verge,

And May with me from head to heel. And now,    80
As tho' 'twere yesterday, as tho' it were
The hour just flown, that morn with all its sound,
(For those old Mays had thrice the life of these,)
Rings in mine ears. The steer forgot to graze,
And, where the hedge-row cuts the pathway, stood,
Leaning his horns into the neighbour field,
And lowing to his fellows. From the woods
Came voices of the well-contented doves.
The lark could scarce get out his notes for joy,
But shook his song together as he near'd    90
His happy home, the ground. To left and right,
The cuckoo told his name to all the hills;
The mellow ouzel fluted in the elm;
The redcap whistled; and the nightingale
Sang loud, as tho' he were the bird of day.

And Eustace turn'd, and smiling said to me,
"Hear how the bushes echo! by my life,
These birds have joyful thoughts. Think you they sing
Like poets, from the vanity of song?
Or have they any sense of why they sing?    100
And would they praise the heavens for what they have?"
And I made answer, "Were there nothing else
For which to praise the heavens but only love,
That only love were cause enough for praise."

Lightly he laugh'd, as one that read my thought,
And on we went; but ere an hour had pass'd,
We reach'd a meadow slanting to the North;
Down which a well-worn pathway courted us
To one green wicket in a privet hedge;
This, yielding, gave into a grassy walk    110
Thro' crowded lilac-ambush trimly pruned;
And one warm gust, full-fed with perfume, blew

Beyond us, as we enter'd in the cool.
The garden stretches southward. In the midst
A cedar spread his dark-green layers of shade.
The garden-glasses shone, and momently
The twinkling laurel scatter'd silver lights.
  "Eustace," I said, "this wonder keeps the house."
He nodded, but a moment afterwards
He cried, "Look! look!" Before he ceased I turn'd,   120
And, ere a star can wink, beheld her there.
  For up the porch there grew an Eastern rose,
That, flowering high, the last night's gale had caught,
And blown across the walk. One arm aloft—
Gown'd in pure white, that fitted to the shape—
Holding the bush, to fix it back, she stood.
A single stream of all her soft brown hair
Pour'd on one side: the shadow of the flowers
Stole all the golden gloss, and, wavering
Lovingly lower, trembled on her waist—   130
Ah, happy shade—and still went wavering down,
But, ere it touch'd a foot, that might have danced
The greensward into greener circles, dipt,
And mix'd with shadows of the common ground!
But the full day dwelt on her brows, and sunn'd
Her violet eyes, and all her Hebe-bloom,
And doubled his own warmth against her lips,
And on the bounteous wave of such a breast
As never pencil drew. Half light, half shade,
She stood, a sight to make an old man young.   140
  So rapt, we near'd the house; but she, a Rose
In roses, mingled with her fragrant toil,
Nor heard us come, nor from her tendance turn'd
Into the world without; till close at hand,
And almost ere I knew mine own intent,

This murmur broke the stillness of that air
Which brooded round about her:
                      "Ah, one rose,
One rose, but one, by those fair fingers cull'd,
Were worth a hundred kisses press'd on lips
Less exquisite than thine."
                  She look'd: but all     150
Suffused with blushes—neither self-possess'd
Nor startled, but betwixt this mood and that,
Divided in a graceful quiet—paused,
And dropt the branch she held, and turning, wound
Her looser hair in braid, and stirr'd her lips
For some sweet answer, tho' no answer came,
Nor yet refused the rose, but granted it,
And moved away, and left me, statue-like,
In act to render thanks.
                I, that whole day,
Saw her no more, altho' I linger'd there     160
Till every daisy slept, and Love's white star
Beam'd thro' the thicken'd cedar in the dusk.
  So home we went, and all the livelong way
With solemn gibe did Eustace banter me.
"Now," said he, "will you climb the top of Art.
You cannot fail but work in hues to dim
The Titianic Flora. Will you match
My Juliet? you, not you,—the Master, Love,
A more ideal Artist he than all."
  So home I went, but could not sleep for joy,     170
Reading her perfect features in the gloom,
Kissing the rose she gave me o'er and o'er,
And shaping faithful record of the glance
That graced the giving—such a noise of life
Swarm'd in the golden present, such a voice

Call'd to me from the years to come, and such
A length of bright horizon rimm'd the dark.
And all that night I heard the watchmen peal
The sliding season: all that night I heard
The heavy clocks knolling the drowsy hours.　180
The drowsy hours, dispensers of all good,
O'er the mute city stole with folded wings,
Distilling odours on me as they went
To greet their fairer sisters of the East.

　Love at first sight, first-born, and heir to all,
Made this night thus. Henceforward squall nor
　　storm
Could keep me from that Eden where she dwelt.
Light pretexts drew me: sometimes a Dutch love
For tulips; then for roses, moss or musk,
To grace my city-rooms; or fruits and cream　190
Served in the weeping elm; and more and more
A word could bring the colour to my cheek;
A thought would fill my eyes with happy dew;
Love trebled life within me, and with each
The year increased.

　　　　　　　The daughters of the year,
One after one, thro' that still garden pass'd:
Each garlanded with her peculiar flower
Danced into light, and died into the shade;
And each in passing touch'd with some new grace
Or seem'd to touch her, so that day by day,　200
Like one that never can be wholly known,
Her beauty grew; till Autumn brought an hour
For Eustace, when I heard his deep "I will,"
Breathed, like the covenant of a God, to hold
From thence thro' all the worlds: but I rose up
Full of his bliss, and following her dark eyes
Felt earth as air beneath me, till I reach'd

The wicket-gate, and found her standing there.
   There sat we down upon a garden mound,
Two mutually enfolded; Love, the third,      210
Between us, in the circle of his arms
Enwound us both; and over many a range
Of waning lime the gray cathedral towers,
Across a hazy glimmer of the west,
Reveal'd their shining windows: from them clash'd
The bells; we listen'd; with the time we play'd;
We spoke of other things; we coursed about
The subject most at heart, more near and near,
Like doves about a dovecote, wheeling round
The central wish, until we settled there.      220
   Then, in that time and place, I spoke to her,
Requiring, tho' I knew it was mine own,
Yet for the pleasure that I took to hear,
Requiring at her hand the greatest gift,
A woman's heart, the heart of her I loved;
And in that time and place she answer'd me,
And in the compass of three little words,
More musical than ever came in one,
The silver fragments of a broken voice,
Made me most happy, faltering "I am thine."      230
   Shall I cease here? Is this enough to say
That my desire, like all strongest hopes,
By its own energy fulfill'd itself,
Merged in completion? Would you learn at full
How passion rose thro' circumstantial grades
Beyond all grades develop'd? and indeed
I had not staid so long to tell you all,
But while I mused came Memory with sad eyes,
Holding the folded annals of my youth;
And while I mused, Love with knit brows went by,      240
And with a flying finger swept my lips,

And spake, "Be wise: not easily forgiven
Are those, who setting wide the doors, that bar
The secret bridal chambers of the heart,
Let in the day." Here, then, my words have end.
  Yet might I tell of meetings, of farewells—
Of that which came between, more sweet than each,
In whispers, like the whispers of the leaves
That tremble round a nightingale—in sighs
Which perfect Joy, perplex'd for utterance,          250
Stole from her sister Sorrow. Might I not tell
Of difference, reconcilement, pledges given,
And vows, where there was never need of vows,
And kisses, where the heart on one wild leap
Hung tranced from all pulsation, as above
The heavens between their fairy fleeces pale
Sow'd all their mystic gulfs with fleeting stars;
Or while the balmy glooming, crescent-lit,
Spread the light haze along the river-shores,
And in the hollows; or as once we met          260
Unheedful, tho' beneath a whispering rain
Night slid down one long stream of sighing wind,
And in her bosom bore the baby, Sleep.
  But this whole hour your eyes have been intent
On that veil'd picture—veil'd, for what it holds
May not be dwelt on by the common day.
This prelude has prepared thee. Raise thy soul;
Make thine heart ready with thine eyes: the time
Is come to raise the veil.
                    Behold her there,
As I beheld her ere she knew my heart,          270
My first, last love; the idol of my youth,
The darling of my manhood, and, alas!
Now the most blessed memory of mine age.

## ULYSSES

It little profits that an idle king,
By this still hearth, among these barren crags,
Match'd with an aged wife, I mete and dole
Unequal laws unto a savage race,
That hoard, and sleep, and feed, and know not me.
I cannot rest from travel: I will drink
Life to the lees: all times I have enjoy'd
Greatly, have suffer'd greatly, both with those
That loved me, and alone; on shore, and when
Thro' scudding drifts the rainy Hyades          10
Vext the dim sea: I am become a name;
For always roaming with a hungry heart
Much have I seen and known; cities of men
And manners, climates, councils, governments,
Myself not least, but honour'd of them all;
And drunk delight of battle with my peers,
Far on the ringing plains of windy Troy.
I am a part of all that I have met;
Yet all experience is an arch wherethro'
Gleams that untravell'd world, whose margin fades   20
For ever and for ever when I move.
How dull it is to pause, to make an end,
To rust unburnish'd, not to shine in use!
As tho' to breathe were life. Life piled on life
Were all too little, and of one to me
Little remains: but every hour is saved
From that eternal silence, something more,
A bringer of new things; and vile it were
For some three suns to store and hoard myself,

And this gray spirit yearning in desire                    30
To follow knowledge, like a sinking star,
Beyond the utmost bound of human thought.
  This is my son, mine own Telemachus,
To whom I leave the sceptre and the isle—
Well-loved of me, discerning to fulfil
This labour, by slow prudence to make mild
A rugged people, and thro' soft degrees
Subdue them to the useful and the good.
Most blameless is he, centred in the sphere
Of common duties, decent not to fail                    40
In offices of tenderness, and pay
Meet adoration to my household gods,
When I am gone.  He works his work, I mine.
  There lies the port: the vessel puffs her sail:
There gloom the dark broad seas.  My mariners,
Souls that have toil'd, and wrought, and thought with
    me—
That ever with a frolic welcome took
The thunder and the sunshine, and opposed
Free hearts, free foreheads—you and I are old;
Old age hath yet his honour and his toil;              50
Death closes all: but something ere the end,
Some work of noble note, may yet be done,
Not unbecoming men that strove with Gods.
The lights begin to twinkle from the rocks:
The long day wanes: the slow moon climbs: the deep
Moans round with many voices.  Come, my friends,
'Tis not too late to seek a newer world.
Push off, and sitting well in order smite
The sounding furrows; for my purpose holds
To sail beyond the sunset, and the baths              60
Of all the western stars, until I die.

It may be that the gulfs will wash us down:
It may be we shall touch the Happy Isles,
And see the great Achilles, whom we knew.
Tho' much is taken, much abides; and tho'
We are not now that strength which in old days
Moved earth and heaven; that which we are, we are;
One equal temper of heroic hearts,
Made weak by time and fate, but strong in will
To strive, to seek, to find, and not to yield.            70


# LOCKSLEY HALL

Comrades, leave me here a little, while as yet 'tis
  early morn:
Leave me here, and when you want me, sound upon
  the bugle horn.

'Tis the place, and all around it, as of old, the curlews
  call,
Dreary gleams about the moorland flying over Locksley
  Hall;

Locksley Hall, that in the distance overlooks the sandy
  tracts,
And the hollow ocean-ridges roaring into cataracts.

Many a night from yonder ivied casement, ere I went
  to rest,
Did I look on great Orion sloping slowly to the West.

Many a night I saw the Pleiads, rising thro' the mellow
  shade,
Glitter like a swarm of fire-flies tangled in a silver
  braid.            10

Here about the beach I wander'd, nourishing a youth
  sublime
With the fairy tales of science, and the long result of
  Time;

When the centuries behind me like a fruitful land
  reposed;
When I clung to all the present for the promise that
  it closed:

When I dipt into the future far as human eye could see;
Saw the Vision of the world, and all the wonder that
  would be.——

In the Spring a fuller crimson comes upon the robin's
  breast;
In the Spring the wanton lapwing gets himself another
  crest;

In the Spring a livelier iris changes on the burnish'd dove;
In the Spring a young man's fancy lightly turns to
  thoughts of love.                                   20

Then her cheek was pale and thinner than should
  be for one so young.
And her eyes on all my motions with a mute observance
  hung.

And I said, "My cousin Amy, speak, and speak the
  truth to me.
Trust me, cousin, all the current of my being sets
  to thee."

On her pallid cheek and forehead came a colour and
  a light,
As I have seen the rosy red flushing in the northern
  night.

L. T.                                                  8

And she turn'd—her bosom shaken with a sudden
storm of sighs—

All the spirit deeply dawning in the dark of hazel eyes—

Saying, "I have hid my feelings, fearing they should
do me wrong;"

Saying, "Dost thou love me, cousin?" weeping, "I
have loved thee long."                           30

Love took up the glass of Time, and turn'd it in his
glowing hands;

Every moment, lightly shaken, ran itself in golden sands.

Love took up the harp of Life, and smote on all the
chords with might;

Smote the chord of Self, that, trembling, pass'd in
music out of sight.

Many a morning on the moorland did we hear the
copses ring,

And her whisper throng'd my pulses with the fullness
of the Spring.

Many an evening by the waters did we watch the
stately ships,

And our spirits rush'd together at the touching of
the lips.

O my cousin, shallow-hearted! O my Amy, mine no
more!

O the dreary, dreary moorland! O the barren, barren
shore!                                           40

Falser than all fancy fathoms, falser than all songs
have sung,

Puppet to a father's threat, and servile to a shrewish
tongue!

Is it well to wish thee happy ?—having known me—
    to decline
On a range of lower feelings and a narrower heart
    than mine !

Yet it shall be: thou shalt lower to his level day by day,
What is fine within thee growing coarse to sympathise
    with clay.

As the husband is, the wife is: thou art mated with
    a clown,
And the grossness of his nature will have weight to
    drag thee down.

He will hold thee, when his passion shall have spent
    its novel force,
Something better than his dog, a little dearer than
    his horse.                  50

What is this ? his eyes are heavy: think not they
    are glazed with wine.
Go to him: it is thy duty: kiss him: take his hand
    in thine.

It may be my lord is weary, that his brain is over-wrought:
Soothe him with thy finer fancies, touch him with thy
    lighter thought.

He will answer to the purpose, easy things to
    understand—
Better thou wert dead before me, tho' I slew thee
    with my hand !

Better thou and I were lying, hidden from the heart's
    disgrace,
Roll'd in one another's arms, and silent in a last
    embrace.

Cursed be the social wants that sin against the
strength of youth!

Cursed be the social lies that warp us from the living
truth!                                                          60

Cursed be the sickly forms that err from honest
Nature's rule!

Cursed be the gold that gilds the straiten'd forehead
of the fool!

Well—'tis well that I should bluster!—Hadst thou
less unworthy proved—

Would to God—for I had loved thee more than ever
wife was loved.

Am I mad, that I should cherish that which bears
but bitter fruit?

I will pluck it from my bosom, tho' my heart be
at the root.

Never, tho' my mortal summers to such length of
years should come

As the many-winter'd crow that leads the clanging
rookery home.

Where is comfort? in division of the records of the mind?

Can I part her from herself, and love her, as I knew
her, kind?                                                     70

I remember one that perish'd: sweetly did she speak
and move:

Such a one do I remember, whom to look at was
to love.

Can I think of her as dead, and love her for the
love she bore?

No—she never loved me truly: love is love for evermore.

Comfort? comfort scorn'd of devils! this is truth
    the poet sings,

That a sorrow's crown of sorrow is remembering
    happier things.

Drug thy memories, lest thou learn it, lest thy heart
    be put to proof,

In the dead unhappy night, and when the rain is
    on the roof.

Like a dog, he hunts in dreams, and thou art staring
    at the wall,

Where the dying night-lamp flickers, and the shadows
    rise and fall.                   80

Then a hand shall pass before thee, pointing to his
    drunken sleep,

To thy widow'd marriage-pillows, to the tears that
    thou wilt weep.

Thou shalt hear the "Never, never," whisper'd by
    the phantom years,

And a song from out the distance in the ringing of
    thine ears;

And an eye shall vex thee, looking ancient kindness
    on thy pain.

Turn thee, turn thee on thy pillow: get thee to
    thy rest again.

Nay, but Nature brings thee solace; for a tender
    voice will cry.

'Tis a purer life than thine; a lip to drain thy trouble dry.

Baby lips will laugh me down: my latest rival brings
    thee rest.

Baby fingers, waxen touches, press me from the
    mother's breast.                 90

O, the child too clothes the father with a dearness
   not his due.
Half is thine and half is his: it will be worthy of
   the two.

O, I see thee old and formal, fitted to thy petty part,
With a little hoard of maxims preaching down a
   daughter's heart.

"They were dangerous guides the feelings—she herself
   was not exempt—
Truly, she herself had suffer'd"—Perish in thy self-
   contempt!

Overlive it—lower yet—be happy! wherefore should
   I care?
I myself must mix with action, lest I wither by despair.

What is that which I should turn to, lighting upon
   days like these?
Every door is barr'd with gold, and opens but to
   golden keys.                                    100

Every gate is throng'd with suitors, all the markets
   overflow.
I have but an angry fancy: what is that which I
   should do?

I had been content to perish, falling on the foeman's
   ground,
When the ranks are roll'd in vapour, and the winds
   are laid with sound.

But the jingling of the guinea helps the hurt that
   Honour feels,
And the nations do but murmur, snarling at each
   other's heels.

Can I but relive in sadness? I will turn that earlier page.
Hide me from my deep emotion, O thou wondrous
Mother-Age!

Make me feel the wild pulsation that I felt before
the strife,
When I heard my days before me, and the tumult
of my life;                                          110

Yearning for the large excitement that the coming
years would yield,
Eager-hearted as a boy when first he leaves his
father's field,

And at night along the dusky highway near and
nearer drawn,
Sees in heaven the light of London flaring like a
dreary dawn;

And his spirit leaps within him to be gone before
him then,
Underneath the light he looks at, in among the
throngs of men;

Men, my brothers, men the workers, ever reaping
something new:
That which they have done but earnest of the things
that they shall do:

For I dipt into the future, far as human eye could see,
Saw the Vision of the world, and all the wonder that
would be;                                            120

Saw the heavens fill with commerce, argosies of magic
sails,
Pilots of the purple twilight, dropping down with
costly bales;

Heard the heavens fill with shouting, and there rain'd
a ghastly dew

From the nations' airy navies grappling in the central
blue;

Far along the world-wide whisper of the south-wind
rushing warm,

With the standards of the peoples plunging thro' the
thunder storm;

Till the war-drum throbb'd no longer, and the battle
flags were furl'd

In the Parliament of man, the Federation of the world.

There the common sense of most shall hold a fretful
realm in awe,

And the kindly earth shall slumber, lapt in universal
law.                                                          130

So I triumph'd, ere my passion sweeping thro' me
left me dry,

Left me with the palsied heart, and left me with
the jaundiced eye;

Eye, to which all order festers, all things here are
out of joint,

Science moves, but slowly slowly, creeping on from
point to point:

Slowly comes a hungry people, as a lion, creeping
nigher,

Glares at one that nods and winks behind a slowly-
dying fire.

Yet I doubt not thro' the ages one increasing purpose
runs,

And the thoughts of men are widen'd with the process
of the suns.

What is that to him that reaps not harvest of his
    youthful joys,
Tho' the deep heart of existence beat for ever like
    a boy's?                                        140

Knowledge comes, but wisdom lingers, and I linger
    on the shore,
And the individual withers, and the world is more
    and more.

Knowledge comes, but wisdom lingers, and he bears
    a laden breast,
Full of sad experience, moving toward the stillness
    of his rest.

Hark, my merry comrades call me, sounding on the
    bugle-horn,
They to whom my foolish passion were a target for
    their scorn:

Shall it not be scorn to me to harp on such a moulder'd
    string?
I am shamed thro' all my nature to have loved so
    slight a thing.

Weakness to be wroth with weakness! woman's
    pleasure, woman's pain—
Nature made them blinder motions bounded in a
    shallower brain:                                150

Woman is the lesser man, and all thy passions, match'd
    with mine,
Are as moonlight unto sunlight, and as water unto wine—

Here at least, where nature sickens, nothing. Ah, for
    some retreat
Deep in yonder shining Orient, where my life began
    to beat;

Where in wild Mahratta-battle fell my father evil-
    starr'd;—
I was left a trampled orphan, and a selfish uncle's
    ward.

Or to burst all links of habit—there to wander far
    away,
On from island unto island at the gateways of the
    day.

Larger constellations burning, mellow moons and
    happy skies,
Breadths of tropic shade and palms in cluster, knots
    of Paradise.                                        160

Never comes the trader, never floats an European
    flag,
Slides the bird o'er lustrous woodland, swings the
    trailer from the crag;

Droops the heavy-blossom'd bower, hangs the heavy-
    fruited tree—
Summer isles of Eden lying in dark-purple spheres
    of sea.

There methinks would be enjoyment more than in
    this march of mind,
In the steamship, in the railway, in the thoughts
    that shake mankind.

There the passions cramp'd no longer shall have
    scope and breathing-space;
I will take some savage woman, she shall rear my
    dusky race.

Iron-jointed, supple-sinew'd, they shall dive, and they
shall run,

Catch the wild goat by the hair, and hurl their lances
in the sun;                                              170

Whistle back the parrot's call, and leap the rainbows
of the brooks,

Not with blinded eyesight poring over miserable
books—

Fool, again the dream, the fancy! but I *know* my
words are wild,

But I count the gray barbarian lower than the
Christian child.

*I*, to herd with narrow foreheads, vacant of our glorious
gains,

Like a beast with lower pleasures, like a beast with
lower pains!

Mated with a squalid savage—what to me were sun
or clime?

I the heir of all the ages, in the foremost files of time—

I that rather held it better men should perish one
by one,

Than that earth should stand at gaze like Joshua's
moon in Ajalon!                                         180

Not in vain the distance beacons. Forward, forward
let us range.

Let the great world spin for ever down the ringing
grooves of change.

Thro' the shadow of the globe we sweep into the
younger day:

Better fifty years of Europe than a cycle of Cathay.

Mother-Age (for mine I knew not) help me as when
     life begun:
Rift the hills, and roll the waters, flash the lightnings,
     weigh the Sun—

O, I see the crescent promise of my spirit hath not
     set.
Ancient founts of inspiration well thro' all my fancy
     yet.

Howsoever these things be, a long farewell to Locksley
     Hall!
Now for me the woods may wither, now for me the
     roof-tree fall.               190

Comes a vapour from the margin, blackening over
     heath and holt,
Cramming all the blast before it, in its breast a
     thunderbolt.

Let it fall on Locksley Hall, with rain or hail, or
     fire or snow;
For the mighty wind arises, roaring seaward, and
     I go.


## THE DAY-DREAM

### PROLOGUE

O, Lady Flora, let me speak:
     A pleasant hour has past away
While, dreaming on your damask cheek,
     The dewy sister-eyelids lay.
As by the lattice you reclined,
     I went thro' many wayward moods

To see you dreaming—and, behind,
　A summer crisp with shining woods.
And I too dream'd, until at last
　Across my fancy, brooding warm,　　　　10
The reflex of a legend past,
　And loosely settled into form.
And would you have the thought I had,
　And see the vision that I saw,
Then take the broidery-frame, and add
　A crimson to the quaint Macaw,
And I will tell it.　Turn your face,
　Nor look with that too-earnest eye—
The rhymes are dazzled from their place,
　And order'd words asunder fly.　　　　20

## THE SLEEPING PALACE

The varying year with blade and sheaf
　Clothes and reclothes the happy plains;
Here rests the sap within the leaf,
　Here stays the blood among the veins.
Faint shadows, vapours lightly curl'd,
　Faint murmurs from the meadows come,
Like hints and echoes of the world
　To spirits folded in the womb.

Soft lustre bathes the range of urns
　On every slanting terrace-lawn.　　　　30
The fountain to his place returns
　Deep in the garden lake withdrawn.
Here droops the banner on the tower,
　On the hall-hearths the festal fires,
The peacock in his laurel bower,
　The parrot in his gilded wires.

Roof-haunting martins warm their eggs:
  In these, in those the life is stay'd.
The mantles from the golden pegs
  Droop sleepily: no sound is made,                40
Not even of a gnat that sings.
  More like a picture seemeth all
Than those old portraits of old kings,
  That watch the sleepers from the wall.

Here sits the Butler with a flask
  Between his knees, half-drain'd; and there
The wrinkled steward at his task,
  The maid-of-honour blooming fair:
The page has caught her hand in his:
  Her lips are sever'd as to speak:               50
His own are pouted to a kiss:
  The blush is fix'd upon her cheek.

Till all the hundred summers pass,
  The beams, that thro' the Oriel shine,
Make prisms in every carven glass,
  And beaker brimm'd with noble wine.
Each baron at the banquet sleeps,
  Grave faces gather'd in a ring.
His state the king reposing keeps.
  He must have been a jovial king.                60

All round a hedge upshoots, and shows
  At distance like a little wood;
Thorns, ivies, woodbine, mistletoes,
  And grapes with bunches red as blood;
All creeping plants, a wall of green
  Close-matted, bur and brake and briar,
And glimpsing over these, just seen,
  High up, the topmost palace-spire.

When will the hundred summers die,
  And thought and time be born again,        70
And newer knowledge, drawing nigh,
  Bring truth that sways the soul of men?
Here all things in their place remain,
  As all were order'd, ages since.
Come, Care and Pleasure, Hope and Pain,
  And bring the fated fairy Prince.

### THE SLEEPING BEAUTY

Year after year unto her feet,
  She lying on her couch alone,
Across the purpled coverlet,
  The maiden's jet-black hair has grown,      80
On either side her tranced form
  Forth streaming from a braid of pearl:
The slumbrous light is rich and warm,
  And moves not on the rounded curl.

The silk star-broider'd coverlid
  Unto her limbs itself doth mould
Languidly ever; and, amid
  Her full black ringlets downward roll'd,
Glows forth each softly-shadow'd arm
  With bracelets of the diamond bright:       90
Her constant beauty doth inform
  Stillness with love, and day with light.

She sleeps: her breathings are not heard
  In palace chambers far apart.
The fragrant tresses are not stirr'd
  That lie upon her charmed heart.
She sleeps: on either hand upswells
  The gold-fringed pillow lightly prest:
She sleeps, nor dreams, but ever dwells
  A perfect form in perfect rest.            100

### The Arrival

All precious things, discover'd late,
   To those that seek them issue forth;
For love in sequel works with fate,
   And draws the veil from hidden worth.
He travels far from other skies—
   His mantle glitters on the rocks—
A fairy Prince, with joyful eyes,
   And lighter-footed than the fox.
The bodies and the bones of those
   That strove in other days to pass,       110
Are wither'd in the thorny close,
   Or scatter'd blanching on the grass.
He gazes on the silent dead:
   "They perish'd in their daring deeds."
This proverb flashes thro' his head,
   "The many fail: the one succeeds."

He comes, scarce knowing what he seeks:
   He breaks the hedge: he enters there:
The colour flies into his cheeks:
   He trusts to light on something fair;     120
For all his life the charm did talk
   About his path, and hover near
With words of promise in his walk,
   And whisper'd voices at his ear.

More close and close his footsteps wind:
   The Magic Music in his heart
Beats quick and quicker, till he find
   The quiet chamber far apart.
His spirit flutters like a lark,
   He stoops—to kiss her—on his knee.     130
"Love, if thy tresses be so dark,
   How dark those hidden eyes must be!"

## THE REVIVAL

A touch, a kiss! the charm was snapt.
  There rose a noise of striking clocks,
And feet that ran, and doors that clapt,
  And barking dogs, and crowing cocks;
A fuller light illumined all,
  A breeze thro' all the garden swept,
A sudden hubbub shook the hall,
  And sixty feet the fountain leapt.     140

The hedge broke in, the banner blew,
  The butler drank, the steward scrawl'd,
The fire shot up, the martin flew,
  The parrot scream'd, the peacock squall'd,
The maid and page renew'd their strife,
  The palace bang'd, and buzz'd and clackt,
And all the long-pent stream of life
  Dash'd downward in a cataract.

And last with these the king awoke,
  And in his chair himself uprear'd,     150
And yawn'd, and rubb'd his face, and spoke,
  "By holy rood, a royal beard!
How say you? we have slept, my lords.
  My beard has grown into my lap."
The barons swore, with many words,
  'Twas but an after-dinner's nap.

"Pardy," return'd the king, "but still
  My joints are something stiff or so.
My lord, and shall we pass the bill
  I mention'd half an hour ago?"     160
The chancellor, sedate and vain,
  In courteous words return'd reply:
But dallied with his golden chain,
  And, smiling, put the question by.

L. T.          9

### THE DEPARTURE

And on her lover's arm she leant,
  And round her waist she felt it fold,
And far across the hills they went
  In that new world which is the old:
Across the hills, and far away
  Beyond their utmost purple rim,     170
And deep into the dying day
  The happy princess follow'd him.

"I'd sleep another hundred years,
  O love, for such another kiss;"
"O wake for ever, love," she hears,
  "O love, 'twas such as this and this."
And o'er them many a sliding star,
  And many a merry wind was borne,
And, stream'd thro' many a golden bar,
  The twilight melted into morn.     180

"O eyes long laid in happy sleep!"
  "O happy sleep, that lightly fled!"
"O happy kiss, that woke thy sleep!"
  "O love, thy kiss would wake the dead!"
And o'er them many a flowing range
  Of vapour buoy'd the crescent-bark,
And, rapt thro' many a rosy change,
  The twilight died into the dark.

"A hundred summers! can it be?
  And whither goest thou, tell me where?"     190
"O seek my father's court with me,
  For there are greater wonders there."
And o'er the hills, and far away
  Beyond their utmost purple rim,
Beyond the night, across the day,
  Thro' all the world she follow'd him.

## MORAL

So, Lady Flora, take my lay,
  And if you find no moral there,
Go, look in any glass and say,
  What moral is in being fair.     200
Oh, to what uses shall we put
  The wildweed-flower that simply blows?
And is there any moral shut
  Within the bosom of the rose?

But any man that walks the mead,
  In bud or blade, or bloom, may find,
According as his humours lead,
  A meaning suited to his mind.
And liberal applications lie
  In Art like Nature, dearest friend;     210
So 'twere to cramp its use, if I
  Should hook it to some useful end.

## L'ENVOI

You shake your head. A random string
  Your finer female sense offends.
Well—were it not a pleasant thing
  To fall asleep with all one's friends;
To pass with all our social ties
  To silence from the paths of men;
And every hundred years to rise
  And learn the world, and sleep again;     220
To sleep thro' terms of mighty wars,
  And wake on science grown to more,
On secrets of the brain, the stars,
  As wild as aught of fairy lore;
And all that else the years will show,
  The Poet-forms of stronger hours,

The vast Republics that may grow,
　The Federations and the Powers;
Titanic forces taking birth
　In divers seasons, divers climes;　　　　　230
For we are Ancients of the earth,
　And in the morning of the times.

So sleeping, so aroused from sleep
　Thro' sunny decads new and strange,
Or gay quinquenniads would we reap
　The flower and quintessence of change.

Ah, yet would I—and would I might!
　So much your eyes my fancy take—
Be still the first to leap to light
　That I might kiss those eyes awake!　　　　240
For, am I right or am I wrong,
　To choose your own you did not care;
You'd have *my* moral from the song,
　And I will take my pleasure there:
And, am I right or am I wrong,
　My fancy, ranging thro' and thro',
To search a meaning for the song,
　Perforce will still revert to you;
Nor finds a closer truth than this
　All-graceful head, so richly curl'd,　　　　250
And evermore a costly kiss
　The prelude to some brighter world.

For since the time when Adam first
　Embraced his Eve in happy hour,
And every bird of Eden burst
　In carol, every bud to flower,
What eyes, like thine, have waken'd hopes?
　What lips, like thine, so sweetly join'd?

Where on the double rosebud droops
  The fullness of the pensive mind;     260
Which all too dearly self-involved,
  Yet sleeps a dreamless sleep to me;
A sleep by kisses undissolved,
  That lets thee neither hear nor see:
But break it. In the name of wife,
  And in the rights that name may give,
Are clasp'd the moral of thy life,
  And that for which I care to live.

### EPILOGUE

So, Lady Flora, take my lay,
  And, if you find a meaning there,     270
O whisper to your glass, and say,
  "What wonder, if he thinks me fair?"
What wonder I was all unwise,
  To shape the song for your delight
Like long-tail'd birds of Paradise,
  That float thro' Heaven, and cannot light?
Or old-world trains, upheld at court
  By Cupid-boys of blooming hue—
But take it—earnest wed with sport,
  And either sacred unto you.     280

## SIR GALAHAD

My good blade carves the casques of men,
  My tough lance thrusteth sure,
My strength is as the strength of ten
  Because my heart is pure.

The shattering trumpet shrilleth high,
　　The hard brands shiver on the steel,
The splinter'd spear-shafts crack and fly,
　　The horse and rider reel:
They reel, they roll in clanging lists,
　　And when the tide of combat stands,　　10
Perfume and flowers fall in showers,
　　That lightly rain from ladies' hands.

How sweet are looks that ladies bend
　　On whom their favours fall!
For them I battle till the end,
　　To save from shame and thrall:
But all my heart is drawn above,
　　My knees are bow'd in crypt and shrine:
I never felt the kiss of love,
　　Nor maiden's hand in mine.　　20
More bounteous aspects on me beam,
　　Me mightier transports move and thrill;
So keep I fair thro' faith and prayer
　　A virgin heart in work and will.

When down the stormy crescent goes,
　　A light before me swims,
Between dark stems the forest glows,
　　I hear a noise of hymns:
Then by some secret shrine I ride;
　　I hear a voice, but none are there;　　30
The stalls are void, the doors are wide,
　　The tapers burning fair.
Fair gleams the snowy altar-cloth,
　　The silver vessels sparkle clean,
The shrill bell rings, the censer swings,
　　And solemn chaunts resound between.

Sometimes on lonely mountain-meres
  I find a magic bark;
I leap on board: no helmsman steers:
  I float till all is dark.     40
A gentle sound, an awful light!
  Three angels bear the holy Grail:
With folded feet, in stoles of white,
  On sleeping wings they sail.
Ah, blessed vision! blood of God!
  My spirit beats her mortal bars,
As down dark tides the glory slides,
  And star-like mingles with the stars.

When on my goodly charger borne
  Thro' dreaming towns I go,     50
The cock crows ere the Christmas morn,
  The streets are dumb with snow.
The tempest crackles on the leads,
  And, ringing, spins from brand and mail;
But o'er the dark a glory spreads,
  And gilds the driving hail.
I leave the plain, I climb the height;
  No branchy thicket shelter yields;
But blessed forms in whistling storms
  Fly o'er waste fens and windy fields.     60

A maiden knight—to me is given
  Such hope, I know not fear;
I yearn to breathe the airs of heaven
  That often meet me here.
I muse on joy that will not cease,
  Pure spaces clothed in living beams,
Pure lilies of eternal peace,
  Whose odours haunt my dreams;

And, stricken by an angel's hand,
  This mortal armour that I wear,     70
This weight and size, this heart and eyes,
  Are touch'd, are turn'd to finest air.

The clouds are broken in the sky,
  And thro' the mountain-walls
A rolling organ-harmony
  Swells up, and shakes and falls.
Then move the trees, the copses nod,
  Wings flutter, voices hover clear:
"O just and faithful knight of God!
  Ride on! the prize is near."     80
So pass I hostel, hall, and grange;
  By bridge and ford, by park and pale,
All-arm'd I ride, whate'er betide,
  Until I find the holy Grail.

## A FAREWELL

Flow down, cold rivulet, to the sea,
  Thy tribute wave deliver:
No more by thee my steps shall be,
  For ever and for ever.

Flow, softly flow, by lawn and lea,
  A rivulet then a river:
No where by thee my steps shall be,
  For ever and for ever.

But here will sigh thine alder tree,
  And here thine aspen shiver;        10
And here by thee will hum the bee,
  For ever and for ever.

A thousand suns will stream on thee,
  A thousand moons will quiver;
But not by thee my steps shall be,
  For ever and for ever.


## THE BEGGAR MAID

Her arms across her breast she laid;
  She was more fair than words can say:
Bare-footed came the beggar maid
  Before the king Cophetua.
In robe and crown the king stept down,
  To meet and greet her on her way;
"It is no wonder," said the lords,
  "She is more beautiful than day."

As shines the moon in clouded skies,
  She in her poor attire was seen:        10
One praised her ancles, one her eyes,
  One her dark hair and lovesome mien.
So sweet a face, such angel grace,
  In all that land had never been:
Cophetua sware a royal oath:
  "This beggar maid shall be my queen!"

## THE EAGLE

### FRAGMENT

He clasps the crag with hooked hands
Close to the sun in lonely lands,
Ring'd with the azure world, he stands.

The wrinkled sea beneath him crawls;
He watches from his mountain walls,
And like a thunderbolt he falls.


## 'COME NOT, WHEN I AM DEAD.'

Come not, when I am dead,
  To drop thy foolish tears upon my grave,
To trample round my fallen head,
  And vex the unhappy dust thou would'st not save.
There let the wind sweep and the plover cry:
      But thou, go by.

Child, if it were thine error or thy crime
  I care no longer, being all unblest:
Wed whom thou wilt, but I am sick of Time,
  And I desire to rest.          10
Pass on, weak heart, and leave me where I lie:
      Go by, go by.

## TO ——

### AFTER READING A LIFE AND LETTERS

"Cursed be he that moves my bones."
*Shakespeare's Epitaph.*

You might have won the Poet's name,
  If such be worth the winning now,
  And gain'd a laurel for your brow
Of sounder leaf than I can claim;

But you have made the wiser choice,
  A life that moves to gracious ends
  Thro' troops of unrecording friends,
A deedful life, a silent voice:

And you have miss'd the irreverent doom
  Of those that wear the Poet's crown:      10
  Hereafter, neither knave nor clown
Shall hold their orgies at your tomb.

For now the Poet cannot die
  Nor leave his music as of old,
  But round him ere he scarce be cold
Begins the scandal and the cry:

"Proclaim the faults he would not show:
  Break lock and seal: betray the trust:
  Keep nothing sacred: 'tis but just
The many-headed beast should know."      20

Ah shameless! for he did but sing
  A song that pleased us from its worth
  No public life was his on earth,
No blazon'd statesman he, nor king.

He gave the people of his best:
  His worst he kept, his best he gave.
  My Shakespeare's curse on clown and knave
Who will not let his ashes rest!

Who make it seem more sweet to be
  The little life of bank and brier,      30
  The bird that pipes his lone desire
And dies unheard within his tree,

Than he that warbles long and loud
  And drops at Glory's temple-gates,
  For whom the carrion vulture waits
To tear his heart before the crowd!


### 'BREAK, BREAK, BREAK.'

Break, break, break,
  On thy cold gray stones, O Sea!
And I would that my tongue could utter
  The thoughts that arise in me.

O well for the fisherman's boy,
  That he shouts with his sister at play!
O well for the sailor lad,
  That he sings in his boat on the bay!

And the stately ships go on
  To their haven under the hill;      10
But O for the touch of a vanish'd hand,
  And the sound of a voice that is still!

Break, break, break,
  At the foot of thy crags, O Sea!
But the tender grace of a day that is dead
  Will never come back to me.

## THE POET'S SONG

The rain had fallen, the Poet arose,
  He pass'd by the town and out of the street,
A light wind blew from the gates of the sun,
  And waves of shadow went over the wheat,
And he sat him down in a lonely place,
  And chanted a melody loud and sweet,
That made the wild-swan pause in her cloud,
  And the lark drop down at his feet.

The swallow stopt as he hunted the bee,
  The snake slipt under a spray,          10
The wild hawk stood with the down on his beak,
  And stared, with his foot on the prey,
And the nightingale thought, "I have sung many songs,
  But never a one so gay,
For he sings of what the world will be
  When the years have died away."

## TITHONUS

The woods decay, the woods decay and fall,
The vapours weep their burthen to the ground,
Man comes and tills the field and lies beneath,
And after many a summer dies the swan.
Me only cruel immortality
Consumes: I wither slowly in thine arms,

Here at the quiet limit of the world,
A white-hair'd shadow roaming like a dream
The ever silent spaces of the East,
Far-folded mists, and gleaming halls of morn.            10

  Alas! for this gray shadow, once a man—
So glorious in his beauty and thy choice,
Who madest him thy chosen, that he seem'd
To his great heart none other than a God!
I ask'd thee, "Give me immortality."
Then didst thou grant mine asking with a smile,
Like wealthy men who care not how they give.
But thy strong Hours indignant work'd their wills,
And beat me down and marr'd and wasted me,
And tho' they could not end me, left me maim'd            20
To dwell in presence of immortal youth,
Immortal age beside immortal youth,
And all I was, in ashes.  Can thy love,
Thy beauty, make amends, tho' even now,
Close over us, the silver star, thy guide,
Shines in those tremulous eyes that fill with tears
To hear me?  Let me go: take back thy gift:
Why should a man desire in any way
To vary from the kindly race of men,
Or pass beyond the goal of ordinance            30
Where all should pause, as is most meet for all?

  A soft air fans the cloud apart; there comes
A glimpse of that dark world where I was born.
Once more the old mysterious glimmer steals
From thy pure brows, and from thy shoulders pure,
And bosom beating with a heart renew'd.
Thy cheek begins to redden thro' the gloom,
Thy sweet eyes brighten slowly close to mine,

Ere yet they blind the stars, and the wild team
Which love thee, yearning for thy yoke, arise,   40
And shake the darkness from their loosen'd manes,
And beat the twilight into flakes of fire.

Lo! ever thus thou growest beautiful
In silence, then before thine answer given
Departest, and thy tears are on my cheek.

Why wilt thou ever scare me with thy tears,
And make me tremble lest a saying learnt,
In days far-off, on that dark earth, be true?
"The Gods themselves cannot recall their gifts."

Ay me! ay me! with what another heart   50
In days far-off, and with what other eyes
I used to watch—if I be he that watch'd—
The lucid outline forming round thee; saw
The dim curls kindle into sunny rings;
Changed with thy mystic change, and felt my blood
Glow with the glow that slowly crimson'd all
Thy presence and thy portals, while I lay,
Mouth, forehead, eyelids, growing dewy-warm
With kisses balmier than half-opening buds
Of April, and could hear the lips that kiss'd   60
Whispering I knew not what of wild and sweet,
Like that strange song I heard Apollo sing,
While Ilion like a mist rose into towers.

Yet hold me not for ever in thine East:
How can my nature longer mix with thine?
Coldly thy rosy shadows bathe me, cold
Are all thy lights, and cold my wrinkled feet
Upon thy glimmering thresholds, when the steam
Floats up from those dim fields about the homes

Of happy men that have the power to die, 70
And grassy barrows of the happier dead.
Release me, and restore me to the ground;
Thou seëst all things, thou wilt see my grave:
Thou wilt renew thy beauty morn by morn;
I earth in earth forget these empty courts,
And thee returning on thy silver wheels.

# THE CAPTAIN

### A LEGEND OF THE NAVY

He that only rules by terror
    Doeth grievous wrong.
Deep as Hell I count his error.
    Let him hear my song.
Brave the Captain was: the seamen
    Made a gallant crew,
Gallant sons of English freemen,
    Sailors bold and true.
But they hated his oppression,
    Stern he was and rash; 10
So for every light transgression
    Doom'd them to the lash.
Day by day more harsh and cruel
    Seem'd the Captain's mood.
Secret wrath like smother'd fuel
    Burnt in each man's blood.
Yet he hoped to purchase glory,
    Hoped to make the name
Of his vessel great in story,
    Wheresoe'er he came. 20

So they past by capes and islands,
    Many a harbour-mouth,
Sailing under palmy highlands
    Far within the South.
On a day when they were going
    O'er the lone expanse,
In the north, her canvas flowing,
    Rose a ship of France.
Then the Captain's colour heighten'd,
    Joyful came his speech:        30
But a cloudy gladness lighten'd
    In the eyes of each.
"Chase," he said: the ship flew forward,
    And the wind did blow;
Stately, lightly, went she Norward,
    Till she near'd the foe.
Then they look'd at him they hated,
    Had what they desired:
Mute with folded arms they waited—
    Not a gun was fired.        40
But they heard the foeman's thunder
    Roaring out their doom;
All the air was torn in sunder,
    Crashing went the boom,
Spars were splinter'd, decks were shatter'd,
    Bullets fell like rain;
Over mast and deck were scatter'd
    Blood and brains of men.
Spars were splinter'd; decks were broken:
    Every mother's son—        50
Down they dropt—no word was spoken—
    Each beside his gun.

On the decks as they were lying,
    Were their faces grim.
In their blood, as they lay dying,
    Did they smile on him.
Those, in whom he had reliance
    For his noble name,
With one smile of still defiance
    Sold him unto shame.        60
Shame and wrath his heart confounded,
    Pale he turn'd and red,
Till himself was deadly wounded
    Falling on the dead.
Dismal error! fearful slaughter!
    Years have wander'd by,
Side by side beneath the water
    Crew and Captain lie;
There the sunlit ocean tosses
    O'er them mouldering,        70
And the lonely seabird crosses
    With one waft of the wing.


## THE FLOWER

Once in a golden hour
    I cast to earth a seed.
Up there came a flower,
    The people said, a weed.

To and fro they went
    Thro' my garden-bower,
And muttering discontent
    Cursed me and my flower.

Then it grew so tall
  It wore a crown of light,                    10
But thieves from o'er the wall
  Stole the seed by night.

Sow'd it far and wide
  By every town and tower,
Till all the people cried,
  "Splendid is the flower."

Read my little fable:
  He that runs may read.
Most can raise the flowers now,
  For all have got the seed.                    20

And some are pretty enough,
  And some are poor indeed;
And now again the people
  Call it but a weed.


## THE SAILOR BOY

He rose at dawn and, fired with hope,
  Shot o'er the seething harbour-bar,
And reach'd the ship and caught the rope,
  And whistled to the morning star.

And while he whistled long and loud
  He heard a fierce mermaiden cry,
"O boy, tho' thou art young and proud,
  I see the place where thou wilt lie.

10—2

"The sands and yeasty surges mix
  In caves about the dreary bay,       10
And on thy ribs the limpet sticks,
  And in thy heart the scrawl shall play."

"Fool," he answer'd, "death is sure
  To those that stay and those that roam,
But I will nevermore endure
  To sit with empty hands at home.

"My mother clings about my neck,
  My sisters crying, 'Stay for shame;'
My father raves of death and wreck,
  They are all to blame, they are all to blame.  20

"God help me! save I take my part
  Of danger on the roaring sea,
A devil rises in my heart,
  Far worse than any death to me."


## LOVE AND DUTY

Of love that never found his earthly close,
What sequel? Streaming eyes and breaking hearts?
Or all the same as if he had not been?
  Not so. Shall Error in the round of time
Still father Truth? O shall the braggart shout
For some blind glimpse of freedom work itself
Thro' madness, hated by the wise, to law
System and empire? Sin itself be found
The cloudy porch oft opening on the Sun?
And only he, this wonder, dead, become    10
Mere highway dust? or year by year alone

Sit brooding in the ruins of a life,
Nightmare of youth, the spectre of himself?
　　If this were thus, if this, indeed, were all,
Better the narrow brain, the stony heart,
The staring eye glazed o'er with sapless days,
The long mechanic pacings to and fro,
The set gray life, and apathetic end.
But am I not the nobler thro' thy love?
O three times less unworthy! likewise thou　　20
Art more thro' Love, and greater than thy years.
The Sun will run his orbit, and the Moon
Her circle. Wait, and Love himself will bring
The drooping flower of knowledge changed to fruit
Of wisdom. Wait: my faith is large in Time,
And that which shapes it to some perfect end.
　　Will some one say, then why not ill for good?
Why took ye not your pastime? To that man
My work shall answer, since I knew the right
And did it; for a man is not as God,　　30
But then most Godlike being most a man.
　　—So let me think 'tis well for thee and me—
Ill-fated that I am, what lot is mine
Whose foresight preaches peace, my heart so slow
To feel it! For how hard it seem'd to me,
When eyes, love-languid thro' half-tears, would dwell
One earnest, earnest moment upon mine,
Then not to dare to see! when thy low voice,
Faltering, would break its syllables, to keep
My own full-tuned,—hold passion in a leash,　　40
And not leap forth and fall about thy neck,
And on thy bosom, (deep-desired relief!)
Rain out the heavy mist of tears, that weigh'd
Upon my brain, my senses and my soul!
　　For Love himself took part against himself

To warn us off, and Duty loved of Love—
O this world's curse,—beloved but hated—came
Like Death betwixt thy dear embrace and mine,
And crying, "Who is this? behold thy bride,"
She push'd me from thee.

               If the sense is hard      50
To alien ears, I did not speak to these—
No, not to thee, but to thyself in me:
Hard is my doom and thine: thou knowest it all.
  Could Love part thus? was it not well to speak,
To have spoken once? It could not but be well.
The slow sweet hours that bring us all things good,
The slow sad hours that bring us all things ill,
And all good things from evil, brought the night
In which we sat together and alone,
And to the want, that hollow'd all the heart,      60
Gave utterance by the yearning of an eye,
That burn'd upon its object thro' such tears
As flow but once a life.

             The trance gave way
To those caresses, when a hundred times
In that last kiss, which never was the last,
Farewell, like endless welcome, lived and died.
Then follow'd counsel, comfort, and the words
That make a man feel strong in speaking truth;
Till now the dark was worn, and overhead
The lights of sunset and of sunrise mix'd      70
In that brief night; the summer night, that paused
Among her stars to hear us; stars that hung
Love-charm'd to listen: all the wheels of Time
Spun round in station, but the end had come.
  O then like those, who clench their nerves to rush
Upon their dissolution, we two rose,
There—closing like an individual life—

In one blind cry of passion and of pain,
Like bitter accusation ev'n to death,
Caught up the whole of love and utter'd it,          80
And bade adieu for ever.
                         Live—yet live—
Shall sharpest pathos blight us, knowing all
Life needs for life is possible to will—
Live happy; tend thy flowers; be tended by
My blessing! Should my Shadow cross thy thoughts
Too sadly for their peace, remand it thou
For calmer hours to Memory's darkest hold,
If not to be forgotten—not at once—
Not all forgotten. Should it cross thy dreams,
O might it come like one that looks content,          90
With quiet eyes unfaithful to the truth,
And point thee forward to a distant light,
Or seem to lift a burthen from thy heart
And leave thee freër, till thou wake refresh'd,
Then when the first low matin-chirp hath grown
Full quire, and morning driv'n her plow of pearl
Far furrowing into light the mounded rack,
Beyond the fair green field and eastern sea.


# EXPERIMENTS IN QUANTITY

## MILTON

### *Alcaics*

O mighty-mouth'd inventor of harmonies,
O skill'd to sing of Time or Eternity,
  God-gifted organ-voice of England,
    Milton, a name to resound for ages;
Whose Titan angels, Gabriel, Abdiel,

Starr'd from Jehovah's gorgeous armouries,
  Tower, as the deep-domed empyrëan
    Rings to the roar of an angel onset—
Me rather all that bowery loneliness,
The brooks of Eden mazily murmuring,     10
  And bloom profuse and cedar arches
    Charm, as a wanderer out in ocean,
Where some refulgent sunset of India
Streams o'er a rich ambrosial ocean isle,
  And crimson-hued the stately palmwoods
    Whisper in odorous heights of even.

### *Hendecasyllabics*

O you chorus of indolent reviewers,
Irresponsible, indolent reviewers,
Look, I come to the test, a tiny poem
All composed in a metre of Catullus,     20
All in quantity, careful of my motion,
Like the skater on ice that hardly bears him,
Lest I fall unawares before the people,
Waking laughter in indolent reviewers.
Should I flounder awhile without a tumble
Thro' this metrification of Catullus,
They should speak to me not without a welcome,
All that chorus of indolent reviewers.
Hard, hard, hard is it, only not to tumble,
So fantastical is the dainty metre.     30
Wherefore slight me not wholly, nor believe me
Too presumptuous, indolent reviewers.
O blatant Magazines, regard me rather—
Since I blush to belaud myself a moment—
As some exquisite rose, a piece of inmost
Horticultural art, or half coquette-like
Maiden, not to be greeted unbenignly.

## ODE ON THE DEATH OF THE DUKE OF WELLINGTON

Bury the Great Duke
  With an empire's lamentation,
Let us bury the Great Duke
  To the noise of the mourning of a mighty nation,
Mourning when their leaders fall,
Warriors carry the warrior's pall,
And sorrow darkens hamlet and hall.

Where shall we lay the man whom we deplore?
Here, in streaming London's central roar.
Let the sound of those he wrought for,          10
And the feet of those he fought for,
Echo round his bones for evermore.

Lead out the pageant: sad and slow,
As fits an universal woe,
Let the long long procession go,
And let the sorrowing crowd about it grow,
And let the mournful martial music blow;
The last great Englishman is low.

Mourn, for to us he seems the last,
Remembering all his greatness in the Past.          20
No more in soldier fashion will he greet
With lifted hand the gazer in the street.
O friends, our chief state-oracle is mute:
Mourn for the man of long-enduring blood,
The statesman-warrior, moderate, resolute,
Whole in himself, a common good.

Mourn for the man of amplest influence,
Yet clearest of ambitious crime,
Our greatest yet with least pretence,
Great in council and great in war,                    30
Foremost captain of his time,
Rich in saving common-sense,
And, as the greatest only are,
In his simplicity sublime.
O good gray head which all men knew,
O voice from which their omens all men drew,
O iron nerve to true occasion true,
O fall'n at length that tower of strength
Which stood four-square to all the winds that blew!
Such was he whom we deplore.                           40
The long self-sacrifice of life is o'er.
The great World-victor's victor will be seen no more.


All is over and done:
Render thanks to the Giver,
England, for thy son.
Let the bell be toll'd.
Render thanks to the Giver,
And render him 'to the mould.
Under the cross of gold
That shines over city and river,                       50
There he shall rest for ever
Among the wise and the bold.
Let the bell be toll'd:
And a reverent people behold
The towering car, the sable steeds:
Bright let it be with his blazon'd deeds,
Dark in its funeral fold.
Let the bell be toll'd:

And a deeper knell in the heart be knoll'd;
And the sound of the sorrowing anthem roll'd          60
Thro' the dome of the golden cross;
And the volleying cannon thunder his loss;
He knew their voices of old.
For many a time in many a clime
His captain's-ear has heard them boom
Bellowing victory, bellowing doom;
When he with those deep voices wrought,
Guarding realms and kings from shame;
With those deep voices our dead captain taught
The tyrant, and asserts his claim                     70
In that dread sound to the great name,
Which he has worn so pure of blame,
In praise and in dispraise the same,
A man of well-attemper'd frame.
O civic muse, to such a name,
To such a name for ages long,
To such a name,
Preserve a broad approach of fame,
And ever-ringing avenues of song.

Who is he that cometh, like an honour'd guest,        80
With banner and with music, with soldier and with priest,
With a nation weeping, and breaking on my rest?
Mighty seaman, this is he
Was great by land as thou by sea.
Thine island loves thee well, thou famous man,
The greatest sailor since our world began.
Now, to the roll of muffled drums,
To thee the greatest soldier comes;
For this is he
Was great by land as thou by sea;                     90

His foes were thine; he kept us free;
O give him welcome, this is he,
Worthy of our gorgeous rites,
And worthy to be laid by thee;
For this is England's greatest son,
He that gain'd a hundred fights,
Nor ever lost an English gun;
This is he that far away
Against the myriads of Assaye
Clash'd with his fiery few and won;                    100
And underneath another sun,
Warring on a later day,
Round affrighted Lisbon drew
The treble works, the vast designs
Of his labour'd rampart-lines,
Where he greatly stood at bay,
Whence he issued forth anew,
And ever great and greater grew,
Beating from the wasted vines
Back to France her banded swarms,                      110
Back to France with countless blows,
Till o'er the hills her eagles flew
Past the Pyrenean pines,
Follow'd up in valley and glen
With blare of bugle, clamour of men,
Roll of cannon and clash of arms,
And England pouring on her foes.
Such a war had such a close.
Again their ravening eagle rose
In anger, wheel'd on Europe-shadowing wings,           120
And barking for the thrones of kings;
Till one that sought but Duty's iron crown
On that loud sabbath shook the spoiler down;

A day of onsets of despair!
Dash'd on every rocky square
Their surging charges foam'd themselves away;
Last, the Prussian trumpet blew;
Thro' the long-tormented air
Heaven flash'd a sudden jubilant ray,
And down we swept and charged and overthrew.  130
So great a soldier taught us there,
What long-enduring hearts could do
In that world's-earthquake, Waterloo!
Mighty seaman, tender and true,
And pure as he from taint of craven guile,
O saviour of the silver-coasted isle,
O shaker of the Baltic and the Nile,
If aught of things that here befall
Touch a spirit among things divine,
If love of country move thee there at all,          140
Be glad, because his bones are laid by thine!
And thro' the centuries let a people's voice
In full acclaim,
A people's voice,
The proof and echo of all human fame,
A people's voice, when they rejoice
At civic revel and pomp and game,
Attest their great commander's claim
With honour, honour, honour, honour to him,
Eternal honour to his name.                          150

A people's voice! we are a people yet.
Tho' all men else their nobler dreams forget,
Confused by brainless mobs and lawless Powers;
Thank Him who isled us here, and roughly set
His Saxon in blown seas and storming showers,

We have a voice, with which to pay the debt
Of boundless love and reverence and regret
To those great men who fought, and kept it ours.
And keep it ours, O God, from brute control;
O Statesmen, guard us, guard the eye, the soul      160
Of Europe, keep our noble England whole,
And save the one true seed of freedom sown
Betwixt a people and their ancient throne,
That sober freedom out of which there springs
Our loyal passion for our temperate kings;
For, saving that, ye help to save mankind
Till public wrong be crumbled into dust,
And drill the raw world for the march of mind,
Till crowds at length be sane and crowns be just.
But wink no more in slothful overtrust.      170
Remember him who led your hosts;
He bad you guard the sacred coasts.
Your cannons moulder on the seaward wall;
His voice is silent in your council-hall
For ever; and whatever tempests lour
For ever silent; even if they broke
In thunder, silent; yet remember all
He spoke among you, and the Man who spoke;
Who never sold the truth to serve the hour,
Nor palter'd with Eternal God for power;      180
Who let the turbid streams of rumour flow
Thro' either babbling world of high and low;
Whose life was work, whose language rife
With rugged maxims hewn from life;
Who never spoke against a foe;
Whose eighty winters freeze with one rebuke
All great self-seekers trampling on the right:
Truth-teller was our England's Alfred named;

Truth-lover was our English Duke;
Whatever record leap to light                         190
He never shall be shamed.

Lo, the leader in these glorious wars
Now to glorious burial slowly borne,
Follow'd by the brave of other lands,
He, on whom from both her open hands
Lavish Honour shower'd all her stars,
And affluent Fortune emptied all her horn.
Yea, let all good things await
Him who cares not to be great,
But as he saves or serves the state.                   200
Not once or twice in our rough island-story,
The path of duty was the way to glory:
He that walks it, only thirsting
For the right, and learns to deaden
Love of self, before his journey closes,
He shall find the stubborn thistle bursting
Into glossy purples, which outredden
All voluptuous garden-roses.
Not once or twice in our fair island-story,
The path of duty was the way to glory:                210
He, that ever following her commands,
On with toil of heart and knees and hands,
Thro' the long gorge to the far light has won
His path upward, and prevail'd,
Shall find the toppling crags of Duty scaled
Are close upon the shining table-lands
To which our God Himself is moon and sun.
Such was he: his work is done:
But while the races of mankind endure,
Let his great example stand                            220

Colossal, seen of every land,
And keep the soldier firm, the statesman pure;
Till in all lands and thro' all human story
The path of duty be the way to glory:
And let the land whose hearths he saved from shame
For many and many an age proclaim
At civic revel and pomp and game,
And when the long-illumined cities flame,
Their ever-loyal iron leader's fame,
With honour, honour, honour, honour to him,     230
Eternal honour to his name.


Peace, his triumph will be sung
By some yet unmoulded tongue
Far on in summers that we shall not see:
Peace, it is a day of pain
For one about whose patriarchal knee
Late the little children clung:
O peace, it is a day of pain
For one, upon whose hand and heart and brain
Once the weight and fate of Europe hung.     240
Ours the pain, be his the gain!
More than is of man's degree
Must be with us, watching here
At this, our great solemnity.
Whom we see not we revere.
We revere, and we refrain
From talk of battles loud and vain,
And brawling memories all too free
For such a wise humility
As befits a solemn fane:     250
We revere, and while we hear
The tides of Music's golden sea

Setting toward eternity,
Uplifted high in heart and hope are we,
Until we doubt not that for one so true
There must be other nobler work to do
Than when he fought at Waterloo,
And Victor he must ever be.
For tho' the Giant Ages heave the hill
And break the shore, and evermore   260
Make and break, and work their will:
Tho' world on world in myriad myriads roll
Round us, each with different powers,
And other forms of life than ours,
What know we greater than the soul?
On God and Godlike men we build our trust.
Hush, the Dead March wails in the people's ears:
The dark crowd moves, and there are sobs and tears:
The black earth yawns: the mortal disappears;
Ashes to ashes, dust to dust;   270
He is gone who seem'd so great.—
Gone; but nothing can bereave him
Of the force he made his own
Being here, and we believe him
Something far advanced in State,
And that he wears a truer crown
Than any wreath that man can weave him.
But speak no more of his renown,
Lay your earthly fancies down,
And in the vast cathedral leave him.   280
God accept him, Christ receive him.

## THE CHARGE OF THE LIGHT BRIGADE

Half a league, half a league,
　Half a league onward,
All in the valley of Death
　Rode the six hundred.
"Forward, the Light Brigade!
Charge for the guns!" he said:
Into the valley of Death
　Rode the six hundred.

"Forward, the Light Brigade!"
Was there a man dismay'd?　　　　10
Not tho' the soldier knew
　Some one had blunder'd:
Their's not to make reply,
Their's not to reason why,
Their's but to do and die,
Into the valley of Death
　Rode the six hundred.

Cannon to right of them,
Cannon to left of them,
Cannon in front of them　　　　20
　Volley'd and thunder'd;
Storm'd at with shot and shell,
Boldly they rode and well,
Into the jaws of Death,
Into the mouth of Hell
　Rode the six hundred.

Flash'd all their sabres bare,
Flash'd as they turn'd in air,
Sabring the gunners there,
Charging an army, while                          30
  All the world wonder'd:
Plunged in the battery-smoke
Right thro' the line they broke;
Cossack and Russian
Reel'd from the sabre-stroke
  Shatter'd and sunder'd.
Then they rode back, but not,
  Not the six hundred.

Cannon to right of them,
Cannon to left of them,                          40
Cannon behind them
  Volley'd and thunder'd;
Storm'd at with shot and shell,
While horse and hero fell,
They that had fought so well
Came thro' the jaws of Death
Back from the mouth of Hell,
All that was left of them,
  Left of six hundred.

When can their glory fade?                        50
O the wild charge they made!
  All the world wonder'd.
Honour the charge they made!
Honour the Light Brigade.
  Noble six hundred!

## THE BROOK

"Here, by this brook, we parted; I to the East
And he for Italy—too late—too late:
One whom the strong sons of the world despise;
For lucky rhymes to him were scrip and share,
And mellow metres more than cent for cent;
Nor could he understand how money breeds,
Thought it a dead thing; yet himself could make
The thing that is not as the thing that is.
O had he lived! In our schoolbooks we say,
Of those that held their heads above the crowd,          10
They flourish'd then or then; but life in him
Could scarce be said to flourish, only touch'd
On such a time as goes before the leaf,
When all the wood stands in a mist of green,
And nothing perfect: yet the brook he loved,
For which, in branding summers of Bengal,
Or ev'n the sweet half-English Neilgherry air,
I panted, seems, as I re-listen to it,
Prattling the primrose fancies of the boy,
To me that loved him; for 'O brook,' he says,          20
'O babbling brook,' says Edmund in his rhyme,
'Whence come you?' and the brook, why not? replies.

> I come from haunts of coot and hern,
>    I make a sudden sally
> And sparkle out among the fern,
>    To bicker down a valley.
>
> By thirty hills I hurry down,
>    Or slip between the ridges,
> By twenty thorps, a little town,
>    And half a hundred bridges.          30

Till last by Philip's farm I flow
  To join the brimming river,
For men may come and men may go,
  But I go on for ever.

"Poor lad, he died at Florence, quite worn out,
Travelling to Naples. There is Darnley bridge,
It has more ivy; there the river; and there
Stands Philip's farm where brook and river meet.

I chatter over stony ways,
  In little sharps and trebles,
I bubble into eddying bays,
  I babble on the pebbles.

40

With many a curve my banks I fret
  By many a field and fallow,
And many a fairy foreland set
  With willow-weed and mallow.

I chatter, chatter, as I flow
  To join the brimming river,
For men may come and men may go,
  But I go on for ever.

50

"But Philip chatter'd more than brook or bird;
Old Philip; all about the fields you caught
His weary daylong chirping, like the dry
High-elbow'd grigs that leap in summer grass.

I wind about, and in and out,
  With here a blossom sailing,
And here and there a lusty trout,
  And here and there a grayling,

And here and there a foamy flake
  Upon me, as I travel
With many a silvery waterbreak
  Above the golden gravel,

60

And draw them all along, and flow
　　To join the brimming river,
For men may come and men may go,
　　But I go on for ever.

"O darling Katie Willows, his one child!
A maiden of our century, yet most meek;
A daughter of our meadows, yet not coarse;
Straight, but as lissome as a hazel wand;　　　70
Her eyes a bashful azure, and her hair
In gloss and hue the chestnut, when the shell
Divides threefold to show the fruit within.

"Sweet Katie, once I did her a good turn,
Her and her far-off cousin and betrothed,
James Willows, of one name and heart with her.
For here I came, twenty years back—the week
Before I parted with poor Edmund; crost
By that old bridge which, half in ruins then,
Still makes a hoary eyebrow for the gleam　　　80
Beyond it, where the waters marry—crost,
Whistling a random bar of Bonny Doon,
And push'd at Philip's garden-gate. The gate,
Half-parted from a weak and scolding hinge,
Stuck; and he clamour'd from a casement, 'run'
To Katie somewhere in the walks below,

'Run, Katie!' Katie never ran: she moved
To meet me, winding under woodbine bowers,
A little flutter'd, with her eyelids down,
Fresh apple-blossom, blushing for a boon.　　　90

"What was it? less of sentiment than sense
Had Katie; not illiterate; neither one
Who dabbling in the fount of fictive tears,

And nursed by mealy-mouth'd philanthropies,
Divorce the Feeling from her mate the Deed.

"She told me. She and James had quarrell'd. Why?
What cause of quarrel? None, she said, no cause;
James had no cause: but when I prest the cause,
I learnt that James had flickering jealousies
Which anger'd her. Who anger'd James? I said.  100
But Katie snatch'd her eyes at once from mine,
And sketching with her slender pointed foot
Some figure like a wizard's pentagram
On garden gravel, let my query pass
Unclaim'd, in flushing silence, till I ask'd
If James were coming. 'Coming every day,'
She answer'd, 'ever longing to explain,
But evermore her father came across
With some long-winded tale, and broke him short;
And James departed vext with him and her.'  110
How could I help her? 'Would I—was it wrong?'
(Claspt hands and that petitionary grace
Of sweet seventeen subdued me ere she spoke)
'O would I take her father for one hour,
For one half-hour, and let him talk to me!'
And even while she spoke, I saw where James
Made toward us, like a wader in the surf,
Beyond the brook, waist-deep in meadow-sweet.

"O Katie, what I suffer'd for your sake!
For in I went, and call'd old Philip out  120
To show the farm: full willingly he rose:
He led me thro' the short sweet-smelling lanes
Of his wheat-suburb, babbling as he went.
He praised his land, his horses, his machines;
He praised his ploughs, his cows, his hogs, his dogs;

He praised his hens, his geese, his guinea-hens;
His pigeons, who in session on their roofs
Approved him, bowing at their own deserts:
Then from the plaintive mother's teat he took
Her blind and shuddering puppies, naming each,    130
And naming those, his friends, for whom they were:
Then crost the common into Darnley chase
To show Sir Arthur's deer.  In copse and fern
Twinkled the innumerable ear and tail.
Then, seated on a serpent-rooted beech,
He pointed out a pasturing colt, and said:
'That was the four-year-old I sold the Squire.'
And there he told a long long-winded tale
Of how the Squire had seen the colt at grass,
And how it was the thing his daughter wish'd,    140
And how he sent the bailiff to the farm
To learn the price, and what the price he ask'd,
And how the bailiff swore that he was mad,
But he stood firm; and so the matter hung;
He gave them line: and five days after that
He met the bailiff at the Golden Fleece,
Who then and there had offer'd something more,
But he stood firm; and so the matter hung;
He knew the man; the colt would fetch its price;
He gave them line: and how by chance at last    150
(It might be May or April, he forgot,
The last of April or the first of May)
He found the bailiff riding by the farm,
And, talking from the point, he drew him in,
And there he mellow'd all his heart with ale,
Until they closed a bargain, hand in hand.

 "Then, while I breathed in sight of haven, he,
Poor fellow, could he help it? recommenced,

And ran thro' all the coltish chronicle,
Wild Will, Black Bess, Tantivy, Tallyho,                160
Reform, White Rose, Bellerophon, the Jilt,
Arbaces, and Phenomenon, and the rest,
Till, not to die a listener, I arose,
And with me Philip, talking still; and so
We turn'd our foreheads from the falling sun,
And following our own shadows thrice as long
As when they follow'd us from Philip's door,
Arrived, and found the sun of sweet content
Re-risen in Katie's eyes, and all things well.

> I steal by lawns and grassy plots,                170
>   I slide by hazel covers;
> I move the sweet forget-me-nots
>   That grow for happy lovers.
>
> I slip, I slide, I gloom, I glance,
>   Among my skimming swallows;
> I make the netted sunbeam dance
>   Against my sandy shallows.
>
> I murmur under moon and stars
>   In brambly wildernesses;
> I linger by my shingly bars;                180
>   I loiter round my cresses;
>
> And out again I curve and flow
>   To join the brimming river,
> For men may come and men may go,
>   But I go on for ever.

Yes, men may come and go; and these are gone,
All gone.  My dearest brother, Edmund, sleeps,
Not by the well-known stream and rustic spire,
But unfamiliar Arno, and the dome
Of Brunelleschi; sleeps in peace: and he,                190

Poor Philip, of all his lavish waste of words
Remains the lean P. W. on his tomb:
I scraped the lichen from it: Katie walks
By the long wash of Australasian seas
Far off, and holds her head to other stars,
And breathes in converse seasons. All are gone."

    So Lawrence Aylmer, seated on a stile
In the long hedge, and rolling in his mind
Old waifs of rhyme, and bowing o'er the brook
A tonsured head in middle age forlorn,       200
Mused, and was mute. On a sudden a low breath
Of tender air made tremble in the hedge
The fragile bindweed-bells and briony rings;
And he look'd up. There stood a maiden near,
Waiting to pass. In much amaze he stared
On eyes a bashful azure, and on hair
In gloss and hue the chestnut, when the shell
Divides threefold to show the fruit within:
Then, wondering, ask'd her "Are you from the farm?"
"Yes" answer'd she. "Pray stay a little: pardon me;
What do they call you?" "Katie." "That were
    strange.                          211
What surname?" "Willows." "No!" "That is my
    name."
"Indeed!" and here he look'd so self-perplext,
That Katie laugh'd, and laughing blush'd, till he
Laugh'd also, but as one before he wakes,
Who feels a glimmering strangeness in his dream.
Then looking at her; "Too happy, fresh and fair,
Too fresh and fair in our sad world's best bloom,
To be the ghost of one who bore your name
About these meadows, twenty years ago."     220

"Have you not heard?" said Katie, "we came back.
We bought the farm we tenanted before.
Am I so like her? so they said on board.
Sir, if you knew her in her English days,
My mother, as it seems you did, the days
That most she loves to talk of, come with me.
My brother James is in the harvest-field:
But she—you will be welcome—O, come in!"

## A WELCOME TO ALEXANDRA

### MARCH 7, 1863

Sea-kings' daughter from over the sea,
                                    Alexandra!
Saxon and Norman and Dane are we,
But all of us Danes in our welcome of thee,
                                    Alexandra!
Welcome her, thunders of fort and of fleet!
Welcome her, thundering cheer of the street!
Welcome her, all things youthful and sweet,
Scatter the blossom under her feet!
Break, happy land, into earlier flowers!          10
Make music, O bird, in the new-budded bowers!
Blazon your mottoes of blessing and prayer!
Welcome her, welcome her, all that is ours!
Warble, O bugle, and trumpet, blare!
Flags, flutter out upon turrets and towers!
Flames, on the windy headland flare!
Utter your jubilee, steeple and spire!
Clash, ye bells, in the merry March air!

Flash, ye cities, in rivers of fire!
Rush to the roof, sudden rocket, and higher        20
Melt into stars for the land's desire!
Roll and rejoice, jubilant voice,
Roll as a ground-swell dash'd on the strand,
Roar as the sea when he welcomes the land,
And welcome her, welcome the land's desire,
The sea-kings' daughter as happy as fair,
Blissful bride of a blissful heir,
Bride of the heir of the kings of the sea—
O joy to the people and joy to the throne,
Come to us, love us and make us your own:        30
For Saxon or Dane or Norman we,
Teuton or Celt, or whatever we be,
We are each all Dane in our welcome of thee,
                                    Alexandra!


# NORTHERN FARMER

## OLD STYLE

Wheer 'asta beän saw long and meä liggin' 'ere aloän?
Noorse? thoort nowt o' a noorse: whoy, Doctor's
    abeän an' agoän:
Says that I moänt 'a naw moor yaäle: but I beänt
    a fool:
Git ma my yaäle, for I beänt a-gooin' to breäk my
    rule.

Doctors, they knaws nowt, for a says what's nawways
    true:
Naw soort o' koind o' use to saäy the things that a do.

I've 'ed my point o' yaäle ivry noight sin' I beän 'ere,
An' I've 'ed my quart ivry market-noight for foorty
    year.

Parson's a beän loikewoise, an' a sittin 'ere o' my
    bed.
"The amoighty's a taäkin o' you to 'issén, my friend,"
    a said,         10
An' a towd ma my sins, an's toithe were due, an' I
    gied it in hond;
I done my duty by un, as I 'a done by the lond.

Larn'd a ma' beä. I reckons I 'annot sa mooch to
    larn.
But a cost oop, thot a did, 'boot Bessy Marris's barn.
Thof a knaws I hallus voäted wi' Squoire an' choorch
    an' staäte,
An' i' the woost o' toimes I wur niver agin the raäte.

An' I hallus comed to 's choorch afoor moy Sally
    wur deäd,
An' 'eerd un a bummin' awaäy loike a buzzard-clock[1]
    ower my yeäd,
An' I niver knaw'd whot a meän'd but I thowt a 'ad
    summut to saäy,
An' I thowt a said whot a owt to 'a said an' I
    comed awaäy.        20

Bessy Marris's barn! tha knaws she laäid it to meä.
Mowt 'a beän, mayhap, for she wur a bad un, sheä.
'Siver, I kep un, I kep un, my lass, tha mun under-
    stond;
I done my duty by un as I 'a done by the lond.

        [1] Cockchafer.

But Parson a comes an' a goos, an' a says it eäsy
    an' freeä
"The amoighty's a taäkin' o' you to 'issén, my friend,"
    says 'eä.
I weänt saäy men be loiars, thof summun said it in
    'aäste:
But a reäds wonn sarmin a weeäk, an' I 'a stubb'd
    Thornaby waäste.

D'ya moind the waäste, my lass? naw, naw, tha was
    not born then;
Theer wur a boggle in it, I often 'eerd un mysen;   30
Moäst loike a butter-bump[1], for I 'eerd un aboot an'
    aboot,
But I stubb'd un oop wi' the lot, an' raäved an'
    rembled un oot.

Keäper's it wur; fo' they fun un theer a-laäid on 'is
    faäce
Doon i' the woild 'enemies[2] afoor I comed to the
    plaäce.
Noäks or Thimbleby—toner 'ed shot un as deäd as
    a naäil.
Noäks wur 'ang'd for it oop at 'soize—but git ma
    my yaäle.

Dubbut looäk at the waäste: theer warn't not feäd
    for a cow:
Nowt at all but bracken an' fuzz, an' looäk at it
    now—
Warnt worth nowt a haäcre, an' now theer's lots o'
    feäd,
Fourscore yows upon it an' some on it doon in seäd.  40

           [1] Bittern.              [2] Anemones.

Nobbut a bit on it's left, an' I meän'd to 'a stubb'd
  it at fall,
Done it ta-year I meän'd, an' runn'd plow thruff it
  an' all,
If godamoighty an' parson 'ud nobbut let ma aloän,
Meä, wi' haäte oonderd haäcre o' Squoire's, an' lond
  o' my oän.

Do godamoighty knaw what a's doing a-taäkin' o'
  meä?
I beänt wonn as saws 'ere a beän an' yonder a
  peä;
An' Squoire 'ull be sa mad an' all—a' dear a'
  dear!
And I 'a monaged for Squoire come Michaelmas
  thirty year.

A mowt 'a taäken Joänes, as 'ant a 'aäpoth o'
  sense,
Or a mowt 'a taäken Robins—a niver mended a
  fence:                                         50
But godamoighty a moost taäke meä an' taäke ma
  now
Wi 'auf the cows to cauve an' Thornaby holms to
  plow!

Looäk 'ow quoloty smoiles when they sees ma a
  passin' by,
Says to thessén naw doot "what a mon a beä
  sewer-ly!"
For they knaws what I beän to Squoire sin fust a
  comed to the 'All;
I done my duty by Squoire an' I done my duty
  by all.

Squoire's i' Lunnon, an' summun I reckons 'ull 'a to
wroite,

For who's to howd the lond ater meä thot muddles
ma quoit;

Sa₁ tin-sewer I beä, thot a weänt niver give it to
Joänes,

Noither a moänt to Robins—a niver rembles the
stoäns.                                                60

But summun 'ull come ater meä mayhap wi' 'is kittle
o' steäm

Huzzin' an' maäzin' the blessed feälds wi' the Divil's
oän teäm.

Gin I mun doy I mun doy, an' loife they says is
sweet,

But gin I mun doy I mun doy, for I couldn abear
to see it.

What atta stannin' theer for, an' doesn bring ma the
yaäle?

Doctor's a 'tottler, lass, an a's hallus i' the owd
taäle;

I weänt breäk rules for Doctor, a knaws naw moor
nor a floy;

Git ma my yaäle I tell tha, an' gin I mun doy I
mun doy.

## NORTHERN FARMER

### NEW STYLE

Inserted by kind permission of Messrs MACMILLAN & Co., LTD.

Dosn't thou 'ear my 'erse's legs, as they canters
    awaäy?

Proputty, proputty, proputty—that's what I 'ears 'em
    saäy.

Proputty, proputty, proputty—Sam, thou's an ass for
    thy paaïns:

Theer's moor sense i' one o' 'is legs nor in all thy
    braaïns.

Woä—theer's a craw to pluck wi' tha, Sam: yon's
    parson's 'ouse—

Dosn't thou knaw that a man mun be eäther a man
    or a mouse?

Time to think on it then; for thou'll be twenty to
    weeäk[1].

Proputty, proputty—woä then woä—let ma 'ear mysén
    speäk.

Me an' thy muther, Sammy, 'as beän a-talkin' o'
    thee;

Thou's beän talkin' to muther, an' she beän a tellin'
    it me.              10

Thou'll not marry for munny—thou's sweet upo'
    parson's lass—

Noä—thou'll marry for luvv—an' we boäth on us
    thinks tha an ass.

[1] This week.

L. T.                            12

Seeä'd her todaäy goä by—Saäint's-daäy—they was
   riuging the bells.
She's a beauty thou thinks—an' soä is scoors o' gells,
Them as 'as munny an' all—wot's a beauty?—the
   flower as blaws.
But proputty, proputty sticks, an' proputty, proputty
   graws.

Do'ant be stunt[1]: taäke time: I knaws what maäkes
   tha sa mad.
Warn't I craäzed fur the lasses mysén when I wur
   a lad?
But I knaw'd a Quaäker feller as often 'as towd ma
   this:
"Doänt thou marry for munny, but goä wheer munny
   is!"                        20

An' I went wheer munny war: an' thy muther coom
   to 'and,
Wi' lots o' munny laaïd by, an' a nicetish bit o' land.
Maäybe she warn't a beauty:—I niver giv it a
   thowt—
But warn't she as good to cuddle an' kiss as a lass
   as 'ant nowt?

Parson's lass 'ant nowt, an' she weänt 'a nowt when
   'e's deäd,
Mun be a guvness, lad, or summut, and addle[2] her
   breäd:
Why? fur 'e's nobbut a curate, an' weänt niver git
   naw 'igher;
An' 'e maäde the bed as 'e ligs on afoor 'e coom'd
   to the shire.

[1] Obstinate.            [2] Earn.

An thin 'e coom'd to the parish wi' lots o' Varsity debt,
Stook to his taaïl they did, an' 'e 'ant got shut on
'em yet.                                                        30
An' 'e ligs on 'is back i' the grip, wi' noän to lend
'im a shove,
Woorse nor a far-welter'd[1] yowe: fur, Sammy, 'e
married fur luvv.

Luvv? what's luvv? thou can luvv thy lass an' 'er
munny too,
Maakin' 'em goä togither as they've good right to do.
Could'n I luvv thy muther by cause o' 'er munny
laaïd by?
Naäy—fur I luvv'd 'er a vast sight moor fur it:
reäson why.

Ay an' thy muther says thou wants to marry the lass,
Cooms of a gentleman burn: an' we boäth on us thinks
tha an ass.
Woä then, proputty, wiltha?—an ass as near as mays
nowt[2]—
Woä then, wiltha? dangtha!—the bees is as fell as
owt[3].                                                         40

Breäk me a bit o' the esh for his 'eäd, lad, out o' the
fence!
Gentleman burn! what's gentleman burn? is it shillins
an' pence?
Proputty, proputty's ivrything 'ere, an', Sammy, I'm
blest
If it isn't the saäme oop yonder, fur them as 'as it's
the best.

[1] Or fow-welter'd,—said of a sheep lying on its back in the furrow.
[2] Makes nothing.        [3] The flies are as fierce as anything.

Tis'n them as 'as munny as breäks into 'ouses an'
steäls,

Them as 'as coäts to their backs an' taäkes their
regular meäls.

Noä, but it's them as niver knaws wheer a meäl's
to be 'ad.

Taäke my word for it, Sammy, the poor in a loomp
is bad.

Them or thir feythers, tha sees, mun 'a beän a laäzy
lot,

Fur work mun 'a gone to the gittin' whiniver munny
was got.                                                    50

Feyther 'ad ammost nowt; leästways 'is munny
was 'id.

But 'e tued an' moil'd 'issén deäd, an 'e died a good
un, 'e did.

Loook thou theer wheer Wrigglesby beck cooms out
by the 'ill!

Feyther run oop to the farm, an' I runs oop to the
mill;

An' I'll run oop to the brig, an' that thou'll live to
see;

And if thou marries a good un I'll leäve the land to
thee.

Thim's my noätions, Sammy, wheerby I means to
stick;

But if thou marries a bad un, I'll leäve the land
to Dick.—

Coom oop, proputty, proputty—that's what I 'ears
'im saäy—

Proputty, proputty, proputty—canter an' canter awaäy.

# IN THE VALLEY OF CAUTERETZ

All along the valley, stream that flashest white,
Deepening thy voice with the deepening of the night,
All along the valley, where thy waters flow,
I walk'd with one I loved two and thirty years ago.
All along the valley while I walk'd to-day,
The two and thirty years were a mist that rolls away;
For all along the valley, down thy rocky bed
Thy living voice to me was as the voice of the dead,
And all along the valley, by rock and cave and tree,
The voice of the dead was a living voice to me.    10

## LYRICS FROM "THE PRINCESS"

### 1

As thro' the land at eve we went,
  And pluck'd the ripen'd ears,
We fell out, my wife and I,
O we fell out I know not why,
  And kiss'd again with tears.

For when we came where lies the child
  We lost in other years,
There above the little grave,
O there above the little grave,
  We kiss'd again with tears.    10

### 2

Sweet and low, sweet and low,
  Wind of the western sea,
Low, low, breathe and blow,
  Wind of the western sea!

Over the rolling waters go,
Come from the dying moon, and blow,
    Blow him again to me;
While my little one, while my pretty one, sleeps.

Sleep and rest, sleep and rest,
    Father will come to thee soon;                     20
Rest, rest, on mother's breast,
    Father will come to thee soon;
Father will come to his babe in the nest,
Silver sails all out of the west
    Under the silver moon:
Sleep, my little one, sleep, my pretty one, sleep.

### 3

The splendour falls on castle walls
    And snowy summits old in story:
The long light shakes across the lakes
    And the wild cataract leaps in glory.          30
Blow, bugle, blow, set the wild echoes flying,
Blow, bugle; answer, echoes, dying, dying, dying.

O hark, O hear! how thin and clear,
    And thinner, clearer, farther going!
O sweet and far from cliff and scar
    The horns of Elfland faintly blowing!
Blow, let us hear the purple glens replying:
Blow, bugle; answer, echoes, dying, dying, dying.

O love, they die in yon rich sky,
    They faint on hill or field or river:          40
Our echoes roll from soul to soul,
    And grow for ever and for ever.
Blow, bugle, blow, set the wild echoes flying,
And answer, echoes, answer, dying, dying, dying.

### 4

Thy voice is heard thro' rolling drums,
    That beat to battle where he stands;
Thy face across his fancy comes,
    And gives the battle to his hands:
A moment, while the trumpets blow,
    He sees his brood about thy knee;      50
The next, like fire he meets the foe,
    And strikes him dead for thine and thee.

### 5

Home they brought her warrior dead:
    She nor swoon'd, nor utter'd cry:
All her maidens, watching, said,
    "She must weep or she will die."

Then they praised him, soft and low,
    Call'd him worthy to be loved,
Truest friend and noblest foe;
    Yet she neither spoke nor moved.      60

Stole a maiden from her place,
    Lightly to the warrior stept,
Took the face-cloth from the face;
    Yet she neither moved nor wept.

Rose a nurse of ninety years,
    Set his child upon her knee—
Like summer tempest came her tears—
    "Sweet my child, I live for thee."

### 6

Ask me no more: the moon may draw the sea;
    The cloud may stoop from heaven and take the shape,
    With fold to fold, of mountain or of cape;    71
But O too fond, when have I answer'd thee?
            Ask me no more.

Ask me no more: what answer should I give?
I love not hollow cheek or faded eye:
Yet, O my friend, I will not have thee die!
Ask me no more, lest I should bid thee live;
   Ask me no more.

Ask me no more: thy fate and mine are seal'd:
I strove against the stream and all in vain:  80
Let the great river take me to the main:
No more, dear love, for at a touch I yield;
   Ask me no more.


# SELECTIONS FROM "IN MEMORIAM"

## A. H. H.

### OBIIT MDCCCXXXIII

#### 1

I held it truth, with him who sings
  To one clear harp in divers tones,
  That men may rise on stepping-stones
Of their dead selves to higher things.

But who shall so forecast the years
  And find in loss a gain to match?
  Or reach a hand thro' time to catch
The far-off interest of tears?

Let Love clasp Grief lest both be drown'd,
  Let darkness keep her raven gloss:  10
  Ah, sweeter to be drunk with loss,
To dance with death, to beat the ground,

Than that the victor Hours should scorn
    The long result of love, and boast:
    "Behold the man that loved and lost,
But all he was is overworn."


## 2

One writes, that "Other friends remain,"
    That "Loss is common to the race"—
    And common is the commonplace,
And vacant chaff well meant for grain.    20

That loss is common would not make
    My own less bitter, rather more:
    Too common! Never morning wore
To evening, but some heart did break.

O father, wheresoe'er thou be,
    That pledgest now thy gallant son;
    A shot, ere half thy draught be done,
Hath still'd the life that beat from thee.

O mother, praying God will save
    Thy sailor,—while thy head is bow'd,    30
    His heavy-shotted hammock-shroud
Drops in his vast and wandering grave.

Ye know no more than I who wrought
    At that last hour to please him well;
    Who mused on all I had to tell,
And something written, something thought;

Expecting still his advent home;
    And ever met him on his way
    With wishes, thinking, here to-day,
Or here to-morrow will he come.    40

O somewhere, meek unconscious dove,
    That sittest ranging golden hair;
    And glad to find thyself so fair,
Poor child, that waitest for thy love!

For now her father's chimney glows
    In expectation of a guest;
    And thinking "this will please him best,"
She takes a riband or a rose;

For he will see them on to-night;
    And with the thought her colour burns;   50
    And, having left the glass, she turns
Once more to set a ringlet right;

And, even when she turn'd, the curse
    Had fallen, and her future Lord
    Was drown'd in passing thro' the ford,
Or kill'd in falling from his horse.

O what to her shall be the end?
    And what to me remains of good?
    To her, perpetual maidenhood,
And unto me, no second friend.   60

### 3

The Danube to the Severn gave
    The darken'd heart that beat no more;
    They laid him by the pleasant shore,
And in the hearing of the wave.

There twice a day the Severn fills;
    The salt sea-water passes by,
    And hushes half the babbling Wye,
And makes a silence in the hills.

The Wye is hush'd nor moved along,
    And hush'd my deepest grief of all,          70
    When fill'd with tears that cannot fall,
I brim with sorrow drowning song.

The tide flows down, the wave again
    Is vocal in its wooded walls;
    My deeper anguish also falls,
And I can speak a little then.

### 4

Now, sometimes in my sorrow shut,
    Or breaking into song by fits;
    Alone, alone, to where he sits,
The Shadow cloak'd from head to foot,          80

Who keeps the keys of all the creeds,
    I wander, often falling lame,
    And looking back to whence I came,
Or on to where the pathway leads;

And crying, how changed from where it ran
    Thro' lands where not a leaf was dumb;
    But all the lavish hills would hum
The murmur of a happy Pan;

When each by turns was guide to each,
    And Fancy light from Fancy caught,          90
    And Thought leapt out to wed with Thought;
Ere Thought could wed itself with Speech:

And all we met was fair and good,
    And all was good that Time could bring,
    And all the secret of the Spring
Moved in the chambers of the blood:

And many an old philosophy
    On Argive heights divinely sang,
    And round us all the thicket rang
To many a flute of Arcady.           100

### 5

I envy not in any moods
    The captive void of noble rage,
    The linnet born within the cage,
That never knew the summer woods:

I envy not the beast that takes
    His license in the field of time,
    Unfetter'd by the sense of crime,
To whom a conscience never wakes;

Nor, what may count itself as blest,
    The heart that never plighted troth    110
    But stagnates in the weeds of sloth,
Nor any want-begotten rest.

I hold it true, whate'er befall;
    I feel it, when I sorrow most;
    'Tis better to have loved and lost
Than never to have loved at all.

### 6

Oh yet we trust that somehow good
    Will be the final goal of ill,
    To pangs of nature, sins of will,
Defects of doubt, and taints of blood:    120

That nothing walks with aimless feet;
    That not one life shall be destroy'd,
    Or cast as rubbish to the void,
When God hath made the pile complete;

That not a worm is cloven in vain;
      That not a moth with vain desire
      Is shrivel'd in a fruitless fire,
Or but subserves another's gain.

Behold, we know not anything;
      I can but trust that good shall fall      130
      At last—far off—at last, to all,
And every winter change to spring.

So runs my dream: but what am I?
      An infant crying in the night:
      An infant crying for the light:
And with no language but a cry.


The wish, that of the living whole
      No life may fail beyond the grave;
      Derives it not from what we have
The likest God within the soul?      140

Are God and Nature then at strife,
      That Nature lends such evil dreams?
      So careful of the type she seems,
So careless of the single life;

That I, considering everywhere
      Her secret meaning in her deeds,
      And finding that of fifty seeds
She often brings but one to bear;

I falter where I firmly trod,
      And falling with my weight of cares      150
      Upon the great world's altar-stairs
That slope thro' darkness up to God;

I stretch lame hands of faith, and grope,
    And gather dust and chaff, and call
    To what I feel is Lord of all,
And faintly trust the larger hope.

### 7

So many worlds, so much to do,
    So little done, such things to be,
    How know I what had need of thee,
For thou wert strong as thou wert true?    160

The fame is quench'd that I foresaw,
    The head hath miss'd an earthly wreath:
    I curse not nature, no, nor death;
For nothing is that errs from law.

We pass: the path that each man trod
    Is dim, or will be dim, with weeds:
    What fame is left for human deeds
In endless age? It rests with God.

O hollow wraith of dying fame,
    Fade wholly, while the soul exults,    170
    And self-infolds the large results
Of force that would have forged a name.

### 8

Sweet after showers, ambrosial air,
    That rollest from the gorgeous gloom
    Of evening over brake and bloom
And meadow, slowly breathing bare

The round of space, and rapt below
    Thro' all the dewy-tassell'd wood,
    And shadowing down the horned flood
In ripples, fan my brows and blow    180

The fever from my cheek, and sigh
    The full new life that feeds thy breath
    Throughout my frame, till Doubt and Death,
Ill brethren, let the fancy fly

From belt to belt of crimson seas
    On leagues of odour streaming far,
    To where in yonder orient star
A hundred spirits whisper "Peace."


I past beside the reverend walls
    In which of old I wore the gown;     190
    I roved at random through the town,
And saw the tumult of the halls;

And heard once more in college fanes
    The storm their high-built organs make,
    And thunder-music, rolling, shake
The prophets blazon'd on the panes;

And caught once more the distant shout,
    The measured pulse of racing oars
    Among the willows; paced the shores
And many a bridge, and all about     200

The same gray flats again, and felt
    The same, but not the same; and last
    Up that long walk of limes I past
To see the rooms in which he dwelt.

Another name was on the door:
    I linger'd; all within was noise
    Of songs, and clapping hands, and boys
That crash'd the glass and beat the floor;

Where once we held debate, a band
   Of youthful friends, on mind and art,   210
   And labour, and the changing mart,
And all the framework of the land;

When one would aim an arrow fair,
   But send it slackly from the string;
   And one would pierce an outer ring,
And one an inner, here and there;

And last the master-bowman, he,
   Would cleave the mark. A willing ear
   We lent him. Who, but hung to hear
The rapt oration flowing free   220

From point to point with power and grace,
   And music in the bounds of law,
   To those conclusions when we saw
The God within him light his face,

And seem to lift the form, and glow
   In azure orbits heavenly-wise;
   And over those ethereal eyes
The bar of Michael Angelo.

### 9

Witch-elms that counterchange the floor
   Of this flat lawn with dusk and bright;   230
   And thou, with all thy breadth and height
Of foliage, towering sycamore;

How often, hither wandering down,
   My Arthur found your shadows fair,
   And shook to all the liberal air
The dust and din and steam of town:

He brought an eye for all he saw;
    He mixt in all our simple sports;
    They pleased him, fresh from brawling courts
And dusky purlieus of the law.        240

O joy to him in this retreat,
    Immantled in ambrosial dark,
    To drink the cooler air, and mark
The landscape winking through the heat:

O sound to rout the brood of cares,
    The sweep of scythe in morning dew,
    The gust that round the garden flew,
And tumbled half the mellowing pears!

O bliss, when all in circle drawn
    About him, heart and ear were fed     250
    To hear him, as he lay and read
The Tuscan poets on the lawn:

Or in the all-golden afternoon
    A guest, or happy sister, sung,
    Or here she brought the harp and flung
A ballad to the brightening moon:

Nor less it pleased in livelier moods,
    Beyond the bounding hill to stray,
    And break the livelong summer day
With banquet in the distant woods;    260

Whereat we glanced from theme to theme,
    Discuss'd the books to love or hate,
    Or touch'd the changes of the state,
Or threaded some Socratic dream;

But if I praised the busy town,
  He loved to rail against it still,
  For "ground in yonder social mill
We rub each other's angles down,

"And merge," he said, "in form and gloss
  The picturesque of man and man."  270
  We talk'd: the stream beneath us ran,
The wine-flask lying couch'd in moss,

Or cool'd within the glooming wave;
  And last, returning from afar,
  Before the crimson-circled star
Had fall'n into her father's grave,

And brushing ankle-deep in flowers,
  We heard behind the woodbine veil
  The milk that bubbled in the pail,
And buzzings of the honied hours.  280

### 10

How pure at heart and sound in head,
  With what divine affections bold
  Should be the man whose thought would hold
An hour's communion with the dead.

In vain shalt thou, or any, call
  The spirits from their golden day,
  Except, like them, thou too canst say
My spirit is at peace with all.

They haunt the silence of the breast,
  Imaginations calm and fair,  290
  The memory like a cloudless air,
The conscience as a sea at rest:

But when the heart is full of din,
   And doubt beside the portal waits,
   They can but listen at the gates
And hear the household jar within.

### 11

The time draws near the birth of Christ;
   The moon is hid, the night is still;
   A single church below the hill
Is pealing, folded in the mist.        300

A single peal of bells below,
   That wakens at this hour of rest
   A single murmur in the breast,
That these are not the bells I know.

Like strangers' voices here they sound,
   In lands where not a memory strays,
   Nor landmark breathes of other days,
But all is new unhallow'd ground.

This holly by the cottage-eave,
   To-night, ungather'd, shall it stand:    310
   We live within the stranger's land,
And strangely falls our Christmas-eve.

Our father's dust is left alone
   And silent under other snows:
   There in due time the woodbine blows,
The violet comes, but we are gone.

No more shall wayward grief abuse
   The genial hour with mask and mime;
   For change of place, like growth of time,
Has broke the bond of dying use.     320

Let cares that petty shadows cast,
    By which our lives are chiefly proved,
    A little spare the night I loved,
And hold it solemn to the past.

But let no footstep beat the floor,
    Nor bowl of wassail mantle warm;
    For who would keep an ancient form
Through which the spirit breathes no more?

Be neither song, nor game, nor feast,
    Nor harp be touch'd, nor flute be blown;   330
    No dance, no motion, save alone
What lightens in the lucid east

Of rising worlds by yonder wood.
    Long sleeps the summer in the seed;
    Run out your measured arcs, and lead
The closing cycle rich in good.


Ring out wild bells to the wild sky,
    The flying cloud, the frosty light:
    The year is dying in the night;
Ring out, wild bells, and let him die.   340

Ring out the old, ring in the new,
    Ring, happy bells, across the snow:
    The year is going, let him go;
Ring out the false, ring in the true.

Ring out the grief that saps the mind,
    For those that here we see no more;
    Ring out the feud of rich and poor,
Ring in redress to all mankind.

Ring out a slowly dying cause,
    And ancient forms of party strife;    350
    Ring in the nobler modes of life,
With sweeter manners, purer laws.

Ring out the want, the care, the sin,
    The faithless coldness of the times;
    Ring out, ring out my mournful rhymes,
But ring the fuller minstrel in.

Ring out false pride in place and blood,
    The civic slander and the spite;
    Ring in the love of truth and right,
Ring in the common love of good.    360

Ring out old shapes of foul disease,
    Ring out the narrowing lust of gold;
    Ring out the thousand wars of old,
Ring in the thousand years of peace.

Ring in the valiant man and free,
    The larger heart, the kindlier hand;
    Ring out the darkness of the land,
Ring in the Christ that is to be.


It is the day when he was born,
    A bitter day that early sank    370
    Behind a purple-frosty bank
Of vapour, leaving night forlorn.

The time admits not flowers or leaves
    To deck the banquet. Fiercely flies
    The blast of North and East, and ice
Makes daggers at the sharpen'd eaves,

And bristles all the brakes and thorns
    To yon hard crescent, as she hangs
    Above the wood which grides and clangs
Its leafless ribs and iron horns         380

Together, in the drifts that pass
    To darken on the rolling brine
    That breaks the coast. But fetch the wine,
Arrange the board and brim the glass;

Bring in great logs and let them lie,
    To make a solid core of heat;
    Be cheerful-minded, talk and treat
Of all things ev'n as he were by:

We keep the day. With festal cheer,
    With books and music, surely we     390
    Will drink to him whate'er he be,
And sing the songs he loved to hear.


### 12

The churl in spirit, up or down
    Along the scale of ranks, thro' all,
    To who may grasp a golden ball
By blood a king, at heart a clown;

The churl in spirit, howe'er he veil
    His want in forms for fashion's sake,
    Will let his coltish nature break
At seasons thro' the gilded pale:     400

For who can always act? but he,
    To whom a thousand memories call,
    Not being less but more than all
The gentleness he seem'd to be,

So wore his outward best, and join'd
    Each office of the social hour,
    To noble manners, as the flower
And native growth of noble mind;

Nor ever narrowness or spite,
    Or villain fancy fleeting by,         410
    Drew in the expression of an eye,
Where God and Nature met in light,

And thus he bore without abuse
    The grand old name of gentleman,
    Defamed by every charlatan,
And soil'd with all ignoble use.

### 13

Love is and was my Lord and King,
    And in his presence I attend
    To hear the tidings of my friend,
Which every hour his couriers bring.     420

Love is and was my King and Lord,
    And will be, tho' as yet I keep
    Within his court on earth, and sleep
Encompass'd by his faithful guard,

And hear at times a sentinel
    That moves about from place to place,
    And whispers to the vast of space
Among the worlds, that all is well.

### 14

Dear friend, far off, my lost desire,
    So far, so near in woe and weal;     430
    O, loved the most when most I feel
There is a lower and a higher;

Known and unknown, human, divine!
    Sweet human hand and lips and eye,
    Dear heavenly friend that canst not die,
Mine, mine, for ever, ever mine!

Strange friend, past, present, and to be,
    Love deeplier, darklier understood;
    Behold I dream a dream of good
And mingle all the world with thee.     440


Thy voice is on the rolling air;
    I hear thee where the waters run;
    Thou standest in the rising sun,
And in the setting thou art fair.

What art thou then? I cannot guess;
    But tho' I seem in star and flower
    To feel thee some diffusive power,
I do not therefore love thee less:

My love involves the love before;
    My love is vaster passion now;     450
    Tho' mix'd with God and Nature thou,
I seem to love thee more and more.

Far off thou art, but ever nigh;
    I have thee still, and I rejoice;
    I prosper, circled with thy voice;
I shall not lose thee tho' I die.


O living will that shalt endure
    When all that seems shall suffer shock,
    Rise in the spiritual rock,
Flow thro' our deeds and make them pure,     460

That we may lift from out of dust
   A voice as unto him that hears,
   A cry above the conquer'd years
To one that with us works, and trust,

With faith that comes of self-control,
   The truths that never can be proved
   Until we close with all we loved,
And all we flow from, soul in soul.

## SELECTIONS FROM "MAUD"

A voice by the cedar tree,
In the meadow under the Hall!
She is singing an air that is known to me,
A passionate ballad gallant and gay,
A martial song like a trumpet's call!
Singing alone in the morning of life,
In the happy morning of life and of May,
Singing of men that in battle array,
Ready in heart and ready in hand,
March with banner and bugle and fife     10
To the death, for their native land.

Maud with her exquisite face,
And wild voice pealing up to the sunny sky,
And feet like sunny gems on an English green,
Maud in the light of her youth and her grace,
Singing of Death, and of Honour that cannot die,
Till I well could weep for a time so sordid and mean,
And myself so languid and base.

Silence, beautiful voice!
Be still, for you only trouble the mind            20
With a joy in which I cannot rejoice,
A glory I shall not find.
Still! I will hear you no more,
For your sweetness hardly leaves me a choice
But to move to the meadow and fall before
Her feet on the meadow grass, and adore,
Not her, who is neither courtly nor kind,
Not her, not her, but a voice.

Birds in the high Hall-garden
    When twilight was falling,            30
Maud, Maud, Maud, Maud,
    They were crying and calling.

Where was Maud? in our wood;
    And I, who else, was with her,
Gathering woodland lilies,
    Myriads blow together.

Birds in our wood sang
    Ringing thro' the valleys,
Maud is here, here, here
    In among the lilies.            40

I kiss'd her slender hand,
    She took the kiss sedately;
Maud is not seventeen,
    But she is tall and stately.

I to cry out on pride
    Who have won her favour!
O Maud were sure of Heaven
    If lowliness could save her.

I know the way she went
   Home with her maiden posy,      50
For her feet have touch'd the meadows
   And left the daisies rosy.

Birds in the high Hall-garden
   Were crying and calling to her,
Where is Maud, Maud, Maud?
   One is come to woo her.

Look, a horse at the door,
   And little King Charles is snarling,
Go back, my lord, across the moor,
   You are not her darling.      60


Come into the garden, Maud,
  For the black bat, night, has flown,
Come into the garden, Maud,
  I am here at the gate alone;
And the woodbine spices are wafted abroad,
  And the musk of the roses blown.

For a breeze of morning moves,
  And the planet of Love is on high,
Beginning to faint in the light that she loves
  On a bed of daffodil sky,      70
To faint in the light of the sun she loves,
  To faint in his light, and to die.

All night have the roses heard
  The flute, violin, bassoon;
All night has the casement jessamine stirr'd
  To the dancers dancing in tune;
Till a silence fell with the waking bird,
  And a hush with the setting moon.

I said to the lily, "There is but one
   With whom she has heart to be gay.        80
When will the dancers leave her alone?
   She is weary of dance and play."
Now half to the setting moon are gone,
   And half to the rising day;
Low on the sand and loud on the stone
   The last wheel echoes away.

I said to the rose, "The brief night goes
   In babble and revel and wine.
O young lord-lover, what sighs are those,
   For one that will never be thine?        90
But mine, but mine," so I sware to the rose,
   "For ever and ever, mine."

And the soul of the rose went into my blood,
   As the music clash'd in the hall;
And long by the garden lake I stood,
   For I heard your rivulet fall
From the lake to the meadow and on to the wood,
   Our wood, that is dearer than all;

From the meadow your walks have left so sweet
   That whenever a March-wind sighs        100
He sets the jewel-print of your feet
   In violets blue as your eyes,
To the woody hollows in which we meet
   And the valleys of Paradise.

The slender acacia would not shake
   One long milk-bloom on the tree;
The white lake-blossom fell into the lake,
   As the pimpernel dozed on the lea;

But the rose was awake all night for your sake,
　Knowing your promise to me;　　　　　110
The lilies and roses were all awake,
　They sigh'd for the dawn and thee.

Queen rose of the rosebud garden of girls,
　Come hither, the dances are done,
In gloss of satin and glimmer of pearls,
　Queen lily and rose in one;
Shine out, little head, sunning over with curls,
　To the flowers, and be their sun.

There has fallen a splendid tear
　From the passion-flower at the gate.　　120
She is coming, my dove, my dear;
　She is coming, my life, my fate;
The red rose cries, "She is near, she is near;"
　And the white rose weeps, "She is late;"
The larkspur listens, "I hear, I hear;"
　And the lily whispers, "I wait."

She is coming, my own, my sweet;
　Were it ever so airy a tread,
My heart would hear her and beat,
　Were it earth in an earthy bed;　　130
My dust would hear her and beat,
　Had I lain for a century dead;
Would start and tremble under her feet,
　And blossom in purple and red.

## ELAINE

Elaine the fair, Elaine the loveable,
Elaine, the lily maid of Astolat,
High in her chamber up a tower to the east
Guarded the sacred shield of Lancelot;
Which first she placed where morning's earliest ray
Might strike it, and awake her with the gleam;
Then fearing rust or soilure fashion'd for it
A case of silk, and braided thereupon
All the devices blazon'd on the shield
In their own tinct, and added, of her wit,        10
A border fantasy of branch and flower,
And yellow-throated nestling in the nest.
Nor rested thus content, but day by day
Leaving her household and good father climb'd
That eastern tower, and entering barr'd her door,
Stript off the case, and read the naked shield,
Now guess'd a hidden meaning in his arms,
Now made a pretty history to herself
Of every dint a sword had beaten in it,
And every scratch a lance had made upon it,        20
Conjecturing when and where: this cut is fresh;
That ten years back; this dealt him at Caerlyle;
That at Caerleon; this at Camelot:
And ah God's mercy, what a stroke was there!
And here a thrust that might have kill'd, but God
Broke the strong lance, and roll'd his enemy down
And saved him: so she lived in fantasy.

How came the lily maid by that good shield
Of Lancelot, she that knew not ev'n his name?

He left it with her, when he rode to tilt          30
For the great diamond in the diamond jousts,
Which Arthur had ordain'd, and by that name
Had named them, since a diamond was the prize.

For Arthur when none knew from whence he came,
Long ere the people chose him for their king,
Roving the trackless realms of Lyonnesse,
Had found a glen, gray boulder and black tarn.
A horror lived about the tarn, and clave
Like its own mists to all the mountain side:
For here two brothers, one a king, had met          40
And fought together; but their names were lost.
And each had slain his brother at a blow,
And down they fell and made the glen abhorr'd:
And there they lay till all their bones were bleach'd,
And lichen'd into colour with the crags:
And one of these, the king, had on a crown
Of diamonds, one in front, and four aside.
And Arthur came, and labouring up the pass
All in a misty moonshine, unawares
Had trodden that crown'd skeleton, and the skull    50
Brake from the nape, and from the skull the crown
Roll'd into light, and turning on its rims
Fled like a glittering rivulet to the tarn:
And down the shingly scaur he plunged, and caught,
And set it on his head, and in his heart
Heard murmurs, "Lo, thou likewise shalt be king."

Thereafter, when a king, he had the gems
Pluck'd from the crown, and show'd them to his knights,
Saying "These jewels, whereupon I chanced
Divinely, are the kingdom's not the king's—         60
For public use: henceforward let there be,

Once every year, a joust for one of these:
For so by nine years' proof we needs must learn
Which is our mightiest, and ourselves shall grow
In use of arms and manhood, till we drive
The Heathen, who, some say, shall rule the land
Hereafter, which God hinder." Thus he spoke:
And eight years past, eight jousts had been, and still
Had Lancelot won the diamond of the year,
With purpose to present them to the Queen,          70
When all were won; but meaning all at once
To snare her royal fancy with a boon
Worth half her realm, had never spoken word.

Now for the central diamond and the last
And largest, Arthur, holding then his court
Hard on the river nigh the place which now
Is this world's hugest, let proclaim a joust
At Camelot, and when the time drew nigh
Spake (for she had been sick) to Guinevere,
"Are you so sick, my Queen, you cannot move          80
To these fair jousts?" "Yea, lord," she said, "you
    know it."
"Then will you miss," he answer'd, "the great deeds
Of Lancelot, and his prowess in the lists,
A sight you love to look on." And the Queen
Lifted her eyes, and they dwelt languidly
On Lancelot, where he stood beside the King.
He thinking that he read her meaning there,
"Stay with me, I am sick; my love is more
Than many diamonds," yielded, and a heart,
Love-loyal to the least wish of the Queen          90
(However much he yearn'd to make complete
The tale of diamonds for his destined boon)

Urged him to speak against the truth, and say,
"Sir King, my ancient wound is hardly whole,
And lets me from the saddle;" and the King
Glanced first at him, then her, and went his way.
No sooner gone than suddenly she began.

"To blame, my lord Sir Lancelot, much to blame.
Why go you not to these fair jousts? the knights
Are half of them our enemies, and the crowd    100
Will murmur, Lo the shameless ones, who take
Their pastime now the trustful king is gone!"
Then Lancelot vext at having lied in vain:
"Are you so wise? you were not once so wise,
My Queen, that summer, when you loved me first.
Then of the crowd you took no more account
Than of the myriad cricket of the mead,
When its own voice clings to each blade of grass,
And every voice is nothing. As to knights,
Them surely can I silence with all ease.    110
But now my loyal worship is allow'd
Of all men: many a bard, without offence,
Has link'd our names together in his lay,
Lancelot, the flower of bravery, Guinevere,
The pearl of beauty: and our knights at feast
Have pledged us in this union, while the king
Would listen smiling. How then? is there more?
Has Arthur spoken aught? or would yourself,
Now weary of my service and devoir,
Henceforth be truer to your faultless lord?"    120

She broke into a little scornful laugh.
"Arthur, my lord, Arthur, the faultless King,
That passionate perfection, my good lord—
But who can gaze upon the Sun in heaven?

He never spake word of reproach to me,
He never had a glimpse of mine untruth,
He cares not for me: only here to-day
There gleam'd a vague suspicion in his eyes:
Some meddling rogue has tamper'd with him—else
Rapt in this fancy of his Table Round,                    130
And swearing men to vows impossible,
To make them like himself: but, friend, to me
He is all fault who hath no fault at all:
For who loves me must have a touch of earth;
The low sun makes the colour: I am yours,
Not Arthur's, as you know, save by the bond.
And therefore hear my words: go to the jousts:
The tiny-trumpeting gnat can break our dream
When sweetest; and the vermin voices here
May buzz so loud—we scorn them, but they sting." 140

   Then answer'd Lancelot, the chief of knights.
"And with what face, after my pretext made,
Shall I appear, O Queen, at Camelot, I
Before a king who honours his own word,
As if it were his God's?"

                "Yea," said the Queen,
"A moral child without the craft to rule,
Else had he not lost me: but listen to me,
If I must find you wit: we hear it said
That men go down before your spear at a touch,
But knowing you are Lancelot; your great name,  150
This conquers: hide it therefore; go unknown:
Win! by this kiss you will: and our true king
Will then allow your pretext, O my knight,
As all for glory; for to speak him true,
You know right well, how meek soe'er he seem,

No keener hunter after glory breathes.
He loves it in his knights more than himself:
They prove to him his work: win and return."

    Then got Sir Lancelot suddenly to horse,
Wroth at himself: not willing to be known,        160
He left the barren-beaten thoroughfare,
Chose the green path that show'd the rarer foot,
And there among the solitary downs,
Full often lost in fancy, lost his way;
Till as he traced a faintly-shadow'd track,
That all in loops and links among the dales
Ran to the Castle of Astolat, he saw
Fired from the west, far on a hill, the towers.
Thither he made and wound the gateway horn.
Then came an old, dumb, myriad-wrinkled man,    170
Who let him into lodging and disarm'd.
And Lancelot marvell'd at the wordless man;
And issuing found the Lord of Astolat
With two strong sons, Sir Torre and Sir Lavaine,
Moving to meet him in the castle court;
And close behind them stept the lily maid
Elaine, his daughter: mother of the house
There was not: some light jest among them rose
With laughter dying down as the great knight
Approach'd them: then the Lord of Astolat:       180
"Whence comest thou, my guest, and by what
     name
Livest between the lips? for by thy state
And presence I might guess thee chief of those,
After the king, who eat in Arthur's halls.
Him have I seen: the rest, his Table Round,
Known as they are, to me they are unknown."

                                    14—2

Then answer'd Lancelot, the chief of knights.
"Known am I, and of Arthur's hall, and known,
What I by mere mischance have brought, my shield.
But since I go to joust as one unknown          190
At Camelot for the diamond, ask me not,
Hereafter you shall know me—and the shield—
I pray you lend me one, if such you have,
Blank, or at least with some device not mine."

Then said the Lord of Astolat, "Here is Torre's:
Hurt in his first tilt was my son, Sir Torre.
And so, God wot, his shield is blank enough.
His you can have." Then added plain Sir Torre,
"Yea since I cannot use it, you may have it."
Here laugh'd the father saying, "Fie, Sir Churl,  200
Is that an answer for a noble knight?
Allow him: but Lavaine, my younger here,
He is so full of lustihood, he will ride
Joust for it, and win, and bring it in an hour
And set it in this damsel's golden hair,
To make her thrice as wilful as before."

"Nay, father, nay good father, shame me not
Before this noble knight," said young Lavaine,
"For nothing. Surely I but play'd on Torre:
He seem'd so sullen, vext he could not go:        210
A jest, no more: for, knight, the maiden dreamt
That some one put this diamond in her hand,
And that it was too slippery to be held,
And slipt and fell into some pool or stream,
The castle-well, belike; and then I said
That *if* I went and *if* I fought and won it
(But all was jest and joke among ourselves)
Then must she keep it safelier. All was jest.

But, father, give me leave, an if he will,
To ride to Camelot with this noble knight:    220
Win shall I not, but do my best to win:
Young as I am, yet would I do my best."

"So you will grace me," answer'd Lancelot,
Smiling a moment, "with your fellowship
O'er these waste downs whereon I lost myself,
Then were I glad of you as guide and friend;
And you shall win this diamond—as I hear,
It is a fair large diamond,—if you may,
And yield it to this maiden, if you will."
"A fair large diamond," added plain Sir Torre,    230
"Such be for Queens and not for simple maids."
Then she, who held her eyes upon the ground,
Elaine, and heard her name so tost about,
Flush'd slightly at the slight disparagement
Before the stranger knight, who, looking at her,
Full courtly, yet not falsely, thus return'd:
"If what is fair be but for what is fair,
And only Queens are to be counted so,
Rash were my judgment then, who deem this maid
Might wear as fair a jewel as is on earth,    240
Not violating the bond of like to like."

He spoke and ceased: the lily maid Elaine,.
Won by the mellow voice before she look'd,
Lifted her eyes, and read his lineaments.
The great and guilty love he bare the Queen,
In battle with the love he bare his lord,
Had marr'd his face, and mark'd it ere his time.
Another sinning on such heights with one,
The flower of all the west and all the world,
Had been the sleeker for it: but in him    250

His mood was often like a fiend, and rose
And drove him into wastes and solitudes
For agony, who was yet a living soul.
Marr'd as he was, he seem'd the goodliest man
That ever among ladies ate in Hall,
And noblest, when she lifted up her eyes.
However marr'd, of more than twice her years,
Seam'd with an ancient swordcut on the cheek,
And bruised and bronzed, she lifted up her eyes
And loved him, with that love which was her doom.  260

Then the great knight, the darling of the court,
Loved of the loveliest, into that rude hall
Stept with all grace, and not with half disdain
Hid under grace, as in a smaller time,
But kindly man moving among his kind:
Whom they with meats and vintage of their best
And talk and minstrel melody entertain'd.
And much they ask'd of court and Table Round,
And ever well and readily answer'd he:
But Lancelot, when they glanced at Guinevere,   270
Suddenly speaking of the wordless man,
Heard from the Baron that, ten years before,
The heathen caught and reft him of his tongue.
"He learnt and warn'd me of their fierce design
Against my house, and him they caught and maim'd;
But I, my sons, and little daughter fled
From bonds or death, and dwelt among the woods
By the great river in a boatman's hut.
Dull days were those, till our good Arthur broke
The Pagan yet once more on Badon hill."   280

"O there, great Lord, doubtless," Lavaine said, rapt
By all the sweet and sudden passion of youth

Toward greatness in its elder, "you have fought.
O tell us; for we live apart, you know
Of Arthur's glorious wars." And Lancelot spoke
And answer'd him at full, as having been
With Arthur in the fight which all day long
Rang by the white mouth of the violent Glem;
And in the four wild battles by the shore
Of Duglas; that on Bassa; then the war          290
That thunder'd in and out the gloomy skirts
Of Celidon the forest; and again
By castle Gurnion where the glorious King
Had on his cuirass worn our Lady's Head,
Carved of one emerald, center'd in a sun
Of silver rays, that lighten'd as he breathed;
And at Caerleon had he help'd his lord,
When the strong neighings of the wild white Horse
Set every gilded parapet shuddering;
And up in Agned Cathregonion too,            300
And down the waste sand-shores of Trath Treroit,
Where many a heathen fell; "and on the mount
Of Badon I myself beheld the King
Charge at the head of all his Table Round,
And all his legions crying Christ and him,
And break them; and I saw him, after, stand
High on a heap of slain, from spur to plume
Red as the rising sun with heathen blood,
And seeing me, with a great voice he cried,
'They are broken, they are broken!' for the King, 310
However mild he seems at home, nor cares
For triumph in our mimic wars, the jousts—
For if his own knight cast him down, he laughs
Saying, his knights are better men than he—
Yet in this heathen war the fire of God

Fills him: I never saw his like: there lives
No greater leader."
                While he utter'd this,
Low to her own heart said the lily maid,
"Save your great self, fair lord;" and when he fell
From talk of war to traits of pleasantry—          320
Being mirthful he but in a stately kind—
She still took note that when the living smile
Died from his lips, across him came a cloud
Of melancholy severe, from which again,
Whenever in her hovering to and fro
The lily maid had striven to make him cheer,
There brake a sudden beaming tenderness
Of manners and of nature: and she thought
That all was nature, all, perchance, for her.
And all night long his face before her lived,          330
As when a painter, poring on a face,
Divinely thro' all hindrance finds the man
Behind it, and so paints him that his face,
The shape and colour of a mind and life,
Lives for his children, ever at its best
And fullest; so the face before her lived,
Dark-splendid, speaking in the silence, full
Of noble things, and held her from her sleep.
Till rathe she rose, half-cheated in the thought
She needs must bid farewell to sweet Lavaine.          340
First as in fear, step after step, she stole
Down the long tower-stairs, hesitating:
Anon, she heard Sir Lancelot cry in the court,
"This shield, my friend, where is it?" and Lavaine
Past inward, as she came from out the tower.
There to his proud horse Lancelot turn'd, and smooth'd
The glossy shoulder, humming to himself.

Half-envious of the flattering hand, she drew
Nearer and stood.  He look'd, and more amazed
Than if seven men had set upon him, saw          350
The maiden standing in the dewy light.
He had not dream'd she was so beautiful.
Then came on him a sort of sacred fear,
For silent, tho' he greeted her, she stood
Rapt on his face as if it were a God's.
Suddenly flash'd on her a wild desire,
That he should wear her favour at the tilt.
She braved a riotous heart in asking for it.
"Fair lord, whose name I know not—noble it is,
I well believe, the noblest—will you wear        360
My favour at this tourney?"  "Nay," said he,
"Fair lady, since I never yet have worn
Favour of any lady in the lists.
Such is my wont, as those, who know me, know."
"Yea, so," she answer'd; "then in wearing mine
Needs must be lesser likelihood, noble lord,
That those who know should know you."  And he turn'd
Her counsel up and down within his mind,
And found it true, and answer'd, "True, my child.
Well, I will wear it: fetch it out to me:         370
What is it?" and she told him "A red sleeve
Broider'd with pearls," and brought it: then he bound
Her token on his helmet, with a smile
Saying, "I never yet have done so much
For any maiden living," and the blood
Sprang to her face and fill'd her with delight;
But left her all the paler, when Lavaine
Returning brought the yet-unblazon'd shield,
His brother's; which he gave to Lancelot,
Who parted with his own to fair Elaine;          380

"Do me this grace, my child, to have my shield
In keeping till I come." "A grace to me,"
She answer'd, "twice to-day. I am your Squire."
Whereat Lavaine said, laughing, "Lily maid,
For fear our people call you lily maid
In earnest, let me bring your colour back;
Once, twice, and thrice: now get you hence to
    bed":
So kiss'd her, and Sir Lancelot his own hand,
And thus they moved away: she stay'd a minute,
Then made a sudden step to the gate, and there—   390
Her bright hair blown about the serious face
Yet rosy-kindled with her brother's kiss—
Paused in the gateway, standing by the shield
In silence, while she watch'd their arms far-off
Sparkle, until they dipt below the downs.

Then to her tower she climb'd, and took the shield,
There kept it, and so lived in fantasy.

Meanwhile the new companions past away
Far o'er the long backs of the bushless downs,
To where Sir Lancelot knew there lived a knight   400
Not far from Camelot, now for forty years
A hermit, who had pray'd, labour'd and pray'd,
And ever labouring had scoop'd himself
In the white rock a chapel and a hall
On massive columns, like a shorecliff cave,
And cells and chambers: all were fair and dry;
The green light from the meadows underneath
Struck up and lived along the milky roofs;
And in the meadows tremulous aspen-trees
And poplars made a noise of falling showers.   410
And thither wending there that night they bode.

But when the next day broke from underground,
And shot red fire and shadows thro' the cave,
They rose, heard mass, broke fast, and rode away:
Then Lancelot saying, "Hear, but hold my name
Hidden, you ride with Lancelot of the Lake,"
Abash'd Lavaine, whose instant reverence,
Dearer to true young hearts than their own praise,
But left him leave to stammer, "Is it indeed?"
And after muttering "The great Lancelot,"          420
At last he got his breath and answer'd, "One,
One have I seen—that other, our liege lord,
The dread Pendragon, Britain's king of kings,
Of whom the people talk mysteriously,
He will be there—then were I stricken blind
That minute, I might say that I had seen."

So spake Lavaine, and when they reach'd the lists
By Camelot in the meadow, let his eyes
Run thro' the peopled gallery which half round
Lay like a rainbow fall'n upon the grass,          430
Until they found the clear-faced King, who sat
Robed in red samite, easily to be known,
Since to his crown the golden dragon clung,
And down his robe the dragon writhed in gold,
And from the carven-work behind him crept
Two dragons gilded, sloping down to make
Arms for his chair, while all the rest of them
Thro' knots and loops and folds innumerable
Fled ever thro' the woodwork, till they found
The new design wherein they lost themselves,       440
Yet with all ease, so tender was the work:
And, in the costly canopy o'er him set,
Blazed the last diamond of the nameless king.

Then Lancelot answer'd young Lavaine and said,
"Me you call great: mine is the firmer seat,
The truer lance: but there is many a youth
Now crescent, who will come to all I am
And overcome it; and in me there dwells
No greatness, save it be some far-off touch
Of greatness to know well I am not great:　　　450
There is the man." And Lavaine gaped upon him
As on a thing miraculous, and anon
The trumpets blew; and then did either side,
They that assail'd, and they that held the lists,
Set lance in rest, strike spur, suddenly move,
Meet in the midst, and there so furiously
Shock, that a man far-off might well perceive,
If any man that day were left afield,
The hard earth shake, and a low thunder of arms.
And Lancelot bode a little, till he saw　　　46c
Which were the weaker; then he hurl'd into it
Against the stronger: little need to speak
Of Lancelot in his glory: King, duke, earl,
Count, baron—whom he smote, he overthrew.

But in the field were Lancelot's kith and kin,
Ranged with the Table Round that held the lists,
Strong men, and wrathful that a stranger knight
Should do and almost overdo the deeds
Of Lancelot; and one said to the other, "Lo!
What is he? I do not mean the force alone,　　　470
The grace and versatility of the man—
Is it not Lancelot?" "When has Lancelot worn
Favour of any lady in the lists?
Not such his wont, as we, that know him, know."
"How then? who then?" a fury seized on them,

A fiery family passion for the name
Of Lancelot, and a glory one with theirs.
They couch'd their spears and prick'd their steeds and
    thus,
Their plumes driv'n backward by the wind they made
In moving, all together down upon him                480
Bare, as a wild wave in the wide North-sea,
Green-glimmering toward the summit, bears, with all
Its stormy crests that smoke against the skies,
Down on a bark, and overbears the bark,
And him that helms it, so they overbore
Sir Lancelot and his charger, and a spear
Down-glancing lamed the charger, and a spear
Prick'd sharply his own cuirass, and the head
Pierced thro' his side, and there snapt, and remain'd.

    Then Sir Lavaine did well and worshipfully;    490
He bore a knight of old repute to the earth,
And brought his horse to Lancelot where he lay.
He up the side, sweating with agony, got,
But thought to do while he might yet endure,
And being lustily holpen by the rest,
His party,—tho' it seemed half-miracle
To those he fought with—drave his kith and kin,
And all the Table Round that held the lists,
Back to the barrier; then the heralds blew
Proclaiming his the prize, who wore the sleeve    500
Of scarlet, and the pearls; and all the knights,
His party, cried "Advance, and take your prize
The diamond;" but he answer'd, "Diamond me
No diamonds! for God's love, a little air!
Prize me no prizes, for my prize is death!
Hence will I, and I charge you, follow me not."

He spoke, and vanish'd suddenly from the field
With young Lavaine into the poplar grove.
There from his charger down he slid, and sat,
Gasping to Sir Lavaine, "Draw the lance-head": 510
"Ah my sweet lord Sir Lancelot," said Lavaine,
"I dread me, if I draw it, you will die."
But he, "I die already with it: draw—
Draw"—and Lavaine drew, and that other gave
A marvellous great shriek and ghastly groan,
And half his blood burst forth, and down he sank
For the pure pain, and wholly swoon'd away.
Then came the hermit out and bare him in,
There stanch'd his wound; and there, in daily doubt
Whether to live or die, for many a week       520
Hid from the wide world's rumour by the grove
Of poplars with their noise of falling showers,
And ever-tremulous aspen-trees, he lay.

But on that day when Lancelot fled the lists,
His party, knights of utmost North and West,
Lords of waste marches, kings of desolate isles,
Came round their great Pendragon, saying to him,
"Lo, Sire, our knight thro' whom we won the day
Hath gone sore wounded, and hath left his prize
Untaken, crying that his prize is death."      530
"Heaven hinder," said the King "that such an one,
So great a knight as we have seen to-day—
He seem'd to me another Lancelot—
Yea, twenty times I thought him Lancelot—
He must not pass uncared for. Gawain, rise,
My nephew, and ride forth and find the knight.
Wounded and wearied needs must he be near.
I charge you that you get at once to horse.

And, knights and kings, there breathes not one
   of you
Will deem this prize of ours is rashly given:    540
His prowess was too wondrous.  We will do him
No customary honour: since the knight
Came not to us, of us to claim the prize,
Ourselves will send it after.  Wherefore take
This diamond, and deliver it, and return,
And bring us what he is and how he fares,
And cease not from your quest, until you find."

  So saying, from the carven flower above,
To which it made a restless heart, he took,
And gave, the diamond: then from where he sat  550
At Arthur's right, with smiling face arose,
With smiling face and frowning heart, a Prince
In the mid might and flourish of his May,
Gawain, surnamed The Courteous, fair and strong,
And after Lancelot, Tristram, and Geraint
And Lamorack, a good knight, but therewithal
Sir Modred's brother, of a crafty house,
Nor often loyal to his word, and now
Wroth that the king's command to sally forth
In quest of whom he knew not, made him leave  560
The banquet, and concourse of knights and kings.

  So all in wrath he got to horse and went;
While Arthur to the banquet, dark in mood,
Past, thinking "Is it Lancelot who has come
Despite the wound he spake of, all for gain
Of glory, and has added wound to wound,
And ridd'n away to die?"  So fear'd the King,
And, after two days' tarriance there, return'd.
Then when he saw the Queen, embracing ask'd,

"Love, are you yet so sick?" "Nay, lord," she said.
"And where is Lancelot?" Then the Queen amazed,
"Was he not with you? won he not your prize?"  572
"Nay, but one like him." "Why that like was he."
And when the King demanded how she knew,
Said, "Lord, no sooner had you parted from us,
Than Lancelot told me of a common talk
That men went down before his spear at a touch,
But knowing he was Lancelot; his great name
Conquer'd; and therefore would he hide his name
From all men, ev'n the king, and to this end  580
Had made the pretext of a hindering wound,
That he might joust unknown of all, and learn
If his old prowess were in aught decay'd:
And added, 'Our true Arthur, when he learns,
Will well allow my pretext, as for gain
Of purer glory.'"
                              Then replied the King:
"Far lovelier in our Lancelot had it been,
In lieu of idly dallying with the truth,
To have trusted me as he has trusted you.
Surely his king and most familiar friend  590
Might well have kept his secret. True, indeed,
Albeit I know my knights fantastical,
So fine a fear in our large Lancelot
Must needs have moved my laughter: now remains
But little cause for laughter: his own kin—
Ill news, my Queen, for all who love him, these!
His kith and kin, not knowing, set upon him;
So that he went sore wounded from the field:
Yet good news too: for goodly hopes are mine
That Lancelot is no more a lonely heart.  600
He wore, against his wont, upon his helm

A sleeve of scarlet, broidered with great pearls,
Some gentle maiden's gift."
                              " Yea, lord," she said,
"Your hopes are mine," and saying that she choked,
And sharply turn'd about to hide her face,
Moved to her chamber, and there flung herself
Down on the great King's couch, and writhed upon it,
And clench'd her fingers till they bit the palm,
And shriek'd out "Traitor" to the unhearing wall,
Then flash'd into wild tears, and rose again,      610
And moved about her palace, proud and pale.


Gawain the while thro' all the region round
Rode with his diamond, wearied of the quest,
Touch'd at all points, except the poplar grove,
And came at last, tho' late, to Astolat:
Whom glittering in enamell'd arms the maid
Glanced at, and cried, "What news from Camelot,
    lord ?
What of the knight with the red sleeve?" "He
    won."
"I knew it," she said. "But parted from the jousts
Hurt in the side," whereat she caught her breath;   620
Thro' her own side she felt the sharp lance go;
Thereon she smote her hand: well-nigh she swoon'd:
And, while he gazed wonderingly at her, came
The lord of Astolat out, to whom the Prince
Reported who he was, and on what quest
Sent, that he bore the prize and could not find
The victor, but had ridden wildly round
To seek him, and was wearied of the search.
To whom the lord of Astolat, "Bide with us,
And ridé no longer wildly, noble Prince!           630

Here was the knight, and here he left a shield;
This will he send or come for: furthermore
Our son is with him; we shall hear anon,
Needs must we hear." To this the courteous Prince
Accorded with his wonted courtesy,
Courtesy with a touch of traitor in it,
And stay'd; and cast his eyes on fair Elaine:
Where could be found face daintier? then her shape
From forehead down to foot perfect—again
From foot to forehead exquisitely turn'd:            640
"Well—if I bide, lo! this wild flower for me!"
And oft they met among the garden yews,
And there he set himself to play upon her
With sallying wit, free flashes from a height
Above her, graces of the court, and songs,
Sighs, and slow smiles, and golden eloquence
And amorous adulation, till the maid
Rebell'd against it, saying to him, "Prince,
O loyal nephew of our noble King,
Why ask you not to see the shield he left,            650
Whence you might learn his name? Why slight your
     King,
And lose the quest he sent you on, and prove
No surer than our falcon yesterday,
Who lost the hern we slipt him at, and went
To all the winds?" "Nay, by mine head," said he,
"I lose it, as we lose the lark in heaven,
O damsel, in the light of your blue eyes:
But an you will it let me see the shield."
And when the shield was brought, and Gawain saw
Sir Lancelot's azure lions, crown'd with gold,            660
Ramp in the field, he smote his thigh, and mock'd;
"Right was the King! our Lancelot! that true man!"

"And right was I," she answer'd merrily, "I,
Who dream'd my knight the greatest knight of all."
"And if _I_ dream'd," said Gawain, "that you love
This greatest knight, your pardon! lo, you know it!
Speak therefore: shall I waste myself in vain?"
Full simple was her answer, "What know I?
My brethren have been all my fellowship,
And I, when often they have talk'd of love,          670
Wish'd it had been my mother, for they talk'd,
Meseem'd, of what they knew not; so myself—
I know not if I know what true love is,
But if I know, then, if I love not him,
Methinks there is none other I can love."
"Yea, by God's death," said he, "you love him well,
But would not, knew you what all others know,
And whom he loves." "So be it," cried Elaine,
And lifted her fair face and moved away:
But he pursued her, calling, "Stay a little!          680
One golden minute's grace: he wore your sleeve:
Would he break faith with one I may not name?
Must our true man change like a leaf at last?
May it be so? why then, far be it from me
To cross our mighty Lancelot in his loves!
And, damsel, for I deem you know full well
Where your great knight is hidden, let me leave
My quest with you; the diamond also: here!
For if you love, it will be sweet to give it;
And if he love, it will be sweet to have it          690
From your own hand; and whether he love or not,
A diamond is a diamond. Fare you well
A thousand times!—a thousand times farewell!
Yet, if he love, and his love hold, we two
May meet at court hereafter: there, I think,

So you will learn the courtesies of the court,
We two shall know each other."

                Then he gave,
And slightly kiss'd the hand to which he gave,
The diamond, and all wearied of the quest
Leapt on his horse, and carolling as he went     700
A true-love ballad, lightly rode away.

Thence to the court he past; there told the King
What the King knew, "Sir Lancelot is the knight."
And added, "Sire, my liege, so much I learnt;
But fail'd to find him tho' I rode all round
The region: but I lighted on the maid,
Whose sleeve he wore; she loves him; and to her,
Deeming our courtesy is the truest law,
I gave the diamond: she will render it;
For by mine head she knows his hiding-place."   710

The seldom-frowning King frown'd, and replied,
"Too courteous truly! you shall go no more
On quest of mine, seeing that you forget
Obedience is the courtesy due to kings."

He spake and parted. Wroth but all in awe,
For twenty strokes of the blood, without a word,
Linger'd that other, staring after him;
Then shook his hair, strode off, and buzz'd abroad
About the maid of Astolat, and her love.
All ears were prick'd at once, all tongues were loosed:
"The maid of Astolat loves Sir Lancelot,   721
Sir Lancelot loves the maid of Astolat."
Some read the King's face, some the Queen's, and all
Had marvel what the maid might be, but most
Predoom'd her as unworthy. One old dame

Came suddenly on the Queen with the sharp news.
She, that had heard the noise of it before,
But sorrowing Lancelot should have stoop'd so low,
Marr'd her friend's point with pale tranquillity.
So ran the tale like fire about the court,          730
Fire in dry stubble a nine days' wonder flared:
Till ev'n the knights at banquet twice or thrice
Forgot to drink to Lancelot and the Queen,
And pledging Lancelot and the lily maid
Smiled at each other, while the Queen who sat
With lips severely placid felt the knot
Climb in her throat, and with her feet unseen
Crush'd the wild passion out against the floor
Beneath the banquet, where the meats became
As wormwood, and she hated all who pledged.          740

But far away the maid in Astolat,
Her guiltless rival, she that ever kept
The one-day-seen Sir Lancelot in her heart,
Crept to her father, while he mused alone,
Sat on his knee, stroked his gray face and said,
"Father, you call me wilful, and the fault
Is yours who let me have my will, and now,
Sweet father, will you let me lose my wits?"
"Nay," said he, "surely." "Wherefore let me hence,"
She answer'd, "and find out our dear Lavaine."          750
"You will not lose your wits for dear Lavaine:
Bide," answer'd he: "we needs must hear anon
Of him, and of that other." "Ay," she said,
"And of that other, for I needs must hence
And find that other, whereso'er he be,
And with mine own hand give his diamond to him,
Lest I be found as faithless in the quest

As yon proud Prince who left the quest to me.
Sweet father, I behold him in my dreams
Gaunt as it were the skeleton of himself,                    760
Death-pale, for lack of gentle maiden's aid.
The gentler-born the maiden, the more bound,
My father, to be sweet and serviceable
To noble knights in sickness, as you know,
When these have worn their tokens: let me hence
I pray you." Then her father nodding said,
"Ay, ay, the diamond: wit you well, my child,
Right fain were I to learn this knight were whole,
Being our greatest: yea, and you must give it—
And sure I think this fruit is hung too high       770
For any mouth to gape for save a Queen's—
Nay, I mean nothing: so then, get you gone,
Being so very wilful you must go."

    Lightly, her suit allow'd, she slipt away,
And while she made her ready for her ride,
Her father's latest word humm'd in her ear,
"Being so very wilful you must go,"
And changed itself and echoed in her heart,
"Being so very wilful you must die."
But she was happy enough and shook it off,        780
As we shake off the bee that buzzes at us;
And in her heart she answer'd it and said,
"What matter, so I help him back to life?"
Then far away with good Sir Torre for guide
Rode o'er the long backs of the bushless downs
To Camelot, and before the city-gates
Came on her brother with a happy face
Making a roan horse caper and curvet
For pleasure all about a field of flowers:

Whom when she saw, "Lavaine," she cried, "Lavaine
How fares my lord Sir Lancelot?" He amazed,    791
"Torre and Elaine! why here? Sir Lancelot!
How know you my lord's name is Lancelot?"
But when the maid had told him all her tale,
Then turn'd Sir Torre, and being in his moods
Left them, and under the strange-statued gate,
Where Arthur's wars were render'd mystically,
Past up the still rich city to his kin,
His own far blood, which dwelt at Camelot;
And her Lavaine across the poplar grove    800
Led to the caves: there first she saw the casque
Of Lancelot on the wall: her scarlet sleeve,
Tho' carved and cut, and half the pearls away,
Stream'd from it still; and in her heart she laugh'd,
Because he had not loosed it from his helm,
But meant once more perchance to tourney in it.
And when they gain'd the cell in which he slept,
His battle-writhen arms and mighty hands
Lay naked on the wolfskin, and a dream
Of dragging down his enemy made them move.    810
Then she that saw him lying unsleek, unshorn,
Gaunt as it were the skeleton of himself,
Uttered a little tender dolorous cry.
The sound not wonted in a place so still
Woke the sick knight, and while he roll'd his eyes
Yet blank from sleep, she started to him, saying
"Your prize the diamond sent you by the King":
His eyes glisten'd: she fancied "Is it for me?"
And when the maid had told him all the tale
Of King and Prince, the diamond sent, the quest    820
Assign'd to her not worthy of it, she knelt
Full lowly by the corners of his bed,

And laid the diamond in his open hand.
Her face was near, and as we kiss the child
That does the task assign'd, he kiss'd her face.
At once she slipt like water to the floor.
"Alas," he said, "your ride has wearied you.
Rest must you have." "No rest for me," she said;
"Nay, for near you, fair lord, I am at rest."
What might she mean by that? his large black eyes,
Yet larger thro' his leanness, dwelt upon her,    831
Till all her heart's sad secret blazed itself
In the heart's colours on her simple face;
And Lancelot look'd and was perplext in mind,
And being weak in body said no more;
But did not love the colour; woman's love,
Save one, he not regarded, and so turn'd
Sighing, and feign'd a sleep until he slept.

Then rose Elaine and glided thro' the fields,
And past beneath the wildly-sculptured gates    840
Far up the dim rich city to her kin;
There bode the night: but woke with dawn, and past
Down thro' the dim rich city to the fields,
Thence to the cave: so day by day she past
In either twilight ghost-like to and fro
Gliding, and every day she tended him,
And likewise many a night: and Lancelot
Would, tho' he call'd his wound a little hurt
Whereof he should be quickly whole, at times
Brain-feverous in his heat and agony, seem    850
Uncourteous, even he: but the meek maid
Sweetly forbore him ever, being to him
Meeker than any child to a rough nurse,
Milder than any mother to a sick child,

And never woman yet, since man's first fall,
Did kindlier unto man, but her deep love
Upbore her; till the hermit, skill'd in all
The simples and the science of that time,
Told him that her fine care had saved his life.
And the sick man forgot her simple blush,        860
Would call her friend and sister, sweet Elaine,
Would listen for her coming and regret
Her parting step, and held her tenderly,
And loved her with all love except the love
Of man and woman when they love their best
Closest and sweetest, and had died the death
In any knightly fashion for her sake.
And peradventure had he seen her first
She might have made this and that other world
Another world for the sick man; but now        870
The shackles of an old love straiten'd him,
His honour rooted in dishonour stood,
And faith unfaithful kept him falsely true.

Yet the great knight in his mid-sickness made
Full many a holy vow and pure resolve.
These, as but born of sickness, could not live:
For when the blood ran lustier in him again,
Full often the sweet image of one face,
Making a treacherous quiet in his heart,
Dispersed his resolution like a cloud.        880
Then if the maiden, while that ghostly grace
Beam'd on his fancy, spoke, he answer'd not,
Or short and coldly, and she knew right well
What the rough sickness meant, but what this meant
She knew not, and the sorrow dimm'd her sight,
And drave her ere her time across the fields

Far into the rich city, where alone
She murmur'd, "Vain, in vain: it cannot be.
He will not love me: how then? must I die?"
Then as a little helpless innocent bird,    890
That has but one plain passage of few notes,
Will sing the simple passage o'er and o'er
For all an April morning, till the ear
Wearies to hear it, so the simple maid
Went half the night repeating, "Must I die?"
And now to right she turn'd, and now to left,
And found no ease in turning or in rest;
And "Him or death," she mutter'd, "death or him,"
Again and like a burthen, "Him or death."

But when Sir Lancelot's deadly hurt was whole,    900
To Astolat returning rode the three.
There morn by morn, arraying her sweet self
In that wherein she deem'd she look'd her best,
She came before Sir Lancelot, for she thought
"If I be loved, these are my festal robes,
If not, the victim's flowers before he fall."
And Lancelot ever prest upon the maid
That she should ask some goodly gift of him
For her own self or hers; "and do not shun
To speak the wish most near to your true heart;    910
Such service have you done me, that I make
My will of yours, and Prince and Lord am I
In mine own land, and what I will I can."
Then like a ghost she lifted up her face,
But like a ghost without the power to speak.
And Lancelot saw that she withheld her wish,
And bode among them yet a little space
Till he should learn it; and one morn it chanced

He found her in among the garden yews,
And said, "Delay no longer, speak your wish,     920
Seeing I must go to-day": then out she brake;
"Going? and we shall never see you more.
And I must die for want of one bold word."
"Speak: that I live to hear," he said, "is yours."
Then suddenly and passionately she spoke:
"I have gone mad. I love you: let me die."
"Ah sister," answer'd Lancelot, "what is this?"
And innocently extending her white arms,
"Your love," she said, "your love—to be your wife."
And Lancelot answer'd, "Had I chos'n to wed,     930
I had been wedded earlier, sweet Elaine:
But now there never will be wife of mine."
"No, no," she cried, "I care not to be wife,
But to be with you still, to see your face,
To serve you, and to follow you thro' the world."
And Lancelot answer'd, "Nay, the world, the world,
All ear and eye, with such a stupid heart
To interpret ear and eye, and such a tongue
To blare its own interpretation—nay,
Full ill then should I quit your brother's love,     940
And your good father's kindness." And she said,
"Not to be with you, not to see your face—
Alas for me then, my good days are done."
"Nay, noble maid," he answer'd, "ten times nay!
This is not love: but love's first flash in youth,
Most common: yea I know it of mine own self:
And you yourself will smile at your own self
Hereafter, when you yield your flower of life
To one more fitly yours, not thrice your age:
And then will I, for true you are and sweet     950
Beyond mine old belief in womanhood,

More specially should your good knight be poor,
Endow you with broad land and territory
Even to the half my realm beyond the seas,
So that would make you happy: furthermore,
Ev'n to the death, as tho' you were my blood,
In all your quarrels will I be your knight.
This will I do, dear damsel, for your sake,
And more than this I cannot."

              While he spoke
She neither blush'd nor shook, but deathly-pale    960
Stood grasping what was nearest, then replied:
"Of all this will I nothing"; and so fell,
And thus they bore her swooning to her tower.

  Then spake, to whom thro' those black walls of yew
Their talk had pierced, her father. "Ay, a flash,
I fear me, that will strike my blossom dead.
Too courteous are you, fair Lord Lancelot.
I pray you, use some rough discourtesy
To blunt or break her passion."

              Lancelot said,
"That were against me: what I can I will";    970
And there that day remain'd, and toward even
Sent for his shield: full meekly rose the maid,
Stript off the case, and gave the naked shield;
Then, when she heard his horse upon the stones,
Unclasping flung the casement back, and look'd
Down on his helm, from which her sleeve had gone.
And Lancelot knew the little clinking sound;
And she by tact of love was well aware
That Lancelot knew that she was looking at him.
And yet he glanced not up, nor waved his hand,  980
Nor bad farewell, but sadly rode away.
This was the one discourtesy that he used.

So in her tower alone the maiden sat:
His very shield was gone; only the case,
Her own poor work, her empty labour, left.
But still she heard him, still his picture form'd
And grew between her and the pictured wall.
Then came her father, saying in low tones,
"Have comfort," whom she greeted quietly.
Then came her brethren saying, "Peace to thee, 990
Sweet sister," whom she answer'd with all calm.
But when they left her to herself again,
Death, like a friend's voice from a distant field
Approaching thro' the darkness, call'd; the owls
Wailing had power upon her, and she mixt
Her fancies with the sallow-rifted glooms
Of evening, and the moanings of the wind.

And in those days she made a little song,
And call'd her song "The Song of Love and Death,"
And sang it: sweetly could she make and sing. 1000

"Sweet is true love tho' given in vain, in vain;
And sweet is death who puts an end to pain:
I know not which is sweeter, no, not I.

"Love, art thou sweet? then bitter death must be:
Love, thou art bitter; sweet is death to me.
O Love, if death be sweeter, let me die.

"Sweet love, that seems not made to fade away,
Sweet death, that seems to make us loveless clay,
I know not which is sweeter, no, not I.

"I fain would follow love, if that could be; 1010
I needs must follow death, who calls for me;
Call and I follow, I follow! let me die."

High with the last line scaled her voice, and this,
All in a fiery dawning wild with wind
That shook her tower, the brothers heard, and thought
With shuddering "Hark the Phantom of the house
That ever shrieks before a death," and call'd
The father, and all three in hurry and fear
Ran to her, and lo! the bloodred light of dawn
Flared on her face, she shrilling, "Let me die!"  1020

As when we dwell upon a word we know,
Repeating, till the word we know so well
Becomes a wonder and we know not why,
So dwelt the father on her face and thought
"Is this Elaine?" till back the maiden fell,
Then gave a languid hand to each, and lay,
Speaking a still good-morrow with her eyes.
At last she said, "Sweet brothers, yesternight
I seem'd a curious little maid again,
As happy as when we dwelt among the woods,  1030
And when you used to take me with the flood
Up the great river in the boatman's boat.
Only you would not pass beyond the cape
That has the poplar on it: there you fixt
Your limit, oft returning with the tide.
And yet I cried because you would not pass
Beyond it, and far up the shining flood
Until we found the palace of the king.
And yet you would not; but this night I dream'd
That I was all alone upon the flood,  1040
And then I said, 'Now shall I have my will':
And there I woke, but still the wish remain'd.
So let me hence that I may pass at last
Beyond the poplar and far up the flood,

Until I find the palace of the king.
There will I enter in among them all,
And no man there will dare to mock at me;
But there the fine Gawain will wonder at me,
And there the great Sir Lancelot muse at me;
Gawain, who bad a thousand farewells to me,    1050
Lancelot, who coldly went nor bad me one:
And there the King will know me and my love,
And there the Queen herself will pity me,
And all the gentle court will welcome me,
And after my long voyage I shall rest!"

  "Peace," said her father, "O my child, you seem
Light-headed, for what force is yours to go
So far, being sick? and wherefore would you look
On this proud fellow again, who scorns us all?"

  Then the rough Torre began to heave and move,    1060
And bluster into stormy sobs and say,
"I never loved him: an I meet with him,
I care not howsoever great he be,
Then will I strike at him and strike him down,
Give me good fortune, I will strike him dead,
For this discomfort he hath done the house."

  To which the gentle sister made reply,
"Fret not yourself, dear brother, nor be wroth,
Seeing it is no more Sir Lancelot's fault
Not to love me, than it is mine to love    1070
Him of all men who seems to me the highest."

  "Highest?" the father answer'd, echoing "highest?"
(He meant to break the passion in her) "nay,
Daughter, I know not what you call the highest;
But this I know, for all the people know it,
He loves the Queen, and in an open shame:

And she returns his love in open shame.
If this be high, what is it to be low?"

Then spake the lily maid of Astolat;
"Sweet father, all too faint and sick am I     1080
For anger: these are slanders: never yet
Was noble man but made ignoble talk.
He makes no friend who never made a foe.
But now it is my glory to have loved
One peerless, without stain: so let me pass,
My father, howsoe'er I seem to you,
Not all unhappy, having loved God's best
And greatest, tho' my love had no return:
Yet, seeing you desire your child to live,
Thanks, but you work against your own desire;     1090
For if I could believe the things you say
I should but die the sooner; wherefore cease,
Sweet father, and bid call the ghostly man
Hither, and let me shrive me clean, and die."

So when the ghostly man had come and gone
She with a face, bright as for sin forgiven,
Besought Lavaine to write as she devised
A letter, word for word; and when he ask'd
"Is it for Lancelot, is it for my dear lord?
Then will I bear it gladly"; she replied,     1100
"For Lancelot and the Queen and all the world,
But I myself must bear it." Then he wrote
The letter she devised; which being writ
And folded, "O sweet father, tender and true,
Deny me not," she said—"you never yet
Denied my fancies—this, however strange,
My latest: lay the letter in my hand
A little ere I die, and close the hand

Upon it; I shall guard it even in death.
And when the heat is gone from out my heart,   1110
Then take the little bed on which I died
For Lancelot's love, and deck it like the Queen's
For richness, and me also like the Queen
In all I have of rich, and lay me on it.
And let there be prepared a chariot-bier
To take me to the river, and a barge
Be ready on the river, clothed in black.
I go in state to court, to meet the Queen.
There surely I shall speak for mine own self,
And none of you can speak for me so well.   1120
And therefore let our dumb old man alone
Go with me, he can steer and row, and he
Will guide me to that palace, to the doors."

She ceased: her father promised; whereupon
She grew so cheerful that they deem'd her death
Was rather in the fantasy than the blood.
But ten slow mornings past, and on the eleventh
Her father laid the letter in her hand,
And closed the hand upon it, and she died.
So that day there was dole in Astolat.   1130

But when the next sun brake from underground,
Then, those two brethren slowly with bent brows
Accompanying, the sad chariot-bier
Past like a shadow thro' the field, that shone
Full-summer, to that stream whereon the barge,
Pall'd all its length in blackest samite, lay.
There sat the lifelong creature of the house,
Loyal, the dumb old servitor, on deck,
Winking his eyes, and twisted all his face.
So those two brethren from the chariot took   1140

And on the black decks laid her in her bed,
Set in her hand a lily, o'er her hung
The silken case with braided blazonings,
And kiss'd her quiet brows, and saying to her
"Sister, farewell for ever," and again
"Farewell, sweet sister," parted all in tears.
Then rose the dumb old servitor, and the dead
Steer'd by the dumb went upward with the flood—
In her right hand the lily, in her left
The letter—all her bright hair streaming down—    1150
And all the coverlid was cloth of gold
Drawn to her waist, and she herself in white
All but her face, and that clear-featured face
Was lovely, for she did not seem as dead
But fast asleep, and lay as tho' she smiled.

That day Sir Lancelot at the palace craved
Audience of Guinevere, to give at last
The price of half a realm, his costly gift,
Hard-won and hardly won with bruise and blow,
With deaths of others, and almost his own,    1160
The nine-years-fought-for diamonds: for he saw
One of her house, and sent him to the Queen
Bearing his wish, whereto the Queen agreed
With such and so unmoved a majesty
She might have seem'd her statue, but that he,
Low-drooping till he wellnigh kiss'd her feet
For loyal awe, saw with a sidelong eye
The shadow of a piece of pointed lace,
In the Queen's shadow, vibrate on the walls,
And parted, laughing in his courtly heart.    1170

All in an oriel on the summer side,
Vine-clad, of Arthur's palace toward the stream,

They met, and Lancelot kneeling utter'd, "Queen,
Lady, my liege, in whom I have my joy,
Take, what I had not won except for you,
These jewels, and make me happy, making them
An armlet for the roundest arm on earth,
Or necklace for a neck to which the swan's
Is tawnier than her cygnet's: these are words:
Your beauty is your beauty, and I sin            1180
In speaking, yet O grant my worship of it
Words, as we grant grief tears. Such sin in words
Perchance, we both can pardon: but, my Queen,
I hear of rumours flying thro' your court.
Our bond, as not the bond of man and wife,
Should have in it an absoluter trust
To make up that defect: let rumours be:
When did not rumours fly? these, as I trust
That you trust me in your own nobleness,
I may not well believe that you believe."          1190

While thus he spoke, half turn'd away, the Queen
Brake from the vast oriel-embowering vine
Leaf after leaf, and tore, and cast them off,
Till all the place whereon she stood was green;
Then, when he ceased, in one cold passive hand
Received at once and laid aside the gems
There on a table near her, and replied.

"It may be, I am quicker of belief
Than you believe me, Lancelot of the Lake.
Our bond is not the bond of man and wife.          1200
This good is in it, whatsoe'er of ill,
It can be broken easier. I for you
This many a year have done despite and wrong
To one whom ever in my heart of hearts

16—2

I did acknowledge nobler.  What are these?
Diamonds for me! they had been thrice their worth
Being your gift, had you not lost your own.
To loyal hearts the value of all gifts
Must vary as the giver's.  Not for me!
For her! for your new fancy.  Only this      1210
Grant me, I pray you: have your joys apart.
I doubt not that however changed, you keep
So much of what is graceful: and myself
Would shun to break those bounds of courtesy
In which as Arthur's queen I move and rule:
So cannot speak my mind.  An end to this!
A strange one! yet I take it with Amen.
So pray you, add my diamonds to her pearls;
Deck her with these; tell her, she shines me down:
An armlet for an arm to which the Queen's      1220
Is haggard, or a necklace for a neck
O as much fairer—as a faith once fair
Was richer than these diamonds—hers not mine—
Nay, by the mother of our Lord himself,
Or hers or mine, mine now to work my will—
She shall not have them."
                      Saying which she seized,
And, thro' the casement standing wide for heat,
Flung them, and down they flash'd, and smote the stream,
Then from the smitten surface flash'd, as it were,
Diamonds to meet them, and they past away.      1230
Then while Sir Lancelot leant, in half disgust
At love, life, all things, on the window ledge,
Close underneath his eyes, and right across
Where these had fallen, slowly past the barge
Whereon the lily maid of Astolat
Lay smiling, like a star in blackest night.

But the wild Queen, who saw not, burst away
To weep and wail in secret; and the barge,
On to the palace-doorway sliding, paused.
There two stood arm'd, and kept the door; to whom,
All up the marble stair, tier over tier,          1241
Were added mouths that gaped, and eyes that ask'd
"What is it?" but that oarsman's haggard face,
As hard and still as is the face that men
Shape to their fancy's eye from broken rocks
On some cliff-side, appall'd them, and they said,
"He is enchanted, cannot speak—and she,
Look how she sleeps—the Fairy Queen, so fair!
Yea, but how pale! what are they? flesh and blood?
Or come to take the King to fairy land?          1250
For some do hold our Arthur cannot die,
But that he passes into fairy land."

While thus they babbled of the King, the King
Came girt with knights: then turn'd the tongueless man
From the half-face to the full eye, and rose
And pointed to the damsel, and the doors.
So Arthur bad the meek Sir Percivale
And pure Sir Galahad to uplift the maid;
And reverently they bore her into hall.
Then came the fine Gawain and wonder'd at her,     1260
And Lancelot later came and mused at her,
And last the Queen herself and pitied her:
But Arthur spied the letter in her hand,
Stoopt, took, brake seal, and read it; this was all:

"Most noble lord, Sir Lancelot of the Lake,
I, sometime call'd the maid of Astolat,
Come, for you left me taking no farewell,
Hither, to take my last farewell of you.
I loved you, and my love had no return,

And therefore my true love has been my death. 1270
And therefore to our lady Guinevere,
And to all other ladies, I make moan.
Pray for my soul, and yield me burial.
Pray for my soul thou too, Sir Lancelot,
As thou art a knight peerless."
      Thus he read,
And ever in the reading, lords and dames
Wept, looking often from his face who read
To hers which lay so silent, and at times,
So touch'd were they, half-thinking that her lips,
Who had devised the letter, moved again. 1280

Then freely spoke Sir Lancelot to them all;
"My lord liege Arthur, and all ye that hear,
Know that for this most gentle maiden's death
Right heavy am I; for good she was and true,
But loved me with a love beyond all love
In women, whomsoever I have known.
Yet to be loved makes not to love again;
Not at my years, however it hold in youth.
I swear by truth and knighthood that I gave
No cause, not willingly, for such a love: 1290
To this I call my friends in testimony,
Her brethren, and her father, who himself
Besought me to be plain and blunt, and use,
To break her passion, some discourtesy
Against my nature: what I could, I did.
I left her and I bad her no farewell.
Tho', had I dreamt the damsel would have died,
I might have put my wits to some rough use,
And help'd her from herself."
      Then said the Queen
(Sea was her wrath, yet working after storm) 1300

"You might at least have done her so much grace,
Fair lord, as would have help'd her from her death."
He raised his head, their eyes met and hers fell,
He adding,
        "Queen, she would not be content
Save that I wedded her, which could not be.
Then might she follow me thro' the world, she ask'd;
It could not be. I told her that her love
Was but the flash of youth, would darken down
To rise hereafter in a stiller flame
Toward one more worthy of her—then would I,    1310
More specially were he, she wedded, poor,
Estate them with large land and territory
In mine own realm beyond the narrow seas,
To keep them in all joyance: more than this
I could not; this she would not, and she died."

He pausing, Arthur answer'd, "O my knight,
It will be to your worship, as my knight,
And mine, as head of all our Table Round,
To see that she be buried worshipfully."

So toward that shrine which then in all the realm
Was richest, Arthur leading, slowly went    1321
The marshall'd order of their Table Round,
And Lancelot sad beyond his wont, to see
The maiden buried, not as one unknown,
Nor meanly, but with gorgeous obsequies,
And mass, and rolling music, like a Queen.
And when the knights had laid her comely head
Low in the dust of half-forgotten kings,
Then Arthur spake among them, "Let her tomb
Be costly, and her image thereupon.    1330
And let the shield of Lancelot at her feet

Be carven, and her lily in her hand.
And let the story of her dolorous voyage
For all true hearts be blazon'd on her tomb
In letters gold and azure!" which was wrought
Thereafter; but when now the lords and dames
And people, from the high door streaming, brake
Disorderly, as homeward each, the Queen,
Who mark'd Sir Lancelot where he moved apart,
Drew near, and sigh'd in passing, "Lancelot,      1340
Forgive me; mine was jealousy in love."
He answer'd with his eyes upon the ground,
"That is love's curse; pass on, my Queen, forgiven."
But Arthur who beheld his cloudy brows
Approach'd him, and with full affection flung
One arm about his neck, and spake and said:

"Lancelot, my Lancelot, thou in whom I have
Most love and most affiance, for I know
What thou hast been in battle by my side,
And many a time have watch'd thee at the tilt   1350
Strike down the lusty and long-practised knight,
And let the younger and unskill'd go by
To win his honour and to make his name,
And loved thy courtesies and thee, a man
Made to be loved;—but now I would to God,
For the wild people say wild things of thee,
Thou could'st have loved this maiden, shaped, it seems,
By God for thee alone, and from her face,
If one may judge the living by the dead,
Delicately pure and marvellously fair,            1360
Who might have brought thee, now a lonely man
Wifeless and heirless, noble issue, sons
Born to the glory of thy name and fame,
My knight, the great Sir Lancelot of the Lake."

Then answer'd Lancelot, "Fair she was, my King,
Pure, as you ever wish your knights to be.
To doubt her fairness were to want an eye,
To doubt her pureness were to want a heart—
Yea, to be loved, if what is worthy love
Could bind him, but free love will not be bound."    1370

"Free love, so bound, were freëst," said the King.
"Let love be free; free love is for the best:
And, after heaven, on our dull side of death,
What should be best, if not so pure a love
Clothed in so pure a loveliness? yet thee
She fail'd to bind, tho' being, as I think,
Unbound as yet, and gentle, as I know."

And Lancelot answer'd nothing, but he went,
And at the inrunning of a little brook
Sat by the river in a cove, and watch'd    1380
The high reed wave, and lifted up his eyes
And saw the barge that brought her moving down,
Far-off, a blot upon the stream, and said
Low in himself, "Ah simple heart and sweet,
You loved me, damsel, surely with a love
Far tenderer than my Queen's. Pray for thy soul?
Ay, that will I. Farewell too—now at last—
Farewell, fair lily. 'Jealousy in love?'
Not rather dead love's harsh heir, jealous pride?
Queen, if I grant the jealousy as of love,    1390
May not your crescent fear for name and fame
Speak, as it waxes, of a love that wanes?
Why did the King dwell on my name to me?
Mine own name shames me, seeming a reproach,
Lancelot, whom the Lady of the lake
Stole from his mother—as the story runs—

She chanted snatches of mysterious song
Heard on the winding waters, eve and morn
She kiss'd me saying, 'Thou art fair, my child,
As a king's son,' and often in her arms          1400
She bare me, pacing on the dusky mere.
Would she had drown'd me in it, where'er it be!
For what am I? what profits me my name
Of greatest knight? I fought for it, and have it:
Pleasure to have it, none; to lose it, pain;
Now grown a part of me: but what use in it?
To make men worse by making my sin known?
Or sin seem less, the sinner seeming great?
Alas for Arthur's greatest knight, a man
Not after Arthur's heart! I needs must break   1410
These bonds that so defame me: not without
She wills it: would I, if she will'd it? Nay,
Who knows? but if I would not, then may God,
I pray him, send a sudden Angel down
To seize me by the hair and bear me far,
And fling me deep in that forgotten mere,
Among the tumbled fragments of the hills."

So groan'd Sir Lancelot in remorseful pain,
Not knowing he should die a holy man.

# NOTES

## TO THE QUEEN

These verses appeared first in 1851 in the seventh and enlarged edition of the *Poems* originally published in two volumes in 1842. Tennyson had been made Poet Laureate on Nov. 19, 1850.

8. **Of him that utter'd nothing base.** Wordsworth died on April 23, 1850.

The question of his successor was much discussed during the following six months, among those mentioned being Robert and Elizabeth Browning, Barry Cornwall, Charles Mackay, and the veterans, Leigh Hunt and Samuel Rogers.

## THE KRAKEN

### From *Poems, chiefly Lyrical* of 1830.

4. **The Kraken sleepeth.** The Kraken was a sea-monster of Norwegian tradition, of enormous size and capable of sinking a man-of-war.

10. **the slumbering green.** Early editions have the misprint "and" for "the."

## MARIANA

### From *Poems, chiefly Lyrical* of 1830.

The suggestion of the poem is in the Duke's description of Mariana in *Measure for Measure*, III. i. 220 and 278. "She lost a noble and renowned brother, in his love toward her ever most kind and natural; with him, the portion and sinew of her fortune, her marriage-dowry; with both, her combinate husband, this well-seeming Angelo...left her in her tears, and dried not one of them with his comfort; swallowed his vows whole...in few, bestowed her or her own lamentation, which she yet wears for his sake....I will presently to Saint Luke's: there, at the moated grange, resides this dejected Mariana." The connexion of the poem with the foregoing consists merely in the suggestion of "Mariana in the moated grange" as a victim of desertion and dreary loneliness. In his volume of poems in 1832 Tennyson added a pendant to *Mariana* called *Mariana in the South*. The scenery of the latter poem was suggested to the poet in the course of his journey with Arthur Hallam to the Pyrenees in 1830.

"**Mariana in the moated grange.**" Not a textual quotation. See previous note.

4. **That held the peach.** In later editions *pear* and *gable* were substituted for *peach* and *garden*.

18. **did trance the sky.** The oblivion of night.

20. **glooming flats.** The adjectives are finely chosen to make the scene harmonise with Mariana's despair. The skilful alliteration of the poem is notable, and also the musical variety of its stanza which is built up of three differing quatrains, the second being in the *In Memoriam* measure.

25. **Upon the middle of the night.** Perhaps it is not mere coincidence that Mariana's meeting with Angelo was to happen "Upon the heavy middle of the night" (*Measure for Measure*, IV. i. 35).

50. **And the shrill winds were up and away.** An example of the poet's skill in varying the melody by employing metrical equivalence. The third foot is here a dactyl. Compare l. 26 which opens with a trochee.

52. **gusty shadow.** Of the wind-shaken poplar.

63. **The blue fly sung in the pane.** In 1845 Bulwer Lytton satirised Tennyson in an anonymous poem, *The New Timon*, in which he dismisses the poet to

> "Chant 'I'm a-weary' in infectious strain,
> And catch 'the blue fly singing i' the pane'."

## RECOLLECTIONS OF THE ARABIAN NIGHTS

From *Poems, chiefly Lyrical* of 1830.

5. **sheeny.** Shining.

7. **fretted gold.** Carved work. Fretted is often used as a synonym for adorned or embossed, e.g. "This majestical roof fretted with golden fire" (*Hamlet*, II. ii. 313).

11. **good Haroun Alraschid.** Haroun Al-Raschid (i.e. "the orthodox"), 763—809, the famous Caliph who maintained a brilliant court at Bagdad. He was a great patron of learning, and lives for ever in the *Arabian Nights* which describe some of his apocryphal adventures. With all his culture he was a ferocious despot and little entitled to the epithet "Good."

19. **sofas.** Divans. The author says of this passage, "I had only the translation—from the French of Galland—of the *Arabian Nights* when this was written, so I talked of sofas, etc."

23. **platans.** Plane trees (Lat. *platanus*).

28. **damask-work.** As if with flowers interwoven.

34. **A motion.** A current.

37. **another night in night.** The evening voyage brought me into a yet darker reach of the stream.

39, 40. **pillar'd palm, imprisoning sweets.** The date-palm rises to a height of about sixty feet.

46. **rivage.** Banks (Lat. *rivus*). Cf. "Think you stand upon the rivage and behold a city on the inconstant billows dancing" (*Hen. V.* III. Chor. 14).

58. **engrain'd.** Literally, dyed in grain, i.e. in kermes, the crimson dye obtained from certain seed-like dried insects.

64. **With disks and tiars.** The disk is the fleshy expansion at the base of the tiara-like flower.

68. **coverture.** Dense cover or shelter. Cf. "Couched in the woodbine coverture" (*Much Ado*, III. i. 30).

69. **airs of middle night.** Cf. "Flowers of middle summer" (*Winter's Tale*, IV. iv. 106).

70. **the bulbul.** The Turkish and Persian name for the nightingale. In India the same name is applied to a species of thrush known also as "the Ceylon nightingale." Moore and Byron introduced the name into English poetry.

81. **A sudden splendour.** See l. 122.

90. **with vivid stars inlaid.** Cf. "to inlay heaven with stars" (*Cymb.* v. v. 352).

114. **the Caliphat.** The successor of Mohammed was called Khalîfat Rasûl Illâh, successor of the Apostle of God. The office became hereditary in 661 A.D. In 1538 the title was assumed by the Sultan of Turkey.

120. **humour of the golden prime.** Humour is used in the older meaning of the word. With Ben Jonson it means idiosyncrasy. Here it is equal to "mode" or "whim."

127. **Upon the mooned domes.** Domes with crescent moons. Tennyson himself points out his mistake of confusing Turkish and Arabian symbols.

134. **the Persian girl.** A well-known story in the *Arabian Nights*. Noureddin, son of the vizier of the King of Balsora, captured the "beautiful Persian" who had been designed for the King. He fled with her to Bagdad, and encountered Haroun in one of his adventures in disguise. He rose high in Haroun's favour, and lived happily ever after with the Persian girl.

## THE POET

### From *Poems, chiefly Lyrical* of 1830.

3. **Dower'd with the hate of hate, etc.** Hating hate, scorning scorn, and loving love.

13. **Indian reeds.** Blow-pipes for arrows.

15. **Calpe unto Caucasus.** From Gibraltar to the Caucasus, the ancient limits of East and West.

19. **arrow-seeds.** The seeds of the dandelion.

29. **their orbs.** Referring back to "the viewless arrows...wing'd with flame" of ll. 11, 12.

39. **When rites and forms.** Ecclesiastical and scholastic domination.

## THE SEA-FAIRIES

### From *Poems, chiefly Lyrical* of 1830.

1. **Slow sailed.** This poem was recast in later editions. The two versions should be compared as they afford an interesting example of Tennyson's drastic methods of revision.

## THE MERMAN

### From *Poems, chiefly Lyrical* of 1830.

**32. Turkis**, etc. *Turkis* is Milton's form for *turquoise* ; *almondine* or *almandine* is the name of varieties of garnets and rubies brought from Alabanda in Asia Minor.

**38. hollow-hung ocean.** In the under-world which the sea arches as heaven does earth. Cf. *The Mermaid*, l. 54.

## THE MERMAID

### From *Poems, chiefly Lyrical* of 1830.

**23. that great sea-snake.** Cf. *The Kraken*.
**54. the hollow sphere.** See note on *The Merman*, l. 38.

## THE LADY OF SHALOTT

### From *Poems* of 1832.

The poem as printed here is in the revised form of 1842. *The Lady of Shalott* is Tennyson's brilliant first essay in Arthurian romance. In the *Poems* of 1842 he resumed that subject in *Sir Galahad* and *Morte d'Arthur*, and in 1859 came the idyll of *Elaine* in which the Lady of Shalott reappears as "the lily maid of Astolat." In the idyll (see p. 206) Tennyson follows the story as told in Malory's *Morte d'Arthur*. To press a coherent allegorical interpretation into this exquisitely wrought poem is doing it a wrong. Its "magic web with colours gay" ill endures the handling of the expositor. The poem is in need of no allegorical side-wind to waft it to fame. It gains that haven by reason of its haunting music and pictorial power, and in the more prosaic region of literary history it has its assured place as an interesting anticipation of the Pre-Raphaelite ideals. Tennyson may be said to have been lucky in having the story of Arthurian romance reserved for him. For the subject was included in the " projects " both of Milton and of Dryden.

3. **the wold.** Weald, or open country. (O.E. weald, a wood.) A favourite word with Tennyson. (Cf. p. 22, l. 36.)

5. **Camelot.** The "Camelot" of romance has many claimants—Winchester, Carlisle, and Queen Camel in Somersetshire. (Cf. *King Lear*, II. ii. 90.)

9. **Shalott.** The name is a variant of Astolat. The poem, Tennyson tells us, was suggested by an Italian novelette, *Donna di Scalotta*. "The Lady of Shalott is evidently the Elaine of the *Morte d'Arthur*, but I do not think that I had ever heard of the latter when I wrote the former" (Tennyson). "Shalott," says the poet, "was a softer sound than Scalott."

12. **for ever.** One of several instances in the poem of a metrical licence rare in the poet's later work. Note the verse beginning at l. 28, and again l. 106.

56. **on an ambling pad.** "Pad" is a form of "path," and a pad-nag meant a road-horse.

71. **I am half-sick of shadows.** Tennyson indicated that these words contain the essence of the poem's significance.

76. **greaves.** leg-armour.

84. **Galaxy.** The Milky Way. (Through the Fr. from Gk. γάλακτος.)

87. **blazon'd baldric.** Shoulder-belt with heraldic devices.

107. **Tirra lirra.** Onomatopoetic words to imitate the song of the lark. Cf. "The lark that tirra-lyra chants" (*Winter's Tale*, IV. iii. 9).

143. **singing her last song.** Compare the description of Ophelia's death (*Hamlet*, IV. vii. 179).

157. **A corse.** For these words the poet later substituted "dead-pale."

## THE TWO VOICES

### From *Poems* of 1842.

In the first edition the poem is dated 1833, and it was written apparently in the end of that year after the death of the poet's friend, Arthur Henry Hallam. The poem originally had the sub-title, "Thoughts of a Suicide." Its subject and the date of its composition make the poem of special interest as a preface to *In Memoriam*.

1. **A still small voice.** 1 Kings xix. 12.

**10. An inner impulse rent the veil.** These lines afford a celebrated instance of Tennyson's accuracy of natural description. Cf. the article "dragon-fly" in *Chambers's Encyclopaedia* where the lines are quoted for their scientific accuracy.

**18. And in the sixth.** The sixth "day" of Genesis.

**21. Dominion in the head and breast.** Superiority of head and heart.

**27. Is boundless better, boundless worse.** All things are to be measured by the standard of infinity.

**28. this mould.** Humanity.

**29. no statelier than his peers.** Superiors.

**39. weep for thy deficiency.** For losing you.

**41. peculiar difference.** Special characteristics.

**51. but thou wilt weep.** Without weeping.

**53. make dark my countenance.** Abandon myself to dejection.

**59. the thorn.** Blossoming hawthorn.

**65. gray prime.** Daybreak.

**66. thy grass.** Grave.

**68. Rapt.** Carried away. The word comes from rap = to snatch, and the meaning is confused by a false derivation from Lat. *raptus*.

**71. fire the dells.** With a blaze of colour.

**79. The highest-mounted mind.** The most soaring intellect cannot probe the mysteries of the skies.

**88. Forerun thy peers.** Even if you could anticipate your contemporaries and benefit by the new knowledge of the ages to come, you would still be no nearer to the secrets of infinity.

**94. 'Twere better not to breathe or speak.** Death would be preferable to praying vainly for power and pretending to have found a solution of what we still investigate. And even this feigned satisfaction demands qualities which you lack.

**101. He dared not tarry.** Had not the courage to live.

**118. Hard task,** etc. Neither intellectual pride nor the thought of annihilation affords any courage for resolving on death.

**127. joyful Pæan.** Pæan (physician of the gods) was an attribute of Apollo. Hence it was used to designate a choral hymn to Apollo, and more generally a song of triumph.

**141. the law within the law.** Ultimate principles.

**158. While thou abodest in the bud.** Your dream was not based on reason but was merely the natural prompting of youth.

**166. Yet hadst thou, etc.** Even if you had devoted years to such speculations (cf. ll. 130—141), it would still all be in vain.

**177. relation to the mind.** In other things the march of knowledge is slow, but there is no discovering the secrets of the unseen.

**181. Cry, faint not.** The still small voice says ironically "suppose you take courage and say."

**192. the fold.** The cloud.

**195. Ixion-like.** Ixion embraced the cloud that Zeus substituted for Hera.

**216. The murmur of the fountain-head.** Came near to discovering the Truth.

**220. He heeded not.** Acts vii. 55.

**227. Not that the grounds of hope.** Stephen's courage and forgiveness were based not on any rational ground for belief but on his guileless character.

**235. this anguish.** I dread lest my misery may haunt me perpetually when I am free from the trammels of the flesh.

**277. The simple senses crown'd his head.** The senses recognise death as the King who overcomes them.

**280. rot in dreamless ease.** If man were to free himself from anxiety by abjuring speculation.

**281. plain fact, as taught by these.** The evidence of the senses that there is "no motion in the dead."

**283. Who forged that other influence.** Whence comes the hope of immortality ?

**286. fatal gift of eyes.** Providence has given him powers of introspection by which he can perceive the wisdom as well as the limitations of his soul.

**292. type of Perfect.** His notions of the ideal come from within : he sets his stamp on everything in nature.

**303. do the thing he would.** His moral sense is innate.

**313. The doubt would rest.** The doubt that I dare not solve would remain though I died. Certainty is the only ground of courage.

**347. one engine bound.** Attached to but one body.

**357. those two likes.** Two incarnations in similar form.

**360. hint of my disgrace.** Any history of a downfall might suffice to remind me of my own degradation in this latest birth.

**365. experience past became.** Though all my past experiences in lower forms of life left their influences on my present nature, yet I might have no recollection of these experiences.

371. **unconfined.** Set free.

372. **lose whole years of darker mind.** Forget their years of derangement.

375. **Incompetent.** Not possessed of.

377. **he with matter.** Time deals only with facts.

378. **material prime.** Beginning as a created thing.

381. **forgotten dreams.** Cf. Wordsworth's *Ode on Intimations of Immortality from Recollections of Early Childhood*, e.g.

> "Whither is fled the visionary gleam?
> Where is it now, the glory and the dream?
> Our birth is but a sleep and a forgetting."

A similar thought is expressed in Henry Vaughan's poem *The Retreat* (1650) :

> "Happy those early days, when I
> Shined in my Angel-infancy !
>
> .    .    .    .
>
> And looking back, at that short space
> Could see a glimpse of His bright face;
> When on some gilded cloud or flower
> My gazing soul would dwell an hour,
> And in those weaker glories spy
> Some shadows of eternity."

392. **This rashness.** Suicide.

394. **crazy sorrow.** Distracted grief.

401. **in quiet scorn.** The voice of the tempter ironically reminds his antagonist that of all days Sunday seems the most incongruous with his despairing mood.

430. **blissful neighbourhood.** Some blessed voice near by.

431. **notice.** Intimation.

432. **the end.** God's design.

436. **Æolian harp.** A simple stringed instrument formed of eight or ten catgut strings of varying thickness stretched across a wooden shell. The wind as it falls and rises produces plaintive notes.

437. **overtakes far thought.** Seems to out-distance our dreamy thoughts.

451. **bounteous hours.** The recent rapid growth.

**457. so variously seem'd.** This line was changed later to "And all so variously wrought."

## THE MILLER'S DAUGHTER

### From *Poems* of 1832.

The version in the text is from the edition ten years later, when the poem was greatly altered and enlarged.

**1. the wealthy miller.** "If I thought at all of any mill it was that of Trumpington, near Cambridge." (Tennyson.)

**25. a happy earth.** Earthly happiness.

**172. trembles at her ear.** *In* was substituted later for *at*.

**221. a many tears.** Cf. *Merchant of Venice*, III. v. 73. The usage is frequent in Shakespeare.

**229. that brought us pain.** *Had* was later substituted for *that*.

## ŒNONE

### From *Poems* of 1832

The poem was recast for the volume of 1842.

**1. Ida.** The range of mountains south of Troy.

**8. the clov'n ravine.** The scenery of the poem was suggested partly by that of the Pyrenees which Tennyson and Hallam visited in 1830.

**10. Gargarus.** One of the peaks of Ida.

**13. Troas and Ilion's column'd citadel.** The Troad or district of Troy, and Troy itself.

**15. Œnone.** The daughter of Cebren, a river god, and beloved of Paris before his passion for Helen. **forlorn of.** Deserted by.

**16. Paris.** The second son of Priam and Hecuba. To avoid the prophecy of his mother that he would be the cause of Troy's destruction, Paris was exposed on Mount Ida and brought up by a shepherd as his son. Paris, after the incident told in this poem, carried off Helen, the wife of Menelaus, and thus fulfilled the prophecy by causing the Trojan war.

**18. to float in rest.** Seemed to have movement although still. An oxymoron.

22. **many-fountain'd Ida.** An instance of Tennyson's use of compound epithets as used by Homer and Theocritus. Tennyson cites *Iliad*, VIII. 47, Ἴδην δ᾽ ἵκανε πολυπίδακα, μητέρα θηρῶν.

24. **For now the noonday.** Cf. Gray's *Elegy*, "And all the air a solemn stillness holds."

27. **the cicala sleeps.** Altered later to "the winds are dead."

28. **The purple flowers droop.** "A misprint for 'flower droops'" (Tennyson).

36. **cold crown'd snake.** Clammy hooded snake.

37. **a River-God.** See note, l. 15.

40. **Rose slowly to a music.** Raised by the music of Apollo's lute. "Phoebeae structa canore lyrae" (Ovid).

51. **Simois.** A small river in Troas flowing into the Scamander. Cf.

> "Quam frigida parvi
> Findunt Scamandri flumina, lubricus et Simois."

> (Hor. *Ep.* XIII. 14.)

55. **virgin snow.** Cf. note on l. 8 *supra*.

60. **foam-bow.** "Formed by the sunshine on the foam" (Tennyson).

65. **Hesperian gold.** The Hesperides were the sisters who guarded the golden apples of Hera in the wonderful gardens of the West.

66. **ambrosially.** Ambrosia, the food of the gods (Gk. ἄμβροτος, immortal).

72. **whatever Oread haunt.** Than any Oread that haunts. Oread, a mountain-nymph.

74. **married brows.** Meeting eyebrows.

77. **cast upon the board.** The apple of discord was thrown among the gods at their feast by Eris, the goddess of strife, who had not been invited.

79. **halls of Peleus.** The gods were present at the marriage-banquet of Peleus and Thetis.

81. **Iris.** The messenger of the gods. **it.** The message.

94. **crocus brake like fire.** This line was a brilliant afterthought in the version of 1842. "It is the flame-like petal of the crocus which is alluded to, not only the colour" (Tennyson—Eversley Ed.).

95. **amaracus.** Marjoram. **asphodel.** A kind of lily.

102. **crested peacock.** Sacred to Hera.

105. **voice of her.** Hera.

125. **king-born.** See note on l. 16 *supra*.

129. **quiet seats.** Cf. Lucretius, *De Rerum Nat.* iii. **18,**

> "sedesque quietae
> Quas neque concutiunt venti."
>
> (Tennyson—Eversley Ed.)

137. **O'erthwarted.** Crossed by.

148. **Were wisdom.** Would be the really wise course no matter what the consequences.

151. **Sequel of guerdon.** Promise of reward to follow would make me no fairer: i.e. cannot affect your impartial and just decision.

155. **frail to judge of fair.** May not be impartial judges of beauty.

161. **until endurance grow.** Until your power is braced by trial, and the developed will, having run the whole circle of human experience, becomes a law unto itself and thus attains to complete freedom.

170. **Idalian...Paphian.** Idalium (or Idalia) and Paphos, both in Cyprus, were places sacred to Aphrodite.

183. **The fairest.** Helen, wife of Menelaus, King of Sparta.

220. **The Abominable.** Eris. See note on l. 77.

259. **wild Cassandra.** The daughter of Priam who was dowered by her lover, Apollo, with the gift of prophecy. As she rejected his suit, the god ordained that her prophecies should not be believed. Thus she foretold in vain the destruction of Troy, and was regarded as " wild " or mad.


# THE PALACE OF ART

### From *Poems* of 1832.

The poem is an allegorical interpretation of the relation between life and art. The key to the meaning is found by comparing the opening and the closing verses. The poet builds for his soul " a lordly pleasure house" made of "all things fair to sate my various eyes," and his soul thinks "in bliss I shall abide." But after three years of this "God-like isolation," God plagued the soul " with sore despair " until

> "She threw her royal robes away.
> 'Make me a cottage in the vale,' she said,
> 'Where I may mourn and pray'."

But the beautiful Palace of Art was not to be destroyed. The fault lay only with the soul not yet chastened and purified for such isolation.

> "Yet pull not down my palace towers, that are
>     So lightly, beautifully built!
> Perchance I may return with others there
>     When I have purged my guilt."

**8. scaled the light.** The rock abruptly towered aloft.

**15. Still as, while Saturn.** Motionless as seems the revolving planet's shadow cast upon its outermost luminous rings.

**26. branch'd like mighty woods.** Arched like forest avenues.

**30. broad verge.** "A broad horizon " (Tennyson—Eversley Ed.).

**33. those four jets.** From "the golden gorge of dragons " in each of the four courts. Cf. l. 22.

**36. a torrent-bow.** Cf. *Œnone*, l. 60.

**46. day.** I.e. the sun.

**49. traced.** With open-work ornament.

**61. arras.** Tapestry (from the name of the French town famous for its manufacture).

**64. wreathed.** Curved, winding.

**75. rims of thunder.** Edge of thunder-clouds.

**80. hoary to the wind.** The white under-sides of the olive leaves as exposed by the wind. For similar accuracy of description cf. *The Lady of Shalott*, l. 10, a line reminiscent of *Hamlet*, IV. vii. 169.

**92. truth design'd.** All true to nature.

**95. branch-work of costly sardonyx.** A canopy of sardonyx so wrought as to imitate clustering vines.

**99. St Cecily.** St Cecilia, the legend runs, was a noble Roman lady who died a Christian martyr in 320 A.D. Credited by tradition with the invention of the organ, she became the patron saint of music. The celebration of her Day was revived in England in 1683, and was the occasion of three well-known Odes—two by Dryden in 1687 and 1697, and one by Pope in 1708.

**100. An angel look'd at her.** Cecilia, after her forced marriage to a pagan noble, Valerian, was visited nightly by an angel. Her husband obtained this privilege on condition of his embracing Christianity, and he shared Cecilia's martyrdom.

**102. Houris.** The brides of the faithful in paradise.

**105. mythic Uther's deeply-wounded son.** King Arthur, the son of Uther and Igerna, received his death-wound from his nephew, Modred, at the fight of Cambula. The story as told in Tennyson's *Idylls* differs largely from Geoffrey of Monmouth's account.

**107. Avalon.** Avalon or Avilion is traditionally located near Glastonbury whither Joseph of Arimathea brought the Holy Grail and planted the famous Thorn.

**111. The wood-nymph.** Refers to the story of the nymph Egeria who instructed her lover, King Numa, in the law. Ausonian = Roman (the Ausones being the name of the primitive inhabitants of Lower Italy).

**113. engrail'd.** Indented.

**115. Indian Cama.** "The Hindu god of young love, son of Brahma" (Tennyson—Eversley Ed.).

**116. fann'd with spice.** Wafted by odorous breezes.

**117. Europa.** The daughter of the Phoenician king, Agenor, whom Zeus, disguised as a bull, carried off to Crete.

**121. Ganymede.** The beautiful youth who was carried off by Jupiter's eagle from Mount Ida to take Hebe's place as the Olympian cup-bearer.

**126. Caucasian mind.** The Indo-European races.

**128. Not less than life.** Cf. l. 92.

**135. grasp'd his song.** Held a scroll.

**137. Ionian father.** Homer.

**138. A million wrinkles.** Homer was represented by tradition as being aged. Cf. Byron's "The blind old man of Scio's rocky isle."

**151. Here play'd, a tiger.** The French revolution.

**153. an athlete.** The labours of Hercules.

**155. like some sick man.** A representation of the torments of Hercules caused by the poisoned shirt of his father-in-law, Nessus.

**157. over these she trod.** Over these mosaic pictures.

**159. Oriels.** Windows with recesses. A word of uncertain origin. (L. Lat. *oriolum*, a portico.)

**161. colour'd flame.** The stained-glass aglow with the sunshine.

**163. Verulam.** Francis Bacon, Baron Verulam and Viscount St Albans.

**164. The first of those who know.** Explained by Tennyson as referring only to Bacon. This is an endorsement of the old-time exaggerated estimate of Bacon's place in the history of experimental science.

**165. in their motion.** By the result of their activities.

**167. slender shafts.** The window traceries.

**172. as morn from Memnon.** The colossal statue of Amenoph III. at Thebes which emitted musical sounds when struck by the rays of the morning sun.

**188. Lit light in wreaths and anadems.** Kindled lamps set in wreaths and crowns and crescents (moons) of precious jewels.

**189. quintessences.** Finest extracts. Literally, the fifth or most etherial essence in the doctrine of the alchemists.

**201. droves of swine.** This—the pride of intellect—marks the beginning of the deterioration of the self-absorbed soul.

**207. moral instinct.** The soul in her pride now claims infallibility and immortality.

**209. full-accomplished Fate.** Having fully achieved her destiny.

**215. Full oft the riddle.** The poem here takes a sudden turn, and introduces the soul beset with doubts and problems.

**221. Like Herod.** "And the people gave a shout, saying, It is the voice of a god, and not of a man. And immediately the angel of the Lord smote him " (Acts xii. 22).

**225. The abysmal deeps of Personality.** The innermost secrets of the human heart. The phrase, Tennyson tells us (Eversley Ed.), occurs in the writings of his friend, Arthur Hallam. "Cave" and " den" are old philosophical metaphors for "personality."

**228. airy hand.** Unseen hand of God.

**229. Mene, mene.** Daniel v. 25. **Divided quite.** Between "scorn of herself " and "laughter at her self scorn."

**241. On white-eyed phantasms.** Governed by " she came " in l. 245.

**244. dim fretted foreheads.** Fretted, Tennyson explains, (Eversley Ed.) means "worm-fretted." "Dim" we may interpret as dulled and lustreless.

**247. A spot of dull stagnation,** etc. My soul, "divided quite the kingdom of her thoughts," is at a standstill amid the general progress of all else in nature towards a pre-ordained goal.

**251. with bars of sand.** The semi-colon after "sand" was changed to a comma in later editions.

**255. choral starry dance.** Referring to the Pythagorean notion of the music of the spheres. This beautiful fancy has for centuries been one of the familiar ornaments of English verse. Compare Addison's well-known lines:

> "In Reason's ear they all rejoice,
> And utter forth a glorious voice;
> For ever singing, as they shine,
> The hand that made us is divine."

This verse and the two preceding ones are notable examples of Tennyson's pictorial power and felicity of illustration. The stranded soul is compared first to "a spot of dull stagnation" past which rushes the stream of evolution: secondly to "a little salt pool" left on the shore by an ebbing tide: and lastly to a lone "star" that cannot join in the choral dance of the spheres.

**256. but stood.** That is, stood still and could not join in the "starry dance."

**257. moving Circumstance.** Tennyson admits this to be "more or less a play on the word" (Eversley Ed.). In the old Ptolemaic system of astronomy the earth was the centre of the universe and was surrounded by seven, eight, or nine moving spheres. In Milton's poems and in all before his time, this theory of the cosmogony is referred to. Milton, who probably acquiesced in the reasonableness of the Copernican theory, adhered to the older as being the more poetical and as best suiting his biblical epic. Tennyson here re-christens one of the spheres as Circumstance—the play on the word being that Circumstance here means Human Progress, while literally it may be called an enwrapping sphere.

**297. return with others.** "Contrast l. 199, 'O God-like isolation which art mine'" (J. H. Fowler).


## LADY CLARA VERE DE VERE

From *Poems* of 1842.

**46. To make him trust.** You behaved so as to give him sufficient confidence to love you.

**51. grand old gardener.** Altered later to "gardener Adam."

52. **Smile at the claims.** Cf. Prior's Epitaph on himself:

"The son of Adam and of Eve,
Can Bourbon or Nassau claim higher?"

## THE LOTOS-EATERS

### From *Poems* of 1832.

The poem is based on the passage in the *Odyssey* (Bk. IX. l. 82) which describes the arrival of Ulysses and his companions in the land of the lotos-eaters. Those mariners who partook of lotos no longer wished to return home.

The first part of the poem is written in the Spenserian stanza, a verse-form elaborated by Spenser from the old rime-royal of seven lines. The scheme of the latter is a b a b b c c: Spenser added two lines b c—thus avoiding the couplet-effect of the concluding lines— and changed the last line into an alexandrine or twelve-syllable line. The stanza, which is the only English verse-form named after a poet, is particularly suitable for slow, languorous movement and gorgeous scenic effects. Cf. Thomson's *Castle of Indolence* and Keats's *The Eve of St Agnes*. In *The Lotos-Eaters* it is noticeable how skilfully Tennyson constantly succeeds in making the sound echo the sense.

1. **he said.** Ulysses.

8. **a downward smoke.** The stream falling in fine spray. Some of the lines were suggested, Tennyson tells us, by notes he made of scenes in the Pyrenees. Cf. *Œnone*, l. 8, *note*.

11. **veils of thinnest lawn.** A variant on the preceding metaphor in l. 8.

19. **charmed.** As if under the prevailing spell.

23. **galingale.** Sedge. "The *Cyperus papyrus* of Linnaeus" (Tennyson—Eversley Ed.).

26. **Dark faces.** Lotos-land was supposed to be on the north coast of Africa.

46. **Choric Song.** An ode of irregular metre. It is after the style of the late seventeenth-century so-called Pindaric Ode as used first by Congreve and Dryden, who set a fashion that lasted for three-quarters of a century. The "Pindaric Ode" was really a reaction against the domination of the couplet of the "classical school." It made no attempt to imitate the regular formation of the Greek choral

ode, and "Pindaric" in this usage means only "irregular." This
meaning is clearly shown in an interesting use of the word in the
*Spectator*, No. 147, where Steele denounces the pulpit elocution of his
time. Some of the clergy, he says, read one part quickly and another
slowly, "whom I call Pindaric readers, as being confined to no set
measure."

**51. tir'd eyelids.** This phrase is an interesting example of
Tennyson's concern for the music of his verse. He put "tir'd" and
not "tired," he says (*vide* Eversley Ed.), in order that the word should
not be pronounced *tirèd* instead of *tiĕrd*. The latter pronunciation
obviously doubles the onomatopoetic effect.

**120. island princes.** The importunate suitors of Penelope.

**128-9. There is confusion, etc.** Cf.

> "With ruin upon ruin, rout on rout,
> Confusion worse confounded."
>
> (*Para. Lost*, **II.** 995.)

**131. with many wars.** Later changed to *by*.

**133. amaranth and moly.** Amaranth = everlasting (Gk. ἀμάραντος). Moly (Gk. μῶλυ), the magic herb that Hermes gave to
Ulysses as a counter-charm to the spells of Circe.

**142. acanthus.** A plant with prickly leaves (Gk. ἄκανθα = a
thorn). The interweaving of its leaves suggested the ornaments of the
Corinthian capital.

**153. an equal mind.** Steadfastly. (Lat. *aequo animo.*)

**154. hollow Lotos-land.** The land full of caves and valleys.
Cf. ll. 7, 140, 148.

**160. Blight and famine.** Here, in the midst of a medley of
rhythmical (Pindaric) irregularity, we catch the trochaic metre of the
future *Locksley Hall*.

**170. beds of asphodel.** The asphodel, or lily, was supposed to
grow in the Elysian fields. Cf. *Œnone*, l. 95.


# A DREAM OF FAIR WOMEN

## From *Poems* of 1832.

**2. The Legend of Good Women.** The unfinished poem in which
Chaucer introduced the heroic couplet into English verse.

**5. Dan.** "Sir," a title of respect. (Lat. *dominus*.) Cf. Dan

Piers, Dan Cupid, Dan Pirrus. In the *Nun's Priest's Tale* Chaucer humorously applies it to Russel the fox.

10. **Held me above the subject.** Hovering in doubt.

17. **far-renowned brides.** Cleopatra and the others mentioned by Chaucer.

27. **the tortoise.** The Roman *testudo*, a protection for advancing troops made of wood or formed by their uplifted shields.

85. **I saw a lady.** Helen of Troy, daughter of Zeus and Leda.

96. **I brought calamity.** She was the cause of the Trojan war by leaving Menelaus for Paris. After the death of Paris she married his brother, Deiphobus, whom she betrayed later to Menelaus.

100. **To one that stood beside.** Iphigenia, the daughter of Agamemnon and Clytemnestra. The Grecian fleet was detained at Aulis (its starting-point for Troy) until Iphigenia was sacrificed to propitiate Artemis. At the last Artemis relented, and substituting a hind on the altar, carried Iphigenia off in a cloud to Tauris.

104. **This woman was the cause.** The indirect cause as the reason for the ships leaving Aulis.

106. **Which yet to name.** To avoid the inversion Tennyson later substituted the line: "Which men call'd Aulis in those iron years."

126. **One sitting.** Cleopatra.

127. **swarthy cheeks.** Tennyson explains that by "swarthy" he meant only "sunburnt" (Eversley Ed.). Chaucer describes her as "fair as is the rose in May." Shakespeare calls her a "gipsy," *Romeo*, II. iv. 44. Cleopatra was the daughter of Ptolemy Auletes and of pure Greek descent. Egypt was a Greek province from its conquest by Alexander the Great in 322 B.C. until the battle of Actium in 31 B.C

130. **I govern'd men by change.** Cf.

> "Age cannot wither her, nor custom stale
> Her infinite variety."
>
> *(Ant. and Cleo. II. ii. 240.)*

139. **cold-blooded Cæsar.** The Emperor Augustus, Cæsar's adopted son and heir. Cf.

> " O, couldst thou speak,
> That I might hear thee call great Cæsar ass
> Unpolicied ! "
>
> *(Ant. and Cleo. v. ii. 309.)*

146. **Canopus.** The ship, Argo, was made a constellation by Minerva. Canopus is its brightest star.

**155. with a worm I balk'd.** By the bite of an asp, a deadly kind of viper.

**158. argent.** Silver.

**178. some one coming.** Jephthah's daughter (Judges xi. 33—40).

**229. When the next moon.** "And she said unto her father, Let this thing be done for me: let me alone two months" (Judges xi. 37).

**243. Thridding the sombre boskage.** Threading the dark thickets. Cf. "Threading dark-eyed night" (*Lear*, II. i. 121), and "My bosky acres" (*Tempest*, IV. 81).

**251. Rosamond.** Rosamond Clifford (*d.* about 1176), daughter of the first Baron Clifford and mistress of Henry II. A century after her death her name had become the centre of an ever-increasing romance, of which the best known episode is her murder by Queen Eleanor.

**258. the Egyptian.** Cleopatra.

**259. Fulvia's waist.** Fulvia was the wife of Cleopatra's lover, Mark Antony. To Cleopatra Fulvia is the generic name for interfering wives.

**263. The captain of my dreams.** Venus, the morning star. Cf. ll. 55, 244.

**266. who clasp'd in her last trance.** Margaret Roper, the daughter of Sir Thomas More, married William Roper, her father's biographer. According to Thomas Stapleton's *Tres Thomae* (1588), Margaret Roper purchased the head of her father after its exposure on London Bridge and preserved it till her death. Margaret Roper was buried in Chelsea parish church. In 1824 a skull in a leaden box was found in William Roper's vault in St Dunstan's, Canterbury.

**269. Or her, who knew that Love.** Eleanor of Castile (*d.* 1290), who is said to have saved the life of her husband, Edward I., by sucking a wound inflicted by a poisoned dagger in 1272. Her husband's gratitude was shown by his erection of nine memorial crosses at the various points at which the funeral cortege stopped on its progress from Nottinghamshire to Westminster Abbey. The last of these was Charing Cross, removed in 1647, the site of which is marked by the present erection.

**275. That glimpses, moving up.** That gleams where the seam touches the surface.

**278. Compass'd.** Enveloped.

**286. the bitter of the sweet.** Words can more easily paint remembered joys than the painful regret attending their recollection.

## THE BLACKBIRD

From *Poems* of 1842.

**5. espaliers and the standards.** Trees or bushes trained on trellis-work or standing singly.

**7. unnetted black-hearts.** Unprotected cherries.

**12. jenneting.** A kind of early apple. Tennyson accepts the popular derivation of "June-eating" which Skeat calls "a miserable jest."

## OF OLD SAT FREEDOM ON THE HEIGHTS

From *Poems* of 1842.

**1. on the heights.** Cf. Milton's *L'Allegro*, 1. 36,

"The mountain nymph, sweet Liberty,"

and Wordsworth's sonnet on Liberty,

"Two voices are there—one is of the sea,
One of the mountains."

**6. Self-gathered.** Absorbed.

**14. isle-altar.** Freedom identified with Britannia.

**15. God-like.** Cf. "Jovis telo trisulco" (Ovid, *Ibis*, 471).

## MORTE D'ARTHUR

From *Poems* of 1842.

This poem was written in 1835, and originally stood as printed in the text. When Tennyson included it in the 1842 volume, he furnished it with an introduction and an epilogue. The former appears in his collected poems under the title of *The Epic* : the epilogue consists of thirty-one lines at the end of the poem. These additions are intended to provide a framework for this isolated incident of Arthurian story. In *The Epic* a festal gathering is described in which Everard Hall, the poet, is persuaded to read a fragment of the Arthurian Epic which he had burned as being merely

> "faint Homeric echoes, nothing-worth,
> Mere chaff and draff, much better burnt.
>
> .     .     .     .     .     .
>
> The poet little urged,
> But with some prelude of disparagement,
> Read, mouthing out his hollow oes and aes,
> Deep-chested music."

The epilogue completes this setting for the poem. It continues the half-apologetic vein of *The Epic*, e.g.

> "Perhaps some modern touches here and there
> Redeem'd it from the charge of nothingness,"

and concludes with the dream of Arthur's return.

The *Morte d'Arthur*, based on Malory's collection of Arthurian romances bearing the same name and printed by Caxton in 1485, was finally incorporated by Tennyson (without, of course, *The Epic* or the epilogue) in the *Idylls of the King*, where it received a new setting and is called *The Passing of Arthur*.

**4. Lyonness.** Later spelled *Lyonnesse.* The fabled land connecting Cornwall and the Scilly Isles.

> "A land of old upheaven from the abyss
> By fire, to sink into the abyss again;
> Where fragments of forgotten peoples dwelt,
> And the long mountains ended in a coast
> Of ever-shifting sand, and far away
> The phantom circle of a moving sea."
>
> *(The Passing of Arthur, l. 82.)*

This was the scene of Arthur's last battle, when he received a mortal wound at the hands of Modred.

**21. Camelot.** See note on p. 256.

**23. Merlin.** The Enchanter who saved Arthur in his childhood.

> "Merlin in our time
> Hath spoken also, not in jest, and sworn
> Tho' men may wound him that he will not die,
> But pass, again to come."
>
> *(Idylls of the King—The Coming of Arthur.)*

25. **smitten thro' the helm.** Cf.

> "Modred smote his liege
> Hard on that helm which many a heathen sword
> Had beaten thin."            (*The Passing of Arthur.*)

27. **Excalibur.** The sword wrought by the Lady of the Lake, cf. ll. 103—106.

29. **In those old days.** The finding of the sword is described in *The Coming of Arthur.*

**An arm.** The Lady of the Lake.

31. **samite.** Rich embroidered silk.

38. **lightly.** Nimbly.

43. **at full.** To the utmost.

46. **in the moon.** Moonshine—on the analogy of "in the sun."

56. **studs.** Altered later to "sparks."

58. **subtlest jewellery.** With the original meaning of the adjective, finely worked or woven.

60. **dividing the swift mind.** A translation of *Aeneid*, IV. 285: "Atque animum nunc huc celerem, nunc dividit illuc." (Tennyson—Eversley Ed.)

70. **I heard the ripple.** The couplet exemplifies Tennyson's skill in adapting sound to sense. Cf. ll. 48, 49, 64.

80. **lief.** Synonymous with dear (O.E. *leóf*, beloved). Shakespeare uses it in the phrase "I had as lief" many times, but only in 2 *Hen. VI*, III. i. 164 is it used as here, "my liefest liege."

110. **clouded with his own conceit.** Troubled by his own notion.

121. **Authority forgets.** Power of command deserts a dying king bereft of the old strength to compel obedience by a glance.

124. **latest-left.** The last.

125. **meet the offices.** Who (being the last) should sum up in himself the loyal service of all my dead knights.

139. **northern morn.** A translation of *Aurora Borealis.*

140. **moving isles of winter.** Icebergs.

**shock.** Collide. Cf. *King John*, v. vii. 116:

> "Come the three corners of the world in arms,
> And we shall shock them."

165. **the margin.** Lat. *margo*, edge or brink. Cf. "Margent of the Sea" (*M. N. D.* II. i. 85).

167. **pavement.** The floor of the chancel (cf. l. 9).

171. **Remorsefully.** Pitifully—the usual Shakespearean sense.

186. **harness.** Armour.

197. **Black-stoled.** Robed in black. Stole is used by Milton both for a robe and for a hood. Cf. *Ode on the Morning of Christ's Nativity*, l. 220, and *Il Penseroso*, l. 35.

198. **Three Queens.**

> "Three fair queens,
> Who stood in silence near his throne, the friends
> Of Arthur, gazing on him, tall, with bright
> Sweet faces, who will help him at his need."
>
> (*The Coming of Arthur.*)

The Queëns are named in Malory's *Morte D'Arthur*. They are generally interpreted as the three Graces, but Tennyson, while admitting this to be partly true, said "they are much more" (Tennyson—Eversley Ed.).

214. **the springing east.** The rising sun.

215. **greaves and cuisses.** Armour for legs and thighs..

223. **a star of tournament.** The cynosure of the lists.

232. **the light that led.** "When they saw the star, they rejoiced with exceeding great joy. And when they were come into the house... they presented unto him gifts; gold, and frankincense, and myrrh" (Matthew, ii. 11).

242. **one good custom.** Any unvarying system such as the order of chivalry.

250. **better than sheep or goats.** Cf. *Hamlet*, iv. iv. 33 :

> "What is a man,
> If his chief good and market of his time
> Be but to sleep and feed? a beast, no more."

255. **Bound by gold chains.** "That excellent and divine fable of the golden chain: That men and gods were not able to draw Jupiter down to the earth; but contrariwise Jupiter was able to draw them up to heaven" (Bacon, *Adv. of Learning*, II. vi. 1). Cf. *Iliad*, VIII. 19 and Plato, *Theaet.* 153.

259. **Avilion.** See note on p. 264.

262. **Deep-meadow'd.** Richly meadowed (Gk. βαθύλειμος).

263. **crown'd with summer sea.** Crowned, i.e. encircled.

267. **fluting a wild carol.** "Swans, a little before their death sing most sweetly" (Pliny, *Nat. Hist.* x. 23).

## THE GARDENER'S DAUGHTER

### From *Poems* of 1842.

16. **The summer pilot.** For some three months the object of my heart's idle fancy.

19. **ere he found.** Before he establishes.

28. **More black than ashbuds.** This line and line 115, instances of Tennyson's closeness of observation and felicitous description, are celebrated in Mrs Gaskell's *Cranford*, where Mr Holbrook is moved by them to call the poet a "wonderful man."

**the front of March.** Cf. "Flora peering in April's front" (*Winter's Tale*, IV. iv. 3).

47. **murmurous wings.** Cf. "And murmuring of innumerable bees" (*The Princess*, VII. 207).

93. **The mellow ouzel.** The blackbird.

94. **The redcap.** The goldfinch (Tennyson—Eversley Ed.).

116. **The garden-glasses shone.** The poet finally substituted "glanced."

133. **greener circles.** Fairy rings.

136. **Hebe bloom.** The daughter of Juno, goddess of youth, and cup-bearer to the gods.

161. **Love's white star.** Venus, "the planet of Love."

178. **the watchmen peal.** The final text reads "watchman."

195. **The daughters of the year.** The months. The poem opens in May (l. 79) and now it is Autumn (l. 202).

202. **brought an hour.** Wedding day.

210. **mutually enifolded.** The erroneous use of mutual for similarly confuses the picture.

236. **Beyond all grades develop'd.** To full completion.

258. **glooming.** Twilight.

## ULYSSES

### From *Poems* of 1842.

*Ulysses*, Tennyson tells us, was composed soon after the death of A. H. Hallam, and expresses his feeling of "the need of going forward, and braving the struggle of life." The poem is based on a passage in Dante's *Inferno*, canto xxvi. ll. 90—120. The further voyaging of Ulysses is foreshadowed in the *Odyssey* in the predictions of Tiresias, Bk. xi. ll. 100—137.

2. **barren crags.** Ithaca.

3. **aged wife.** Penelope.

4. **Unequal.** Arbitrary government for "a savage race."

10. **rainy Hyades.** Seven stars ("the rainers") in the head of Taurus, the rising and setting of which were supposed to threaten rain.

13. **Much have I seen,** etc. One of many lines in the poem that echo the *Odyssey*.

17. **ringing plains.** Resounding with the noise of battle.

18. **I am a part of all that I have met.** I have been an actor in all the experiences of my life.

29. **three suns.** Three years.

**hoard myself.** Cf. *The Gardener's Daughter*, l. 48.

35. **discerning.** Having discernment.

39, 40. **centred in the sphere of common duties.** Left in charge of a position of ordinary responsibility.

40. **decent not to fail.** Becomingly observant of filial regard.

45. **My mariners.** Homer makes Ulysses return alone.

48. **opposed.** Confronted fate with.

49. **Free.** Happy, resolute.

53. **strove with Gods.** The various gods who took sides in the Trojan war.

60. **the baths.** Referring to the old notion of the spheres revolving round the earth. The eighth sphere (the Firmament) contained the fixed stars, so that with its revolution the stars dipped into the western seas.

63. **the Happy Isles.** The Isles of the Blessed (Gk. τῶν Μακάρων νῆσοι), were vaguely located by the Greeks in the West.


## LOCKSLEY HALL

### From *Poems* of 1842.

The poem, which is in no sense autobiographical, voices the eternal protest of youth against the tyranny of social conventions. The speaker, smarting under a disappointment in love, after describing his boyish dreams and first passion, inveighs against woman's inconstancy and paints a scornful picture of his favoured rival. He predicts that his faithless cousin will grow to resemble her mother, and in turn crush her daughter's affections "with a little hoard of maxims." He cannot find forgetfulness in deeds of arms, because chivalry is dead. He will return to his earlier love of books and find consolation in the march of civilisation and knowledge, but even as he philosophises his heart cries out, "What is that to him that reaps not harvest of his youthful joys?" Can he find the remedy in a return to nature in savage lands? He rejects this notion, and concludes with a paean to progress and an anathema on the scene of his disappointment. The argument is incoherent and the sentiment egotistic and hyperbolical as well befits a jilted youth.

3. **'Tis the place.** The first half of the poem is full of Lincoln-shire landscapes.

4. **Locksley Hall.** An imaginary situation.

6. **hollow ocean-ridges.** The trough of the sea presently rising into mountain billows.

14. **closed.** Held.

19. **a livelier iris.** A brighter plumage of mingled hues.

35. **the copses ring.** With the melody of birds.

42. **a shrewish tongue.** Amy's worldly-wise mother. Cf. ll. 93—96.

75. **the poet sings.** Dante's *Inferno*, v. 121.

82. **widow'd.** As good as widow'd.

84. **a song from out the distance.** An echo of her first love.

85. **an eye...looking ancient kindness.** Her first lover looking tenderly as of old.

94. **preaching down a daughter's heart.** Crushing her daughter's romance with prudential advice.

97. **lower yet.** To find happiness in degradation is even worse than apathetically to outlive it.

100. **barr'd with gold.** Defended with the power of wealth.

104. **roll'd in vapour.** Encompassed with the smoke of powder.
**laid with sound.** Silenced by the louder sound of artillery.

107. **Can I but relive, etc.** Is there no course open to me but to live a life of sorrowful retrospect? I will return to my first love of knowledge (cf. ll. 11—16).

108. **Mother-Age.** The present time that is so fruitful of progress and discovery.

109. **before the strife.** Anticipating the battle of life.

113. **along the dusky highway.** On the stage-coach journey to London.

115. **to be gone before him.** To arrive forthwith at his destination.

121. **fill with commerce.** Crowded with aërial merchantmen.

**argosies.** Ships of Ragusa. Ragusa in the 15th and 16th centuries was an important port on the Adriatic and famous for her merchantmen. "Raguses" formed a part of the Armada. The term was used poëtically for a fleet partly owing to association with the mythological *Argo* of Jason.

123. **a ghastly dew.** Rain of blood.

125. **world-wide whisper.** Governed by "heard" in l. 123.

127. **flags were furl'd.** Furled to be laid aside among emblems of the past.

129. **common sense of most.** The wisdom of the majority.

133. **all order festers.** The whole world is "out of joint" to the disappointed lover.

134. **Science.** All knowledge, in the literal sense of science.

135. **as a lion.** The simile was derived, the present Lord Tennyson tells us (Eversley Ed.), from Thomas Pringle's *Narrative of a Residence in South Africa*, 1835. Pringle was one of the two joint-editors of the magazine which, after they left it, was transformed in 1817 into the familiar *Blackwood*. Lord Tennyson also tells us that this couplet and ll. 33, 34 "my father considered two of his finest similes."

138. **the process of the suns.** The progress of the years.

150. **made them blinder motions.** Bestowed on them more irrational impulses.

153. **Here, at least, where nature sickens.** Here, where Nature's dictates are stifled, thy passions are as nothing.

157. **to burst all links of habit.** To break away from familiar associations.

175. **vacant of our glorious gains.** Ignorant of our progress.

180. **Joshua's moon.** Joshua x. 12, 13.

181. **the distance.** The distant prospect.

182. **the ringing grooves of change.** "When I went by the first train from Liverpool to Manchester (1830) I thought that the wheels ran in a groove. It was a black night, and there was such a vast

crowd round the train at the station that we could not see the wheels. Then I made this line " (*Life of Tennyson*, I. p. 195).

183. **the shadow of the globe.** Night.

184. **Cathay.** The medieval name for China—from *Khitan*, the name of the first historical conquerors of China.

185. **for mine I knew not.** Cf. l. 156.

186. **Rift the hills,** etc. The marvels of science such as tunnelling and dam-building, electricity, and astronomy.

191. **a vapour from the margin.** A cloud from the edge of the horizon.


## THE DAY-DREAM

*The Sleeping Beauty,* the nucleus of the poem, appeared in *Poems, chiefly Lyrical* of 1830. The rest of the poem, with the exception of the Prologue and the Epilogue, was finished by 1835. The complete poem was published in the *Poems* of 1842, Tennyson having added the Prologue and the Epilogue as a framework in the same way as he added *The Epic* and the terminal lines to the *Morte D'Arthur.*

2. **past.** Tennyson altered this form later to *passed* in order to avoid ambiguity as in l. 11.

7. **behind.** The garden seen through the window at which Lady Flora sits dreaming.

23. **Here rests the sap.** In the Sleeping Palace all vitality is arrested. The key-line is l. 38, "In these, in those the life is stay'd."

34. **the festal fires.** "Droop" and "droops" are to be understood from the previous line.

55. **prisms.** Prismatic hues.

61. **a hedge upshoots.** The story of *The Sleeping Beauty* owes its celebrity chiefly to the French fabulist, Perrault. In his version an impenetrable wood grew up and surrounded the palace during the hundred-years sleep.

91. **Her constant beauty,** etc. Her unchanging beauty fills the silence and the day with love and light.

103. **in sequel.** In the end.

110. **to pass.** To penetrate the wood.

111. **close.** Enclosure.

126. **Magic Music.** The familiar children's game in which the searcher for a hidden article is told by quick or slow playing of the piano whether he is "hot" or "cold" in his search.

157. **Pardy.** *Par Dieu.*

158. **something.** Altered finally to "somewhat."

168. **that new world which is the old.** "The world of Love" (Tennyson—Eversley Ed.).

169. **Across the hills, and far away.** "Over the hills and far away" was a popular refrain at the beginning of the 18th century. It occurs in Gay's *The Beggar's Opera* and in Farquhar's *The Recruiting Officer.*

186. **vapour buoy'd the crescent-bark.** The young moon riding on the clouds.

209. **liberal applications.** Free interpretations.

226. **The Poet-forms of stronger hours.** The stuff of poetry of a wiser age.

231. **we are Ancients.** A conceit on the double meaning of "ancient." We are "ancients" because the world hourly grows older, "And to speak truly, *Antiquitas saeculi juventus mundi.* These times are the ancient times, when the world is ancient, and not those which we account ancient *ordine retrogrado*, by a computation backward from ourselves" (Bacon, *Adv. of Learning*, I. v. 1). The same thought occurs in Bacon's *Novum Organum*, I. 84, "Illa enim aetas, respectu nostri antiqua et major, respectu mundi ipsius nova et minor fuit." Whewell traces the paradox back to Giordano Bruno's *La Cena de le Ceneri*, 1584.

234, 235. **decads...quinquenniads.** Periods of ten and five years.

236. **quintessence.** See note on *Recollections of the Arabian Nights*, l. 123.

275. **and cannot light.** From the way in which the skins were sent to Europe the myth arose that the birds had no legs. The myth is said to have been fostered by the natives of New Guinea so as to raise the value of their export.


## SIR GALAHAD

### From *Poems* of 1842.

This poem, like *The Lady of Shalott* and the *Morte D'Arthur*, is of special interest as one of Tennyson's early adventures in the

region of Arthurian romance.   Sir Galahad received fuller treatment
later in *The Holy Grail* in the *Idylls of the King.*

4.  **my heart is pure.**  Sir Galahad is the pattern of purity, the
"clean maiden" of Malory's romance.

25.  **the stormy crescent.**  The moon presenting the appearance
associated with impending storm.  Cf. *The Ballad of Sir Patrick Spens*:

> "I saw the new moon, late yestreen,
>   Wi' the auld moon in her arm;
> And if we gang to sea, master,
>   I fear we'll come to harm."

42.  **the holy Grail.**

> "The cup, the cup itself, from which our Lord
> Drank at the last sad supper, with his own.
> This, from the blessed land of Aromat—
> After the day of darkness, when the dead
> Went wandering o'er Moriah—the good saint
> Arimathæan Joseph, journeying brought
> To Glastonbury, where the winter thorn
> Blossoms at Christmas, mindful of our Lord.'
>                         (*The Holy Grail*, ll. 45—52.)

The *Grail* or cup (the derivation is uncertain, but the word is
usually explained as being connected ultimately with the L. Lat.
*cratella*) was adopted into Christian legend from Celtic mythology.
The magic cup of plenty became the vessel in which Joseph of
Arimathæa received the blood of Christ on the cross (hence called the
Sangreal or sacred cup).

54.  **spins.**  Finally altered to "springs."


## A FAREWELL

### From *Poems* of 1842.

1.  **rivulet.**  The brook at the poet's old home at Somersby which
Mrs Tennyson left in 1837.  This brook is also celebrated in his
earlier *Ode to Memory*:

> "The brook that loves,
> To purl o'er matted cress and ribbed sand,
> Or dimple in the dark of rushy coves."

The stream described in *The Brook* is purely imaginary.

## THE BEGGAR MAID

From *Poems* of 1842.

**4. Cophetua.** A legendary African king. "The magnanimous and most illustrate king Cophetua set eye upon the pernicious and indubitate beggar Zenelophon" (*Love's Labour's Lost*, IV. i. 65).

## THE EAGLE

Added in 1851 to the seventh edition of *Poems* of 1842.

**1. with hooked hands.** The adjective later was changed to "crooked"—a doubtful improvement.

**4. The wrinkled sea beneath him crawls.** A much and justly praised line. The whole fragment is one of Tennyson's most masterly verse pictures.

## COME NOT, WHEN I AM DEAD

Added in 1851 to the seventh edition of *Poems* of 1842.

**4. thou would'st not save.** The poem is the cry of a rejected lover.

## TO ——

First published in the *Examiner*, 24th March, 1849, and added to the eighth edition of *Poems* of 1842.

The letters, the publication of which the poet condemns, are the love-letters of Keats. Lord Houghton's *Letters and Literary Remains* of Keats appeared in 1848. The present Lord Tennyson tells us (Eversley Ed.) that the poet meant his reflections to be considered as quite general and not as an indictment of any particular book.

## BREAK, BREAK, BREAK

### From *Poems* of 1842.

"The process of identification, however, has led more than one writer into difficulties. Poetry is not always inspired by its surroundings. 'Break, Break, Break,' for instance, has been generally ascribed to the influence of Clevedon. But we have Tennyson's own denial. 'It was made,' he said, 'in a Lincolnshire lane at five o'clock in the morning'" (*Alfred, Lord Tennyson*, by Arthur Waugh, p. 6).

## THE POET'S SONG

### From *Poems* of 1842.

9. **the bee.** Later changed to "fly."

## TITHONUS

### First published in the second number of *The Cornhill Magazine*, Feb. 1860.

Aurora obtained from Zeus the gift of immortality for her lover, Tithonus, the son of Laomedon, king of Troy. The gift proved to be a curse as it did not also confer eternal youth. Eventually he was transformed into a cicada.

7. **limit.** The eastern boundary of the sky, Aurora's mansion.

18. **Hours.** The daughters of Jupiter and Themis.

25. **the silver star.** Venus.

29. **kindly race.** Natural.

30. **goal of ordinance.** Appointed limit.

34. **old mysterious glimmer.** The rise of dawn personified.

51. **with what other eyes.** Tithonus now describes Dawn as he used to see her when he was a mortal.

62. **that strange song.** See note on *Œnone*, l. 40.

71. **barrows.** An ancient burial mound.

75. **forget.** Will forget.

## THE CAPTAIN

### From *Selections* of 1865.

The poem was possibly suggested, the author tells us (Eversley Ed.), by an incident in the naval mutiny of 1797.

## THE FLOWER

### From *Enoch Arden* volume of 1864.

**3. flower.** The particular flower in the poet's mind was love-in-idleness (Eversley Ed.).

## THE SAILOR BOY

### Published in 1861 in Miss Emily Faithfull's Christmas miscellany *Victoria Regia*.

**4. morning star.** Venus.

**12. the scrawl.** "The young of the dog-crab" (Author's note in Eversley Ed.).

## LOVE AND DUTY

### From *Poems* of 1842.

**4. Shall Error**, etc. From this to the end of l. 13 is to be read as a single period. "Can truth be born of error; can law and empire arise from anarchy; can sweetness and light derive from sin—and yet can unfulfilled love produce nothing but dust and ashes?" The motive of the poem is to justify the negative answer.

**10. this wonder, dead.** Love unfulfilled.

**18. apathetic end.** *Apathetic* still retains the original notion of "indifferent," "unfeeling." *Pathetic* and *pathos* are now used only in the active sense as "causing emotion." At l. 82 Tennyson uses *pathos* in the older sense of "suffering" to balance this use of *apathetic*.

21. **greater than thy years.** The line originally ended with a full-stop. Later the period was deleted, and finally a comma was substituted. The later readings give the true sense. The Sun and Moon, representing time infinite, will see the rectifying and real purpose of the trials of the finite human life.

27. **ill for good.** Pleasure instead of renunciation.

34. **Whose foresight preaches peace.** How hard is my task to preach an acquiescence at which my heart rebels.

39. **would break its syllables.** Would stifle its love so as not to move me from my resolution.

56. **that bring us all things good.** Cf. *The Gardener's Daughter*, l. 181.

74. **in station.** Fixed, stationary.

82. **pathos.** Suffering. Cf. l. 18.

97. **the mounded rack.** The embanked clouds. *Rack* (from O.E. *réc*, smoke) was a frequent sixteenth-century term for the light clouds of the upper air.

## EXPERIMENTS IN QUANTITY

First published in *The Cornhill Magazine* for December, 1863.

"My Alcaics are not intended for Horatian Alcaics, nor are Horace's Alcaics the Greek Alcaics...the Greek Alcaic, if we may judge from the two or three specimens left, had a much freer and lighter movement." (From Author's note in the Eversley Ed.)

## ODE ON THE DEATH OF THE DUKE OF WELLINGTON

First published in pamphlet form on the day of Wellington's funeral, Nov. 18, 1852.

The poem was coldly received. Tennyson at the time wrote of "the all but universal depreciation of my Ode by the Press." The second edition in 1853 contained numerous additions and emendations.

9. **Here.** St Paul's Cathedral.

23. **chief state-oracle.** Wellington on various occasions became a member of the Government. In 1828 he was Prime Minister, and in 1834 took office as Home Secretary under Peel.

42. **World-victor's victor.** Napoleon's conqueror.

49. **the cross of gold.** Surmounting the dome of St Paul's.

55. **The towering car.** Still to be seen in the crypt of St Paul's.

56. **his blazon'd deeds.** His chief victories are inscribed on the sides of the car.

79. **ever-ringing.** Changed finally to *ever-echoing*.

80. **Who is he that cometh.** The question is asked by the spirit of Nelson who was buried in the crypt forty-seven years earlier.

99. **myriads of Assaye.** The battle in which Wellington crushed the Mahratta power on August 23, 1803. The two forces numbered about 50,000 and 7,000. Of the latter more than a third was lost.

104. **The treble works.** The triple line of earthworks of Torres Vedras which Wellington caused to be built during the winter of 1809 to protect his base at Lisbon.

119. **eagle rose.** Napoleon escaped from Elba in March, 1815.

123. **loud sabbath.** The battle of Waterloo, Sunday, June 18, 1815.

126. **Their surging charges.** Attacks of the French cavalry on the British squares.

127. **the Prussian trumpet.** It was not till about 6 p.m. that any considerable portion of Blücher's force was engaged.

153. **brainless mobs.** Referring to the year 1848 when there were insurrections in Austria, Italy, Hungary, Poland, Prussia, Spain, etc.

155. **Saxon.** Finally altered to *Briton*.

160. **the eye...Of Europe.** Cf. "Athens, the eye of Greece." Milton, *Para. Reg.* iv. 240.

232. **will be sung.** The prediction so far is unfulfilled.

248. **brawling memories.** Thoughts of "battles long ago."

278. **But speak no more.** In the final form of the poem *but* is omitted.


## THE CHARGE OF THE LIGHT BRIGADE

This poem was published in *The Examiner*, Dec. 9, 1854.

There are some general resemblances in the poem to Drayton's *Ballad of Agincourt*, but Tennyson tells us that he had not this in mind, and that the poem was built up on the *Times* report of

Lord Cardigan's speech to the survivors that "Some one had blundered."

1. **Half a league.** The actual distance was a mile and a half.

5. **Light Brigade.** Composed of the 13th Light Dragoons, the 17th Lancers, the 11th Hussars, the 8th Hussars, and the 4th Light Dragoons.

6. **he said.** The order to charge was given by Lord Cardigan acting on the orders of Lord Lucan.

12. **Some one had blunder'd.** The blunder has been variously attributed to Lord Lucan, General Airey and Captain Nolan.

38. **Not the six hundred.** In twenty minutes twelve officers and a hundred and forty-seven men were killed, and four officers and a hundred and ten men wounded.

## THE BROOK

First published in the *Maud* volume of 1855.

The brook of the poem is purely imaginary. The blank verse of the poem betrays some of Tennyson's characteristic mannerisms which are to be found later in the *Idylls*. Parodists have accordingly given attention to it. The best known skit is that of C. S. Calverley, but Tennyson's blank verse was never more happily travestied than in General Sir Edward B. Hamley's *Sir Tray: an Arthurian Legend*, which was published in *Blackwood's Magazine* in 1873. Though this diverting rendering of *Mother Hubbard* is ostensibly "an Arthurian Legend," it might quite well have been inspired by *The Brook* alone. Hamley's verses belong to that rare order of parody that illuminates and criticises as well as gives amusement.

2. **too late.** Cf. l. 33, "He died at Florence."

4. **scrip and share.** As good as gold. Scrip, a certificate of stock.

8. **as the thing that is.** Cf.

> "As imagination bodies forth
> The forms of things unknown, the poet's pen
> Turns them to shapes, and gives to airy nothing
> A local habitation and a name."
>
> (*Mid. Night's Dream*, v. i. 14.)

12. **be said to flourish.** His life was nipped in the bud.

16. **branding.** Scorching.

17. **half-English Neilgherry air.** Ootacamund, the chief town in the Neilgherry Hills, is the sanatorium of the Madras Presidency, standing more than seven thousand feet above the sea.

19. **Prattling the primrose fancies.** The brook seems to voice his boyish conceits. For the use of " primrose " as signifying early and unfulfilled, cf.

> " Primrose, first-born child of Ver,
>     Merry springtime's harbinger."
> > *(The Two Noble Kinsmen,* i. i.);

and

> > " Pale primroses,
> > That die unmarried, ere they can behold
> > Bright Phoebus in his strength."
> > > *(Winter's Tale,* iv. iv. 122.)

29. **thorps.** Hamlets.

80. **eyebrow.** Arch.

92. **neither one.** Altered finally to *nor of those.*

103. **wizard's pentagram.** Final reading is *wizard.* A pentagram or pentacle was a five-pointed star-shaped figure used as a mystic sign in astrology.

105. **Unclaim'd.** As not applying to her.

128. **Approved.** Confirmed, bore out.

189. **dome of Brunelleschi.** The dome of the cathedral Santa Maria del Fiore by the great Florentine architect, Filippo Brunelleschi. He died in 1446, having all but completed the work.

196. **converse seasons.** Changed in final form to *April-autumns.*

197. **stile.** Earlier editions read *style.*


## A WELCOME TO ALEXANDRA

Originally appeared as a four-page pamphlet published on March 7, 1863, the day on which the Princess arrived in England.

20. **Rush to the roof.** This line and the following four were not in the poem in its first form.

# NORTHERN FARMER

## OLD STYLE

From *Enoch Arden* volume of 1864.

Numerous changes in the spelling were made in later editions. Only a few of these it has been thought necessary to indicate here.

1. **liggin'.** Lying.
2. **thoort.** Finally changed to *thourt*.
3, 4. **yaäle.** Final reading is *aäle*.
4. **a-gooin'.** Final reading is *a-gawin'*.
12. **I done, etc.** Final reading is *I done moy duty boy 'um, as I 'a done boy the lond.*
14. **a cost oop.** He brought up. **barn.** Altered to *barne* (= a child).
15. **Thof.** Altered to *thaw*.
23. **my lass.** The nurse, cf. ll. 1 and 2.
27. **summun.** Psalm cxvi. 11.
28. **stubb'd.** Cleared.
30. **boggle.** Evil spirit.
32. **raäved an' rembled.** Rove and bundled them out.
35. **toner.** Altered to *toaner* (= one or other of them).
36. **at 'soize.** At the assizes.
41. **Nobbut.** Only.
42. **ta-year.** This year.
45. **Do godamoighty knaw.** A saying resembling this, attributed to a dying farm-bailiff, Tennyson tells us was the nucleus of the poem (Eversley Ed.).
49. **A mowt 'a taäken Joänes.** Final reading is *A mowt 'a taäen owd Joänes, as 'ant not a 'aäpoth o' sense.*
53. **quoloty.** Gentry.
61. **kittle.** Kettle.
63. **Gin.** Gin (= if) was altered to *sin'* (= since)
66. **a 'tottler.** A teetotaler, and is always at the same old story.

## NORTHERN FARMER

### New Style

From *The Holy Grail and Other Poems*, 1869.

(The poem appears in the text by the kind permission of Messrs Macmillan & Co.)

**2. Proputty.** This saying, Tennyson tells us, was the germ of the poem.

**27. git naw 'igher.** Final reading is *git hissen clear.*

## IN THE VALLEY OF CAUTERETZ

From *Enoch Arden* volume of 1864.

" Here, thirty-two years before, he and Arthur Hallam had passed in their exciting expedition to the revolutionists ; and here, during that time, he had conceived the notion of ' Œnone.' It was the sight of the Pyrenees and their scenery that suggested the description of Ida. At this second visit with Clough he recalled the first journey with a painful pleasure....This was in September, and two months later Arthur Hugh Clough died at Florence. The valley of Cauteretz must, from that day, have had a dual message for Tennyson " (*Tennyson : A Study of his Life and Work*, by A. Waugh, p. 149).

## SONGS FROM THE PRINCESS: A MEDLEY

*The Princess* was first published in 1847, but underwent much revision up to the fifth edition of 1853. The songs were first added in the third edition of 1850.

## IN MEMORIAM

First published in 1850, the year in which Tennyson became Poet Laureate. The sections of the poem were composed at various dates between 1833 and 1850 ; most of them there is reason for thinking were drafted by 1842. They do not appear in the poem in the order of their composition. "I did not write them with any view of weaving them into a whole, or for publication, until I found that I had written so many." On this definite statement of the poet Professor Bradley comments, " what is of consequence is the order in which the sections now stand. For although the poet 'did not write them with a view of weaving them into a whole,' he found that when they were written they were capable of being thus woven into a whole, and it seems quite clear that he endeavoured, by arrangement and possibly by writing new pieces, to give the collection a certain amount of definite and significant structure " (*A Commentary on Tennyson's In Memoriam*, p. 18).

*In Memoriam* is partly biographical and partly general. The poet's reflections travel far beyond their biographical starting-point. The immediate occasion of the poem, as its title indicates, was the sudden death at Vienna on September 15, 1833, of the poet's friend and brilliant contemporary at Cambridge, Arthur Henry Hallam, the elder son of Henry Hallam, the historian. Arthur Hallam was engaged to be married to the poet's sister, Emily Tennyson.

1. **I held it truth.** Section I. of the complete poem.

**with him who sings.** Stated by Tennyson to be Goethe. The thought has been traced to St Augustine, cf. Longfellow,

> " Saint Augustine ! well hast thou ·said
>
>> That of our vices we can frame
>
> A ladder, if we will but tread
>
>> Beneath our feet each deed of shame."
>
>> *(The Ladder of St Augustine.)*

13. **victor Hours.** Conquering Time.

17. Section VI. of *In Memoriam*.

32. **vast and wandering.** Cf. "Vast and wandering air" (*Rich. III.* I. iv. 39), and " Wild and wandering flood " (*Troilus*, I. i. 105).

61. Section XIX. of the poem.

**The Danube to the Severn gave.** Refers to Hallam's death at Vienna and his burial at Clevedon on the Wye, an affluent of the Severn.

67. **half the babbling Wye.** "As the tide passes up the Wye, its silent flood deepens and hushes the river; but as it ebbs again, the river, growing shallower, becomes vocal and ' babbles.'...The Wye is tidal for about half its course " (Bradley).

73. **the wave.** The normal stream as contrasted with the tide.

77. Section XXIII. of the poem.

80. **The Shadow.** Death.

101. Section xxvii.

112. **want-begotten rest.** A tranquillity due to the want of some natural human feeling.

115. **'Tis better to have loved and lost.** Cf. "Better to love amiss than nothing to have loved" (Crabbe, *Tales*, xiv.).

117. Section liv.

137. Section lv.

139. **Derives it not,** etc. Does it not spring from that in us that is most godlike?

143. **the type.** Nature is so careful of the species as opposed to the individual.

156. **the larger hope.** Cf. *The Vision of Sin*, l. 18. " He means by ' the larger hope ' that the whole human race would through, perhaps, ages of suffering be at length purified and saved, even those who ' better not with time '; so that at the end of this *Vision* we read ' God made Himself an awful rose of dawn ' " (Editor's note on *The Vision of Sin*, l. 18, Eversley Ed.).

157. Section lxxiii.

159. **what had need of thee.** What greater cosmic purpose required thee.

164. **nothing is.** Nothing exists that is not governed by the laws of nature.

169. **hollow wraith.** Cf. "Hollow as a ghost" (*K. John*, iii. iv. 84).

171. **And self-infolds.** The soul gathers up in itself the unspent energies that would have won earthly renown.

173. Section lxxxvi.

176. **breathing bare.** Clearing with its breath.

177. **rapt.** Carried.

179. **shadowing.** Pursuing. **horned.** Winding.

185. **crimson seas.** "Eastern seas" (Tennyson).

187. **orient star.** Venus when visible at night.

189. Section lxxxvii.

196. **prophets.** Finally altered to *prophet*.

203. **long walk of limes.** At Trinity College, Cambridge.

209. **a band of youthful friends.** A literary society founded about 1820 at Trinity called "The Apostles." Besides Hallam and Tennyson it included many men distinguished later, e.g. Maurice, Trench, Spedding, Monckton Milnes, Lushington and Kennedy.

222. **music in the bounds of law.** Eloquence tempered by art.

226. **orbits.** Eyes.

228. **The bar of Michael Angelo.** "These lines I wrote from what Arthur Hallam said after reading of the prominent ridge of bone over the eyes of Michael Angelo : 'Alfred, look over my eyes; surely I have the bar of Michael Angelo " (*Memoirs of Lord Tennyson*, vol. I., p. 38).

229. Section LXXXIX. **counterchange the floor.** Chequer. Cf. *Recollections of the Arabian Nights*, l. 84.

239. **brawling courts.** Hallam entered at the Inner Temple the year before his death.

240. **dusky.** Finally altered to *dusty*.

244. **winking through the heat.** Shimmering.

254. **happy sister.** Emily Tennyson, betrothed to Hallam.

259. **livelong.** The form *lifelong* was substituted later.

270. **The picturesque.** Lose distinctive personality under the smooth veneer of fashion.

275. **Before the crimson-circled star.** "Before Venus, surrounded by the crimson of sunset, had set after the sun" (Bradley). Professor Bradley justly remarks that these lines " surely mar a beautiful passage." They take us back to the " conceits " of the Jacobean poets or to that later example in Milton's ode *On the Morning of Christ's Nativity*, l. 229.

281. Section XCIV.

282. **affections.** In the older sense of "disposition," "impulses." Cf. " Has he affections in him ? " (*Meas. for Meas.* III. i. 108).

289. **They.** Equivalent to *these* anticipating the subjects presently enumerated.

297. Section CIV. **the birth of Christ.** The third Christmas since Arthur Hallam's death. " Tennyson himself tells us (*Memoirs*, I. 305) that the divisions of the poem are made by the Christmas-tide sections (XXVIII., LXXVIII., CIV.) " (Bradley).

299. **A single church.** Waltham Abbey. In 1837 Mrs Tennyson left Somersby and moved to High Beech, Essex. This removal explains the subsequent lines in this section.

309. Section CV.

309, 310. **This holly**, etc. The final reading runs :

> "To-night ungather'd let us leave
> This laurel, let this holly stand."

312. **strangely.** Used with something of the force of the word in

*The Winter's Tale*, II. iii. 182, referring to the abandonment of Perdita, "Commend it strangely to some place," which Schmidt aptly paraphrases "as a thing belonging to another country or to other people."

**314. other snows.** The poet's father, the Rev. George Clayton Tennyson, died in 1831 and was buried at Somersby, Lincolnshire.

**317. abuse.** Wrong, disfigure. Cf. "Thy face is much abused with tears" (*Romeo and Juliet*, IV. i. 29).

**320. dying use.** Ceremonious commemoration of death. Cf. Section LXXVIII., l. 20 and "Still use of grief makes wild grief tame" (*Rich. III.* IV. iv. 229).

**322. proved.** Put to the test.

**325. beat the floor.** Dance.

**327. ancient form.** Who would keep up an old family custom which has now lost its original motive and zest?

**335. your measured arcs.** The allotted courses of the "rising worlds" (stars).

**336. closing cycle.** "Cf. Virgil, *Ecl.* IV. 4, *Ultima* Cymaei venit jam carminis *aetas*. Time is said to have been divided in the books of the Cumaean Sybil into cycles or saecula, and Virgil makes the golden age return with the closing cycle" (Bradley).

**337.** Section CVI.

**369.** Section CVII. **the day.** Hallam was born on February 1, 1811.

**372. night forlorn.** An inversion = desolate night.

**378. To yon hard crescent.** The ice-bound spinules point upwards towards the frosty moon.

**379. grides.** Creaks harshly. Spenser and Milton use the word in the sense of *piercing* (from O.E. *girden*, to pierce). Professor Bradley suggests that the Tennysonian use of the word is due to Shelley's *Prometheus Unbound*, III. 1,

> "Hear ye the thunder of the fiery wheels
> Griding the winds."

**381. the drifts.** The storm clouds becoming blacker as they drift to sea. "Drifts" is otherwise interpreted (by Gatty) as "drifts of snow," and (by Bradley) as "squalls of wind."

**383. breaks.** Frets, indents.

**393.** Section CXI.

**395. To who may grasp.** Finally changed to *him who grasps*.

**398. His want in forms for fashion's sake.** However much he conceals his unsociableness for fashion's sake.

400. **gilded pale.** Bounds of sham refinement.

401. **act.** Play an unreal part.

402. **a thousand memories call.** Whom I recall by a thousand memories.

405. **So wore his outward best.** The final reading is *Best seem'd the thing he was.*

413. **without abuse.** Without doing it wrong.

417. Section CXXVI.

426. **That.** Altered later to *who.*

427. **vast.** Changed to *worlds.*

428. **Among the worlds.** Changed to *In the deep night.*

429. Section CXXIX. **my lost desire.** Object of desire. Cf. "Lycidas your sorrow is not dead" (*Lycidas*, 166).

441. Section CXXX.

449. **involves.** Includes.

457. Section CXXXI. **O living will.** "That which we know as Free-will, the higher and enduring part of man" (*Tennyson: A Memoir*, vol. I. 319).

459. **spiritual rock.** 1 Corinthians, x. 4.

463. **conquer'd years.** Friendship and love defeat the passing of time.

## MAUD

The poem was published in 1855 in the volume containing amongst other poems *The Brook, The Charge of the Light Brigade*, the *Ode on the Death of Wellington*. The nucleus of the poem is the famous quatrain (*Maud*, pt. II. iv. 1):

> "O that 'twere possible
> After long grief and pain
> To find the arms of my true love
> Round me once again."

These lines were contributed by Tennyson in 1836 to Lord Northampton's charity annual, *The Tribute*. At the suggestion of his friend, Sir John Simeon, in whose garden at Swainston *Maud* was written, Tennyson made the old verses the foundation of his new poem. *Maud* was very unfavourably received by the critics and by the public.

27. **neither courtly nor kind.** The lover changes his mind when his suit succeeds, cf. ll. 45—48.

29. **Birds.** "A story is told of yet another reading of *Maud*, when Tennyson turned to a lady at his elbow in the midst of the passage—

> 'Birds in the high Hall-garden
> When twilight was falling,
> Maud, Maud, Maud, Maud,
> They were crying and calling.'—

with the question, 'What birds were calling?' The lady, willing to justify her taste for poetry, replied: 'Nightingales, I imagine.' 'Ugh!' said the poet, with a shiver, 'what a cockney you are! Do Nightingales cry 'Maud'? Certainly not. But rooks do: 'Caw, caw, caw, caw.' It's very like it, at any rate'" (*Alfred, Lord Tennyson*, by A. Waugh. p. 124).

58. **little King Charles.** The black-and-tan toy spaniel was made fashionable by Charles II.

59. **my lord.** The suspected rival lover.

65. **woodbine spices.** Scent of the honeysuckle.

68. **planet of Love.** Venus.

83. **to the setting moon,** etc. West and east.

## ELAINE

*The Lady of Shalott* (1832) and *Sir Galahad* and the *Morte d'Arthur* (1842) represent Tennyson's earlier handling of Arthurian romance. "The epic, as we have it, however, took time in its growth. The original *Idylls*, which appeared in 1859, were but four in number, *Enid, Vivien, Elaine* and *Guinevere*. Three years later the dedication was added, and in 1869 *The Coming of Arthur, The Holy Grail, Pelleas and Ettarre* and *The Passing of Arthur*. In 1871 *The Last Tournament* appeared in *The Contemporary Review*, and in 1885 *Balin and Balan* was added to *The Round Table*. Subsequently *Geraint and Enid* was split into two parts, the first part being entitled *The Marriage of Geraint*, the second, which begins with the passage

> 'O purblind race of miserable men,'

retaining the old name of *Geraint and Enid*" (*Alfred, Lord Tennyson*, by A. Waugh. p. 128).

2. **the lily maid of Astolat.** "Shalott and Astolat are the same

words. The Lady of Shalott is evidently the Elaine of the *Morte d'Arthur*, but I do not think that I had . ver heard of the latter when I wrote the former " (from Tennyson's note, Eversley Ed.).

7. **soilure.** Stain. The word is once used by Shakespeare, *Troilus*, IV. i. 56, " Not making any scruple of her soilure."

10. **their own tinct.** In their true colours. **of her wit.** Of her own fancy.

11. **fantasy.** Design.

16. **read.** Perused.

22. **Caerlyle.** Carlisle.

23. **Caerleon.** Caerleon-upon-Usk, S. Wales. **Camelot.** See note, p. 256.

27. **fantasy.** Dreamland.

36. **Lyonnesse.** See note, p. 272.

38. **horror.** Tragedy.

45. **lichen'd.** Covered with rock moss.

60. **Divinely.** Providentially.

92. **tale.** Number.

95. **lets.** Hinders.

111. **allow'd.** Acknowledged.

116. **this union.** Coupled together in this toast.

119. **devoir.** Duty, cf. *endeavour*.

123. **passionate perfection.** Sorrowful paragon. Cf. " Poor forlorn Proteus, passionate Proteus " (*Two Gent. of Ver.* I. ii. 124).

130. **Rapt.** Engrossed.

135. **The low sun.** Compared with the pure white light of the sun at its zenith, l. 124.

162. **rarer.** Less frequent.

168. **Fired from the west.** Illumined by the setting sun.

173. **Lord of Astolat.** Sir Bernard.

202. **Allow him.** Pardon him.

204. **Joust for it.** For the ninth diamond.

253. **a living soul.** Had yet an accusing conscience.

264. **as in a smaller time.** Without the scornful pride he might have shewn in time and circumstances of less account.

270. **glanced.** Spoke in passing.

280. **Badon hill.** Bannerdown, the Hill of Bath, the scene of the last of Arthur's twelve victories over the Saxons.

288. **the violent Glem.** Arthur's first victory in Northumberland.

290. **Duglas...Bassa.** The Duglas, which falls into the estuary of the Ribble, witnessed four of Arthur's victories. The Bassa is said to be Bashall Brook which flows into the Ribble.

292. **Celidon.** Conjectured to be in Tweeddale.

293. **Gurnion.** Caer Wen, in Wedale, Stow.

297. **Caerleon.** Caerleon-upon-Usk.

300. **Agned Cathregonion.** Edinburgh.

301. **Trath Treroit.** In Anglesey.

329. **all was nature.** His change of moods was his natural disposition or perhaps due to her presence.

332. **Divinely.** By inspiration pierces the mask.

339. **rathe.** Early. **half-cheated.** Half-deceiving herself by thinking of Lavaine's departure, her heart being really with Lancelot.

358. **asking for it.** It = his wearing of her favour.

378. **yet-unblazon'd.** With no victory yet inscribed on it.

412. **next day.** The sun rising in the east below the cliff.

423. **Pendragon.** Arthur, the son of Uther, the Pendragon (great leader).

430. **like a rainbow.** The variously attired ladies.

441. **Yet all with ease.** The dragons fitted harmoniously into the delicately wrought design.

443. **the nameless king.** Cf. l. 41.

447. **Now crescent.** Now growing to maturity. Cf.

> "My powers are crescent, and my auguring hope
> Says it will come to the full."
>
> *(Ant. and Cleop.* II. i. 10).

458. **afield.** In the fields and not witnessing the tourney.

471. **versatility.** Agility.

490. **worshipfully.** Worthy of honour.

494. **thought to do.** Thought to achieve victory. Cf. "Let us do or die" (Fletcher, *The Island Princess*, II. 4).

535. **Gawain.** The son of King Lot and Morgause, Arthur's sister.

549. **restless.** Flashing.

557. **Sir Modred.** King Arthur's nephew, who mortally wounded the King in "the great battle of the West." Tennyson's account of Modred differs from that of Geoffrey of Monmouth and from Malory's account of Sir Mordred.

568. **tarriance.** Stay. Cf. "I am impatient of my tarriance" *(Two Gent.* II. vii. 90).

577. **Lancelot told me.** Cf. 1. 148 *et seq.*

592. **fantastical.** Full of romantic fancies.

593. **So fine a fear.** So delicate a scruple.

654. **hern.** Heron.

716. **strokes of the blood.** Heart beats.

729. **Marr'd her friend's point.** Blunted the edge of her unkind friend's satisfaction by feigning calmness.

808. **battle-writhen.** Twisted in pain.

841, 843. **dim.** Cf. 1. 845.

858. **simples.** Specifics.

873. **faith unfaithful.** His guilty love for the Queen. A celebrated example of oxymoron.

881. **ghostly grace.** Dream beauty.

884. **rough sickness.** His unconscious discourtesy in his delirium. Cf. 1. 850.

965. **a flash.** Repeating Lancelot's overheard words in 1. 945.

970. **against me.** Contrary to my inclination.

1093. **ghostly man.** Confessor.

1131. **next sun.** Cf. 1. 412.

1143. **silken case.** Cf. 1. 984.

1169. **vibrate.** Over her heaving breast.

1218. **her pearls.** Cf. 1. 602.

1391. **crescent fear.** See note on 1. 447.

1395. **Lady of the lake.** Vivien stole Lancelot, the son of Ban, King of Brittany.

1419. **a holy man.** Sir Lancelot, in Malory's story, became a hermit. A year after Arthur's death Lancelot was summoned to attend the dying Queen, who expired half-an-hour before his arrival. Lancelot himself did not long survive, and was buried at Joyeuse-Garde.

For EU product safety concerns, contact us at Calle de José Abascal, 56–1°,
28003 Madrid, Spain or eugpsr@cambridge.org.

www.ingramcontent.com/pod-product-compliance
Ingram Content Group UK Ltd.
Pitfield, Milton Keynes, MK11 3LW, UK
UKHW020321140625
459647UK00018B/1951